I Am Liberty

One Mind's Journey Through Ascension

By

Libby Maxey

authorHOUSE™

1663 LIBERTY DRIVE, SUITE 200
BLOOMINGTON, INDIANA 47403
(800) 839-8640
WWW.AUTHORHOUSE.COM

First published by AuthorHouse 12/09/04

ISBN: 1-4184-9955-2 (e)
ISBN: 1-4184-9954-4 (sc)

Library of Congress Control Number: 2004096894

Printed in the United States of America
Bloomington, Indiana

This book is printed on acid-free paper.

"It is your mission to express all that you can imagine God to be." Charles Fillmore

Dedicated to the soul who has traveled many lifetimes with me.
Who in this lifetime asked me and over again -
Who are you? I accepted the challenge to fully explore who I am,
so I found out! I also realize who you are,
and who we are becoming, even
while already being that.

Dedicated and consecrated to Aaron, Laura and Isaac,
co-creators of heaven on earth with me, a place
where we are all fully free to practice our Christ selves.
Or not.

Given as a kiss of soul-joy to my beloved friends
on this path into His Arms, my co-prodigals, way wards all:
my spirit-family at Unity Church for Positive Living,
my teachers, in flesh and in spirit,
to all the beloved Christ-beings who have believed with me.
Namaste'

Before we begin, courtesy of Krishna

Immersed in an intense Presence, I sat, transfixed, as Krishna blossomed before my inner eyes. He sat, lotus-fashion, smiling his beneficence. His knees touched mine as we sat together in meditation. He appeared larger than life; perhaps seven feet tall, about 350 pounds, beautifully proportioned, comfortably fleshy. His skin is translucent with a velvety bluish tone. Just as I began to notice his beautiful golden crown of Light, a crown of Light became apparent on my own head, and I lifted my hand to feel the peacock feather perched on the right side. I remembered then a recent inner conversation with Yeshua. "Yeshua, why am I so magnetized by Krishna, by images of Krishna, by the Sanskrit chants?" Yeshua replied "Why, beloved? Krishna was my teacher. Now he teaches you. He guides you to be the child of God you are, completely. He plays with you!"

Krishna's blissful gaze drew my attention. I looked at him, inner eyes wide to see all of his beauty. His own eyes were crinkly with suppressed laughter, then his mirth burst forth in a great cloud of Divine Joy that enveloped us instantaneously. White Light filled with stars surrounded me and filled me, satisfying and comforting as mother's milk, so safe and carefree I felt. Krishna's eyes conveyed a thought, and I understood. This is the "Ocean of Milk", the rapturous Divine Joy that is our birthright as children of the Mother. Tingling, drunk with Joy, I giggled a questioning thought, clumsily projecting it to Krishna with my eyes. Is this how heaven feels? His eyes glowed. Waves of ecstasy billowed from his wonderful being. He breathed forth Ahhhh, and it felt like a spring breeze, fragrant with freshness, pregnant with possibilities. Divine Life.

I fell further into bliss, losing awareness, floating. I could feel something surrounding my being, like a tube or column or Light. I recalled the image of my completed DNA from another visionary experience. It looked then like a cylinder of light, intricately woven in twelve strands. Now it appeared in similar fashion, except the strands were now also woven through me, through the center of my being. Now the strands were no longer simply woven around me, but are also spiraling through me, creating now an intricate cylindrical mandala of energies.

You know about the DNA, Krishna conveyed. Somewhat, I thought back. His eyes responded: *enough to explain what is coming known to you now.* I could feel him nod inside my consciousness. He was being very firm. I knew he wanted me to get this, whatever it was. Inner eyes riveted to his gaze, the idea of shapeshifting, of changing forms at will, ran through my consciousness. I could feel his nod again. He breathed in, and on his outbreath, my consciousness was filled with images. Images of life danced around me, competing for my attention. I saw the rocks and the soil, the matter of the earth, the plants and trees and growing things; I saw the birds and animals, the insects and the sea creatures. I could see all the people, the beautiful children of God. I could feel my oneness with all life, and there was something more. Realize, he breathed. I remembered that human DNA contains all the DNA of every living thing on the earth. Ah! I realized. Since I contain the pattern of every living earth creation, I have within me all the created forms. Shapeshifting calls forth a pattern of creation, a DNA coding already within my being!

Beaming broadly, Krishna breathed out again. Again, my consciousness was filled with images, images of people I have revered in my life. Paintings and photographs of spiritual masters and saints cascaded through my inner vision. I felt profoundly grateful that I have followed my curiosity, collecting these images in my mind. Krishna conveyed his thanks to me. Oh! Krishna has amplified this curiosity! Thank you indeed! Watching the slideshow, beings of Light gathered around me, and I knew I was surrounded by my own personal spiritual cheering section. Expand the realization, he commanded. I knew. I already knew. Just as I am all those created beings contained within my human DNA, I am also all created beings contained within the rewoven, reconnected, re-membered DNA that is the One God. DNA is a continuum, a process. It is the blueprint of evolution. Oh! I *am* God also.

Krishna looked at me with infinite tenderness. I felt newly born. We breathed in simultaneously. I could feel myself within Him. I could feel Him, feeling me within him. I looked at my skin, not the least surprised by its' bluish tone, yet astounded to realize that he lives within me, patterned there in my DNA since the beginning of time. My consciousness was so expanded I could only maintain the ability to observe. All control or ideas of control were surrendered, useless. Shifting my inner awareness, I realized that Yeshua too lives within me. Shifting again, my vision alighted upon Mary, the Cosmic Mother, holding the Terra and every living being in her tender devotion. She lives in me as well. The gargantuan enormity of this realization, of this potential, of this Truth left me in complete awe.

So what is your desire, my darling child? Krishna breathed, returning my attention to my own individualized part of the Whole. I knew he was asking which shape I desired…which being…who I wanted to be. I knew the answer. I knew my deepest desire. I desire to manifest my Self. I desire to manifest, completely, the Self God created. The image and likeness of God's desire: that's my desire. I desire to reflect the full Glory of God, as me, Liberty, the Word made flesh.

Chuckling deeply, tenderly, pleased beyond measure, Krishna breathed out again. A haze of blue light enveloped my consciousness, and I rested.

Introduction

From the moment I connected the concepts of resurrection and ascension to my own self, I knew these were my reasons for being in this human flesh. One beautiful autumn day God challenged me to imagine how it would look and feel on my first day as a quickened, evolving being living in the world we know. God urged me to know everything that level of beingness would bring to my life. Write it, He commanded. Since to me hearing and obeying are the same activity, I began writing! As I wrote, God would actually take over, turning on the italics icon when She wanted to be heard as God. Marvelous understandings appeared on the screen; fully developed concepts not of this world. I am continually awestruck by God's Presence as He writes through me, as me, and as I AM.

Happily writing what I am pretending about ascended mastery, my own experiences build and transform me, until one day a major open-eyed revelatory vision of "the treasure house of God" appeared right on my front lawn! I had a spiritual breakdown after that, now knowing completely that what I was imagining was Truth. From that point, the writing becomes a day-to-day process following my own birthing in Light. Jesus frequently shows up to delight me or to open a new can of spiritual worms, often both. God's Presence occurs with greater and greater frequency and I attempt, with our limiting language, to describe that deliciousness. Openly I depict my wilderness times when I again embrace separation, even while knowing Unity.

God awakened me to my purpose: to follow Jesus all the way **through** the valley of the shadow of death, and to prove Jesus correct with my own life. With ever increasing regularity, I experienced total understanding of puzzling concepts, such as "eye single to God", "...if I be lifted up" and even "Ye are Gods". I read and re-read God's word in many of the forms it has taken throughout human history, and became of vessel of understanding and connection. I want it all. I want all of the All.

During my study of the idea "the Word made flesh" Jesus began to address me as "Liberty". Gently he opened my mind to the fullness of meaning in that word, softly he blew on the embers of hope the idea aroused in me. Today I know that I know: I am the word Liberty made flesh. I live to demonstrate liberty, the fully evolved maturation of freedom that is God's plan for humankind. It is our revolutionary evolution to totality, while simultaneously our return to who we have always been. The dual extremes of darkness and light we are experiencing in our world today leave no doubt for me that our collective birthing in Light is near, even at the gates. And I, if I be lifted up, will draw all of humankind up with me. Will you come?

MAY THE FORCE BE EVER WITH YOU. I AM LIBERTY.

Table of Contents

Part One – Imagination

What was that dream?

mmmmm, I'm waking up, back in my body again. I have the feeling that the dream I was having was so wondrous, beautiful, but it is gone. There are tears running down my cheeks. It must be pretty late, it's so light in here, and my eyes are still closed. Why did everyone let me sleep so long? It must be 10:00 o'clock already, it's so light. Maybe the blinds are open. What a beautiful day it must be today. My body is soooo relaxed, so still, so peaceful, as if I've been on vacation at a spa with whirlpools, saunas, great sex, massages and someone else to do the cooking for a change! My skin is tingling. Maybe I'm still dreaming, because I don't think I have ever felt this good. What was that dream about, anyway?

My eyelids are fluttering open, and I'm looking around the bedroom. Gil must have had an early meeting - his wallet and keys are already gone. The blinds are still closed after all. It is a <u>very</u> bright day, brilliantly bright and sparkling for some reason, like it's been digitally enhanced. My spider plant hanging at the window is so enchanting, so lush and alive; the green and white stripes on the leaves seem lighted from within. The little plantlets dance on tiny breezes. Looking at this creation I am captivated, I weep with the joy of this beauty. Oh look, a spider has made a web from one plantlet to another and the web has minuscule droplets of dew with little rainbows shining from each droplet! I feel like I will explode with joy if I don't look away this minute! What was that dream???

I'd better get up. My legs are wobbly; I've been sleeping so long. I can feel the blood pouring into my arms and legs, like a rushing river. How strange. I have goose bumps all over. Okay God, I'm paying attention. Actually I feel like I've never paid attention before. My consciousness is so profoundly alive, so intensely here and now and I'm not even trying! Maybe I'm dead and now I'm spirit without a body. But my body feels like my body, different, but the same as well. Better have a look in the bathroom mirror. GEEZ! Where is all that light coming from? There's a white glowing light so bright I can only see an outline of myself in the mirror. Yeah right - I just had a crazy thought that I look like an angelic being from one of my meditations, oh yeah, sure, and it's first thing in the morning. But there I am. THAT IS I!!! Oh my God Oh my God Oh Father Mother God the DREAM!

~~~

There are beings like the one in the mirror all around me, hundreds of them, thousands. They all smile at me with looks of joyous love, holding me with their gazes. There is silence filled with laughter. We are in a beautiful room without walls, like a platform suspended in space. The platform is circular but curiously without edges. There is the most gorgeous design of a majestic lion inlaid in all the colors of wood on the floor. Each hair of the lion's face is an individual piece in the mosaic. The beings dance and float about me, blending with each other and with me. My feelings of love and joy and peace are intensified each time we blend in consciousness. This is exquisite. This is bliss. I feel totally known and totally knowing, without fear of any kind.

Now I am standing on a creamy white marble balcony overlooking a meadow. I see the grasses and flowers laughing and giggling, jostling one against the other as the breeze whispers above them. Their colors are marvelous, glowing. I can see the buds opening like eyes, smiling at God as they awaken. A blue white bubble of light with someone inside is to my left. Jesus Himself is there, looking out at the lawns of Heaven with me.

~~~

Wow. He's gone. It feels like the dream has given me an experience of tremendous importance in human life and my spiritual life, but my mind can't assimilate it just yet. My image in the mirror is looking more normal now, but there is still a beautiful light emanating from my third eye area, causing a glow all around my head.

The baby is still quiet. He loves to be alone, talking and playing in his bed. GEEZ! It's only 7:30 after all. The older kids must have gone to school. I hope they ate some breakfast. It was certainly sweet (and uncharacteristic!) of them to be so quiet.

~~~

How strange! I'm outside the house, looking down on the roof, going down our street toward the main road. There's the school bus. Aaron and Laura are on that bus. Somehow I am enabled to see within the bus and there they are! Laura is looking up and smiling - she sees me! Aaron is further back, talking to another boy. He looks up and sees me too! They are so beautiful. Actually all these young people are shining, beautiful beings. All of them have light glowing from their foreheads. Ouch! Laura's being has merged with mine. This merging feels similar to how I felt when I realized I was pregnant with her. I knew her as her spirit first, and her name was and is Laura. I never even chose a boy's name. Now Aaron is merging with me. I feel the love that he is rush into my being. "Aaron" means "enlightened one" and he really is; all he needs to do is remember. I love these two beings of light.

Back. Instantaneously - no return trip, no uncomfortable "snap" back into the body. In fact, I was standing in the kitchen starting to prepare the coffee when I "left" and the coffee is now rapidly dripping into the pot. I remember every step in making the coffee (I don't usually pay enough attention to remember) so I must have been in both locations, consciously! Bi-location! Surely I am a new person today. I have only dreamed of this possibility before. There are several accounts of Jesus bi locating, and I remember too that yogis have also displayed this gift. I have most certainly entered a new phase of my beingness. How strangely normal to have these thoughts! But I feel normal, too. I'm still walking on my two feet, still seeing with my two eyes. The coffee smells so good. The aroma wraps around me like a warm cloud.

~~~

I am lying on wonderfully soft and fragrant grass, watching the clouds pass the sun. My vision is so expanded that I can see the dome of sky all at once. Suddenly my vision shifts and I am the sun, looking back at the earth, my benevolent rays caressing her oceans, dancing over the mountains, blessing her people. My vision shifts again and becomes one ray of the sun's light traveling toward earth to touch one cloud. I seek a perfect raindrop within the cloud, one that makes a tiny rainbow as I shine through it. I touch and become that raindrop, tumbling through the sky, falling, falling to earth. I land on the lush green bough of a fir tree as the tree sways in the breeze. I drop further, onto the soft creamy whiteness of a dogwood blossom. A butterfly comes along, hello beautiful one, and she drinks me!! I travel along the curling swoop of her incredibly long tongue and now I am the butterfly. I flutter to a dazzling yellow flower, dancing with a honeybee in a contest to claim the flower's nectar. The flower is so intricate in design, such perfection, and such a velvety softness to her petals. I allow the honeybee to claim the nectar and fly back to the dogwood blossoms. Now I am a dogwood blossom and oh! I am blown apart by a strong gust of wind. I float down, down to the forest floor, landing gently on the soft decay of leaves. The smell of the good earth is wonderful, living. A raindrop falls onto me, and I am again my true self, the spirit of my own being, while still becoming the raindrop, burrowing and penetrating the soil. I feel and see the layers of the rich earth, sand and sediment and rock. I travel down, down, further and further into the Earth Mother. I am extremely heavy; I can feel it in my body and in spirit as gravity is pulling me into the center of the beloved Earth. Suddenly Light explodes in my consciousness; the heaviness is gone, I am bliss. I AM AN ANCHOR OF THE LIGHT OF GOD WITHIN AND UPON THE EARTH. There are beings of Light surrounding me, beaming Joy upon me.

~~~

Consciousness returns to my human mind and I become aware of my body again. I am sitting comfortably at the kitchen table, gazing at the grassy backyard, watching the pine trees swaying in the morning breeze. There is tiny lightning blazing all over my skin; I am on fire with the Holy Spirit. Maybe this is how the "new wine" makes a human feel.... My ego mind is screaming: **This is not real!** My experiences this morning and in what I was calling a dream can't be true! But I KNOW THAT I KNOW THAT I KNOW this is REAL and it is TRUTH and it is LIGHT.

"I WILL TELL TO YOU ALL TRUTH," a mighty voice thunders soundlessly in my consciousness. There is a magnificent Being of Light, dressed in a creamy white robe, graceful toes bare. There are white rose petals under His feet. The rose petals become roses, rosebushes; there is a beautiful rose garden created as I focus and expand my gaze. The Being is very pleased with the development of spiritual imaging and manifestation in me. I feel a great wave of Love flow from His heart as He extends this thought to me. I

am sitting with this Wonderful Being on soft white banks of rose petals, and the garden expands to hold a stone well, very crude, but of wondrous design at once; the water shines iridescently. *"All possibilities occur simultaneously in the Creation. Do you not receive great thoughts, filled with Goodness and Light? You are aware in those moments that these thoughts came not from your own human mind. RECEIVE the thought, EXPAND upon the thought, IMAGE-IN the thought, SPEAK the thought and the thought is made manifest. GOD the GOOD provides all that is needed for manifestation of each thought. He needs His holy thinkers to manifest all thoughts of goodness. This process is instantaneous, just as the rose petals blossomed into a garden as you thought."*

It would be great if I could manifest instant income, like a gigantic check in the mail to pay off all my bills! With this so human thought I am back as human being, Libby, in mid-sip of coffee. How about manifesting my body as I was at 25? What do You say to instant spiritual wholeness for everyone in my family? Nashville? The US? The world?

"It is done already, my beloved child. All possibilities occur simultaneously in the Creation. You have received thoughts about prosperity, re-claiming your human body of 25 years, and spiritual wholeness for all humankind. These seem to be thoughts of goodness, don't you agree?"

I love You, God. I am engulfed in a wave of inexpressible bliss. My body is like Jell-O, vibrating at a tremendous rate, wave upon wave of sensation. I feel my body as a part of the whole, with no boundaries to mark where my skin touches the air around me.

The baby cries out "Mommy, come back!" He is so funny, such goodness in a cute little package. In his little world I just put him in his bed and now he wants me to come right back and get him out. He has a wonderful grasp of timelessness, of being in the present moment. I'm coming, Isaac. Now if I can just get my Jell-O-legs to motivate. What a day. The clock says 7:45. In a way I hope that the revelations and visions kind of slack off so I can function in the world!

~~~

6

I am standing near the end of what appears to be a driveway, but I realize it is a flight path, kind of a flying guide for beginners. My entire earth family stands at the other end, although there is no real ending, either. Sometimes these visions are so puzzling. I feel a wonderful, fragrant breeze coming directly toward me. I raise my arms as if they are wings and the wind lifts me up! I am so surprised and delighted; this is such fun! I am following the flight path, but I am also going up at a tremendous rate of speed. My family is watching me. Some of them are very frightened by the spectacle of me levitating overhead. I send them thoughts of comfort and understanding. Now they are smiling! The flight path has become a great cone of white Light. I look toward the center of the Light and focus my attention on going to the center of the Light. I know the Christ of God is this Light. The Christ appears in this Light as a human form, neither male nor female. The Christ is not the personality of Jesus, yet the presence of Jesus is within the perfect Light. The Christ is in a white, white robe, all colors shimmering in the whiteness. The hair is softly brown, shining (in fact it looks very much like my own hair) yet all other hair colors as well. The face is beautiful, loving, intense and powerful. The Christ presence drifts down the cone of Light and the Light pulses energy toward my being. The Christ Presence, the total energy field, becomes enmeshed with the energy field I know as my being.

~~~

So much for slacking off! Here I am, trying to write it all down, and I cannot begin to explain how any of this feels. There are truly no words; human language cannot describe things that are not of the human experience. I am still human, however, functioning fully in my role, completely aware of all my body is doing. My hands have changed Isaac's diaper and my human voice has answered his questions, smiling and laughing with him all the while this wild experience is happening in full consciousness. This is more than bi-location; or maybe I never realized that bi-location was a function of consciousness and not of the body. It's all utterly fascinating.

Breakfast. Maybe something solid would make me more of this world. This is the place where I have to function today. There is laundry to do, there are bills to pay, I probably need to get at least some milk at the grocery store, the baby needs to be played with and hugged and fed and changed and chased...I need some normal about now. C'mon Isaac let's go gather up the laundry. I chase him down the hallway and he laughs!! His laughter is a joyful burst of energy; he is such a wonderful gift.

The whites are sloshing around merrily in the hot water of the washing machine. Let's have cinnamon toast, Isaac. How about a banana?

Breakfast is finished: the dishwasher is humming. Isaac is dressed and playing cars in his room. Maybe a second cup of coffee and a phone call to a friend. I wonder if anyone else is experiencing something like me this morning? How will I ask? Maybe Marcia. She will at least feel a new energy this morning and she has never judged what I have revealed to her. This is tough, though. This is so real and so true and so of God that I cannot hear anything negative. It would hurt too much. Maybe Maureen. I told her once that I would let her know when ascension came so she would be ready. I don't want to blow anyone's mind, though. This could do it. But I remember my beloved teacher Ernestine always said that people only hear what they are able to understand. There are many levels to understanding. What about Gil? I have kept quiet about so much of my spiritual life for such a long time, how will he react? I can't call him at work, anyway.

The phone is ringing. Oh! I had completely forgotten about the closing on our new house! It must be the mortgage company on the phone right now. Yes! Our closing is Friday at 2:30 in Lebanon. Wonderful. After some rather frustrating delays, it is happening. The closing was supposed to happen three days ago, and this has caused some schedule changes. This has not affected me, because I just go with whatever is happening to stay in the flow with God. I think that is God's will, just that we stay in the flowing rush of His Love for us. Whenever we are outside of that flow we can know it because we feel disconnected, angry, frustrated, depressed, alone, out of sorts, or any number of other negative states, all describing fear in some way.

My relatives have incessantly asked "Is there going to be a closing? Are you going to get the house?" But I have known since we first saw the house that this was to be ours. God made that clear to me. This house fulfills all the needs of those who are to dwell in it, and then some. There is a spring at the front of the property where we will dig out a pond. There is a willow that will gladly bow down over the pond; and there God will teach me more and more. And so I knew that God's will would not be thwarted. It is our house.

The angst that others in this housing transaction have been feeling is theirs. I have been an observer of the human consciousness from the awareness of the Christ consciousness. This is liberty. I watch, I comment occasionally, I do whatever actions are necessary, like make the phone calls, run to the post office, dash to the bank for signed bank statements: I do my part to make the transaction happen. I observe that I am dependent on others, who are dependent on others, who are dependent on me. We are all dependent on God. We cannot move a muscle, think a thought, breathe a breath, look around, love, be - we are not, without God. This was all His deal. I love You, my own Father Mother God.

I need to get busy and do some errands! First I'll call Gil and leave a message about the closing on his voice mail. I'd better concentrate on my human affairs and take a quick shower. Isaac, do you want to watch a video while I shower? Which one? He wants "Toy Story" and so it is. Ahh, the warm cascading water....

~~~

I am lifted up and out of my body with a whoosh; I am traveling at a tremendous rate of speed. The light around me changes rapidly with the changes in atmosphere; I am above the earth, looking down at the spinning globe enveloped in velvety indigo blackness. I see the beautiful Earth Mother surrounded by the loving thoughts of her inhabitants and her Divine Protectors. My attention is drawn away and I look at the constellation Orion. The sight is awesome; I see the cloudy nebula in reality instead of in a Discovery magazine with staples in the middle! I see the energy formations as geometric designs, somehow. I remember once looking at Orion from the ground, when it appeared as a warrior spirit emblazoned with stars.

I am here. I know I have come to my destination. A marble temple stands before me, with very wide steps leading up to the temple. There are lions made of living gold at each corner. They have beautiful, compassionate faces. I am climbing the steps. I am aware there are others also climbing the steps. I am wearing a garment made of shimmering blue-white light. It is actually woven light - it is a seamless garment. Oh what beauty, what majesty surrounds me. In a state of pure awe, I feel like an infant child seeing for the first time. I look down at the marble, pure whiteness with golden veins; my God my God the veins are pulsing with life! Surely even the rocks will cry out! Suddenly I can look up, and it is as if my consciousness is that of a single eye... I see my life as Libby being one viewpoint of a far greater consciousness. My entire life view has been one of looking outward onto Libby's life, endeavoring to look inward to God. Now I am the inward view. I am not what the eye sees; I am the consciousness behind the eye.

I am standing in awe, and in absolute awareness. I am standing on a raised platform of the white gold marble. This is an ancient place. There are columns of stone surrounding me. Suddenly great obelisks of stone in various colors come rushing at me, each obelisk bearing a story of God in a different language of the Earth. The stones rush at me from the right and from the left. I know that I am reading and understanding each story. I am learning of God in the continuum of language and I am given new understanding of the written and spoken Word. I am given the gift of languages, the gift of a seer. The ability to interpret and speak in all languages, an apostle directed by the Holy Spirit. I am filled with immense gratitude. Again before my God I bow down in surrender.

~~~

Speaking in tongues? God, do You mean out loud? But I am a dreaded "New Age" Christian! Pat Robertson will never approve! God, please prepare my mind and heart for this one. I know, I know, I have known it, but the experience.... well, please prepare me. Thank You.

It's astounding, but I was able to wash my hair through that experience! The water feels like it is running into my very pores, cleansing every atom of my body. Warm and tingling; it feels as if my body is a musical instrument, somehow, the vibration of the tingling water makes a harmonious sound. This is the greatest body rush! Beats the shit out of any drug that comes to mind!

Toweling off is kind of calming the rush down. Good. I need to get it together! Better check the baby. Good. He's fine. Buzz Lightyear has just fallen "accidentally" out the window, courtesy of Woody. Music. Turn on the radio.

How long have I been listening to Christian radio? Must be five years or so. I love it now more than ever before. I remember how I started listening - a Buddhist monk was visiting the town where we lived then and I happened to be listening to an interview with him on talk radio. He recommended that everyone listen to positive music - classical, jazz/new age, or **Christian radio**. I could barely believe what he, a Buddhist monk, was saying, but he went on to explain that the messages of Christian radio are positive and uplifting. The monk found Christian radio and the messages in the lyrics to be very much the same as the messages of Buddhism. He spoke of his love for Jesus and all masters from all religious traditions. He challenged the talk radio audience to listen to Christian radio for an hour, then listen to any other station, and decide which programming made the listener feel better; which programming provided more opportunities for agreement. Christian radio was the winner for me. The music is wonderful and God uses the lyrics to speak to my heart every day. I don't always agree with the announcers or the opinion of the station, but I often find ways in which we do agree. My heart has been softened again and again.

"Awesome God" is playing. He truly is awesome.

Errands

I'm ready; I'm dressed. My body vehicle has never felt better! Time to gather up my boy and his time to go bye-bye supplies. Better make a list and plan my drive. Let's see - the bank to make a deposit and get some cash, Kroger's, what else? Oh yeah, I need to drop off those papers at the realty office in Lebanon. Good, I wanted to know how to get there before the closing anyway.

Off we go, little Isaac. You are properly strapped into your car seat, juice in one hand, and blankie in the other. It is such a beautiful bright day. The sky has that intense, saturated blueness that I so love. The clouds in their whiteness seem super-imposed on the blue screen. Such a cinematographer you are, God, oh great and glorious Producer and Director. A lovely autumn day in Tennessee, golden oak leaves, red-orange maples. Now if I can only focus on the road. Please God, no special effects while I'm driving today, okay?

Ahh good, hardly anyone in the drive-thru teller lines. In and out without a hitch. That was a lovely young woman who handled my transaction. Was she 17 or am I getting old? Please God; bless her and all those she loves with health and prosperity, and most of all with knowing You. Thanks!

On to the realty office. I'll shoot over to the interstate. God thank you so much for music! Another great song on the radio titled "The Concert of the Age". It's about the Great I AM appearing live in concert and what a show that will be. Very new age for Christian radio. It is my fervent prayer that all who love Christ come into agreement about our inherent unity - all the Christian religions, Muslims, Hindus, Buddhists, Native Americans - to see that the gospel of God's goodness has in fact been spread to the nations - we just need to recognize the Truth of our oneness! Thank you God for your fabulous Plan. Thanks too for letting me see these glimpses! Here's I-40, heading toward Lebanon and points east. Hmm. What is that in the road? It looks like tumbleweed, sort of. There's another piece. *Watch for a large piece in the road.* What? Is that You, God? Better keep an eye out, for what I don't know. Anyone back there behind me? No one to my left and nope, nobody in the right lane either. Geez! Half a retread truck tire in the middle of my lane! Thank you God that I knew I could safely swerve around it! Thank you! God protect those who come along in this lane! You are so with me, God. I love You so much. Here come the tears again.

Here we are. That was easy to find - and there is a Kroger's just beyond the office! That will be our new grocery-shopping destination when we move, little Isaac. I will come right back, baby; I need to drop off these papers. See! Here I am and off we go to get our shopping done.

Yes Isaac, the car is parked and here I come to get you out! Hold my hand in the parking lot. Shopping cart, list; okay Isaac, produce first. Let's see, apples, bananas - what a beautiful soul! Such whiteness surrounds that woman over by the lettuce. Maybe I can catch her eye! She looks very sad, even with such a magnificent spirit. *Oh!* Just in an instant, I was able to see her whole story, the one misunderstanding with God that keeps her from Him. She had an abortion as a teen, and her Baptist upbringing has branded her as evil and unclean. Her trust has been stolen by a mistake in understanding, for God does not label His children. She has been trashing herself for many years, and her self-esteem is at an all time low, in this busy-ness before the holiday season begins. She needs you, God. Oh God my God please lift her up! Please give her the knowing, the absolute KNOWING, that You are with her and have never ever left her! Give her health and wholeness in the name of Christ, who lived as Jesus and who is reborn in us. Thank you for loving her and for giving me this gift of seeing. Amen.... there! She smiled at me! Oh geez I'm going to cry.... she is crying, too, and laughing! God we must look like idiots, crying for no apparent reason in the produce aisle of Kroger's. And Isaac is happily waving his blanket at her. I wonder what she has perceived from our encounter? But I know that I know she is forever changed.

That experience reminds me of what happened with so many of my relatives when we all gathered for Grandma's funeral. My wonderful granny, happy to go to her Jesus. She was so ready, so prepared. When I heard the news that she had exited her body, my immediate reaction was joyous excitement for her and I have not been sad, just happy for her, ever since. I have felt sorrow for others in the family, because they do not have such an understanding with God. Grandma was concerned, as I am, about many of our relatives, her children and grandchildren and my aunts and uncles, cousins.

We want them to know God as we know God, because knowing God is the only satisfaction. The Presence of God alone can satisfy the cravings of our souls. As I stood at the cemetery, I glanced at my dear uncle, and in the briefest of instants, saw a movie of his life, a story that told about his first perception of separation from God. He was about five years old when he was told that black children don't go to "our" heaven. My uncle's best friend was a black child! He decided then that he didn't like a God that didn't want his buddy in heaven with him. That mistake in thinking was the temple that his deception of separation from our Creator was built on! I realized in that instant how easily God could erase all deception in his consciousness, by elimination of that first thought of separation. So in that moment, God revealed how very close She is to all Her beloved children - only one thought away.

At the cemetery and then later at the dinner gathering, I would glance at persons and see their stories, but I could not remember details about any of them. God was confirming that we all are only one thought away from Him, even when we seem so far beyond Her reach. God has blessed me so much with these visions.

On to the apple juice aisle, Isaac my boy; then it's milk, cottage cheese and ice cream and we're out of here. Good, great, checkout is going to be a breeze. What's the headline of today's *Star*? Aah, more Bible prophecies coming true. Duh!

Here's your tip, my bagger friend. I love it when the stores hire these wonderful mentally challenged boys to bag and carry out my groceries. This young man, Adam, is so wonderfully sweet and patient, so friendly. He is so easy to love.

Home again, home again, jiggety jig, little Isaac. The trees are changing colors with such drama! Perhaps I will paint in my next lifetime. Great! It's only 10:15. We will put the groceries away and go for a walk with the stroller, okay little chum? He's delighted with that news!

Groceries handled, wet laundry in the dryer, a new load in the washer, water bottles filled, and keys – let's put on your hat, Isaac. Lock the door and put you in the stroller – isn't God great to give us such a day together, Isaac? By his laughter he must know it, too! This walk will give me a chance to put my thoughts in order. And just what am I thinking, "my" thoughts? That's pretty arrogant. Yet I *do* claim these Wondrous Thoughts as my own, because I so identify with the Thinker. *How about if you and I write down all this stuff? As I have said to you before, the greater your imaginings, the grander your visions. Whenever you stretch your mind toward Me I fill the gap you have created with My Glory; and together we progress from glory to glory. Do you see?* My knees are buckling. God, please avoid knocking me down with realizations while I'm pushing the stroller, okay? *You fill me with such joy when you speak to Me with such honesty, to Me as your friend. You also make me laugh! My laughter can heal the world, you know.* Okay, I'm sitting down here on this rock. Isaac, can you watch the birdies and the doggies? Mommy is going to just freak out right now. Damn! No tissues! Okay, God. I do so love You with all my heart, all my soul, and all my mind. I will write all of it down with your help. You do the remembering, okay? And find the time for me, too. I imagine I will need a good measure of Divine Courage. But I also want the Grander Vision, the Greater Experience. Is this how I draw down my ascension? By imagining it? <u>That</u> sounds like a Plan!

~~~

Let's walk again, Isaac. Let's look at the trees and the sky and all of Creation that stands before us. Such a fabulous Creation it is. The trees reach up their leaves, each swaying a song of thanksgiving. Each tree so perfect in design, so glorious in full autumn dress with the midday sun glowing. Look there, Isaac. That is a sugar maple, brilliant yellow-gold. See? Yellow! Or ye-wo, that's good! And look here! This forsythia bush is turning red and blooming again at the same time! How can that be? *I will make all things new.* God, please. I'm not asking You to leave me alone, but please, no more revelations just now. *My child, my promises I cannot break. You asked, I answered. You have cleared your internal sending and receiving instrument, and so you hear My voice in response whenever you send to Me your signal. When you ask, I will answer.* Well, then, is it possible to turn You down? **I can hear God laughing!** *Yes, my child! Simply busy your mind with your everyday thoughts; tune yourself down to the mundane matters of your human existence. These things I have given to you also; your human responsibilities. These "matters" will maintain your split mind. The split mind, still perceiving opposites, is useful for you while you live in a material dimension.*

Here I go again; I am "watching" my consciousness going toward God-mind while at the same time I am fully conscious of walking on the blacktop pavement, pushing the stroller, chatting with Isaac. I am willing, God. I want it ALL. *Ahhh, my sweet beloved child. It is my great delight to give it ALL to you.* In God-consciousness, my hands are lifted and my body posture is of total surrender. I feel my consciousness "self" tumbling in the great river of consciousness, backwards, forwards, bobbing to the surface and finally face-up to the Light that bathes the river and is unified with the river. All the sparkling glints of light upon the water are faces! Faces of others breaking free of the darkness and turbulence that is also one with the water and the Light. My human body is gasping for air but my spirit self is laughing! The water is getting smoother and glassier, all the faces coming together into the One Great Light. Still, we are all individual Lights of this Great Light. The water has become an infinite pool of Peace. There are no edges, yet there are trees and ferns, marvelous water flowers creating "shade" of a sort. *My children hide from the Light beneath the flowers. Sometimes, even in the bliss of Oneness, you too will feel the need to shelter yourself from MY INTENSITY. I tell you, my child, it is My Will to flood you with Love beyond your wildest imaginings.* God, how does this work? How is it that I can see this Light as One, yet still as millions, trillions of individual lights?

My darling child, don't you see? This is the end of opposites I have discussed in so many of your books! You particularly appreciate the description of the end of opposites in "A Course in Miracles", remember? When you, in your sweet delight, notice that there are no edges, yet curiously you still perceive a shape, what you are really noticing is that there is no before and no after. There is only One. Your human perceptions will not serve (except to delight) in the dimensions you seek to know. Do you remember the meditation wherein you walked a path of black and white tiles that became one marvelous whole Light that astounded you? Yes. Completely indescribable, yet so very real. *Remember too the time you hugged my child Wanda in Chattanooga?* Oh Yes!! Wanda is a beautiful black woman, a wonderful Christ spirit. That day I realized the fantastic "white" light that she is, and the light was so wonderfully radiating from her smooth dark skin. The image was so striking. The "opposites" made for a greater wholeness, somehow.

16

These opposites have been the human mind game. The end of separation naturally is the ending of all opposing thought. Such a game we have played! You remember I am quoted as saying "God's promises are YEA and AMEN" and this is Truth. The "Yea" is such wonderful word - one of My favorites. For YEA includes All Things, the visible and invisible: all the Good I have stored up for you. I draw you relentlessly, I pursue you with all My Might, that you will come into the realizations and revelations, the visions and the knowings of My Unimaginable Love for you, for the YEA will draw you into complete knowing of Me. AMEN! This is the knowable beginning and the end that you travel in consciousness - from separation to Unity. You go away and come back, and I meet you at the gate with a wink and a hug. Then we have a FEAST. My Beloved Child, I AM the high, I AM the thrill, I AM All you have ever wanted. Once you grasp the Idea that All is Consciousness, your innate ability to approach Christ Mind is activated. Then is the quickening upon you.

The quickening! That is ascension! My body is vibrating with a new energy; this energy is pulsing into my physical body from above and below; I am drawing this energy into my body with my very breaths, my very steps upon the pavement. It is blueness and whiteness, glistening energy glowing on me and in me and upon every thing I see! Oh the vividness of the colors! The brilliance - I feel that I need to squint against this Light but I want to see it all so my eyes are wide open - oh! It is not just my physical eyes that are wide open but my third eye is also fully functioning...I just realized that! There is **so much more, so much more, to see!** And Thank You God, I can still walk, even with You trying to knock me to my knees again! I feel as if I am fully present in my body for the first time in my life. You are Holiness, God: Kodoish, kodoish, kodoish, Adonai T'sebayoth. I think I will turn this stroller around and head back home. I think we have walked a little over a mile now, Isaac. Water. Let's break for water, little boy, sweet little creation.

I don't see how it is possible, but the sunlight is more brilliant from this angle, heading back the way we came. The trees are swaying in the wonderful fragrant breeze, each with arms uplifted, each tree a magnificent, individual creation. We are so silly in our lives! Thinking for one nanosecond that God cannot love us, when She has made for us such a gorgeous Creation, just for our pleasure! Totally for our use!

17

Oh look Isaac, the doggies! There is the mama retriever, and the puppy. He's getting bigger, isn't he Isaac? They are licking Isaac's legs and he giggles. Dogs love this kid and have always come up to him in the stroller, even when he was an infant. It is his total trust, I think, that the dogs find appealing. I don't project negative energy, either, but they come to him. Come with us, dogs. The mother retriever has jet-black fur. She has some gray on her muzzle and wonderfully wise eyes. I think she is an angel being.

Here we go, up the hill and a little further to home. These Tennessee hills do get to a girl's legs, when she's pushing a stroller with a big little boy inside! When we get home you may play in the sandbox for a while, okay, Isaac? Then we will have lunch, you will have your nap, and I will have my meditation time. Ahh! What in Heaven can God possibly have in store today? What I would like is a replay of the dream that eludes me still. I wonder if I am unable to recall the dream because I have no frame of perceptual reference to describe it to myself. That has happened before; and only later, with expanded awareness, could meaning come through in a definable way. God knows. There's the driveway. Under the oak trees, around back. Isaac, you are free from the stroller straps, climb out and play in your sand. Mom is going to relax in the swing chair for a minute....

I feel God drawing my mind closer, closer to His consciousness. Maybe if I think of something mundane, something ordinary; maybe a list? Nothing mundane will stay in my head! Now what? My spirit self rides along in a curling spiral of the angel Michael's golden hair. His great wings lift us higher, and higher. I am left at the doorstep of a golden doorway. I am encased and surrounded by an ellipse of soft white light. I look at the door. It is of purest gold, with a velvety patina created by the touch of angels for eternity. The door is shaped as an oval rectangle, and is above me as if it were an angled attic door in a gabled roof, even though the door is not attached to anything. Indigo space surrounds the door. I am reaching for the door, but my hand does not move. I gather my faith about me, aware that my human consciousness has joined with the consciousness of spirit in this Holy place, and pray with full power GOD! I AM the open door! I **know** that the Image of God is behind that door. The door is gone! I am standing in the threshold of the open doorway, a stone doorway of emerald and

18

gold-veined stones. I feel a rush of Love Energy explode through my spine, chakra colors spinning all around my physical being. I see my Holy Self, standing upon white roses. A crown of Light is placed on my head, appearing where it already was. I can see this Self of Grace from all angles at once. There is an engraved sign on the stones above my head. It says "Christos Victorios".

Oh my God! My God! I need to breathe, breathe. Just look at the earth scenery for a minute. Breathe. That has to be a preview of things to come in meditation! Maybe I won't meditate after all. This is a too much even for me, God. Please. I know I have said I am ready, but.... no, I **do** desire to be of maximum use to Our Divine Will, Abba. Please be gentle. *Do you remember, My Child, how gently I broke it to you that you are one of my healers? Gently I piqued your interest, gently I blew the embers of that interest into full desire to do this service, gently I developed your physical, intellectual and emotional natures until that day when you commanded Me to Heal! And Our Will was done...and how gently we wept together in Joy.* Oh God, my God, you have melted me again.

Breathe with me, now...

It's great, isn't it, to read God's wonderful words of joy? Yeah, I didn't always feel that way, either. In my thirties I was using my talent with words to be cynical and sarcastic. I worked in a fairly large law office as a paralegal. Cynical and sarcastic worked extremely well in that environment! I want you to know that I'm just like you. I am completely human and I've made plenty of mistakes. I've blown relationships and wrecked cars and sabotaged plans and screamed and hollered; I've gossiped and cussed (still do that some) and cursed. I've also wondered and wandered, looking for "something". During the time I worked for the law firm, my husband and I had been happily married for several years, had two young healthy children, a nice home and all material comforts. The one thing I knew I was lacking was time, time for myself. Being supermom wasn't working for me at all. I slid into a fog of meaninglessness. I was numb. It was my own hell, because to me, there had to be meaning or life was pointless. God had me just where She wanted me. This is where everyone's story is the same. We get to the point where we are so low all we can do is reach up. And when you reach up, God is there; expectant, excited, delighted to see your face, finally looking to Her.

At lunchtime one day in 1991, I walked over to a musty old bookstore downtown, about two blocks from the law firm. The title "A Return to Love" by Marianne Williamson grabbed my attention. The title triggered something deep within me; I could feel it when I touched the paperback book. I bought it, feeling a little light-headed, and walked back to the office in a daze. At the time, I had no idea it was a best seller; reading about the relative popularity of books was way down on my list of things to do, and I wasn't home in time to watch Oprah, either.

I began reading in my office upon my return. I had the distinct feeling that I already knew this material. As I read it seemed as if the words were directly placed in my mind, and sometimes it was like reading a mirror of my own thoughts! Marianne's life was similar in many ways to my own, but she had found a way to figure it out and be happy. But she wasn't just happy in a way I could understand; she was truly, wholly, fully happy. How did she "get" that? She maintained that her peace had come from the experiences gained from taking a special course. "A Course in Miracles", that is. She quoted this source with regularity. These quotes were like lightning; like shouts in my mind. These passages had a life of their own. I realized I would be taking this course.

God was pleased with this decision (this being His will, after all) so very rapidly things began to happen to make taking the course possible. Gil, my husband, had found his calling, working with a hospice and received raises and commendations that made the need for me to work full time disappear. When I gave my notice at the law firm and the questions began, the people were amazingly envious of my intentions. I told them I was going to learn to meditate and quiet my mind, and to explore my spirituality, and that I was going to be mom to my children again.

After I left the law firm it took a little time for me to learn to stop and breathe, and when I did, I summoned up all my courage, went to the bookstore and bought a large blue book with onionskin pages, like a Bible. "A Course in Miracles". I arrogantly thought I could dive in and start reading the text portion. Wrong!! For the first time in my life, I was reading something I could not readily understand (we're not counting the Bible here). It was not because the words or even the concepts were difficult, but because every phrase spoke volumes of its' own. Every sentence opened pages in my mind long since dusty with dis-use. I gave up on the text and began dutifully reading the lessons alone. The lessons lead me through days and weeks and months of introspection, of emptying heart and mind and soul of old patterns of guilt and blame and unforgiveness and attack. About halfway through the lessons there is lesson 185: **I want the Peace of God.** This was my turning point. I most surely did (and do) want the Peace of God. From then on, I was keenly aware of the "Mighty Companions" promised by the course, to help guide the Way. I believe and thank God that "A Course in Miracles" is a direct gift from our God to all His children who have been wounded by the religions of the world.

Yeah, me too. I was wounded by religion. It seems rare in our world when a person is not wounded in this way. Our work is to stop perpetuating this wounding and to heal the wounded! The first church I remember well was a large, granite building with Gothic wood doors. It was a Presbyterian church in Indianapolis. This church was big enough to have a lovely children's chapel with a large stained glass window of Jesus with the children and baby animals. It was my favorite place. Mom attended services off and on but Dad rarely ever went to church. He was a believer, but couldn't stand hypocrisy. He probably would have embarrassed my mother if he had gone with her! My brother Jake and I passed the church every day on the way to school. Life was good. But then first Mom got sick, then just as she was getting better Dad got sick. Pretty soon my little brother Kurt, Jake and I were being shuttled back and forth to stay with relatives so that Mom could be at the hospital with Dad. We were young - Jake 10, me 9 and Kurt just 4. Nobody told us anything, just that Dad was sick and Mom needed time to be with him. We were sure Dad would get better and we would go home and life would resume. My Dad died of cancer one hot August day, that summer when I was 9. Then everyone had plenty to say! "Only the good die young." "God loved your Daddy so much that He called him home." "It's God's will that your Dad died." "You have to be strong for your Mommy. Remember, she's been sick too." Bewildered brother Jake heard this one, too – "You are the man of the family now."

Please don't misunderstand. The people who said these things to us are people who loved us dearly. This is what they were taught to say! They did not know what else to say. They did not realize that God would speak through them to us, to comfort us, if they had only believed. "Father, forgive them, for they know not what they do." Still, the words were deeply wounding. My little child's mind reeled and rebelled - the God who loves the children in the window wouldn't take away my beloved Daddy! But Daddy is gone - what kind of God are You? Is this Love? How can this be God? My questions brought me more platitudes. I cried, all right, but they were tears of anger, confusion and frustration. All the adults who said they loved me had betrayed me, and my Dad had abandoned me. I wanted to hate God. But I couldn't.

Lunchtime with God

It's 11:45. I'm going to head inside and fix my boy his lunch. Grilled cheese, little one? Some apple slices, a cup of milk. I think there are a small head of romaine lettuce and some leftover grilled chicken for me. Isaac, come inside and you can sit on the counter and watch me. Yes, you can play with the big bowls. Why do we buy him toys?

Oh my, here comes my neighbor up the driveway. He is a sweet man, but God, today? Sometimes I wish I could disappear. I don't know if I can bring my consciousness under control enough to deal with his life right now! What is he doing? Chuck has looked right at me (or was that through me?), standing on the back steps, and is now turning around and walking away...what is that about? Oh well. I will visit with him later and see what's up. Yeah sure, maybe I did disappear. *You were not visible to his eyes. That is truth.* Oh yeah, I have just dematerialized. *We need to work on this...simply wishing not to speak to someone is not the greatest use of this gift. However, since your underlying intent is to stay here in consciousness with Me....* God? You really are not being serious here. *Oh yes, my darling child! I am most sincere. Your physical body was not visible to Chuck. Libby, know this. Today you are the Living Christ. Today you have achieved the great goal of humankind. Today you are the Evolution. Today you are the Revolution. Today is My Day to be fully human in you; and your day to be fully Christ in Me. Today is the Word made Flesh once more. We have arrived; and We are One. Here and now.*

Oh God - ISAAC! Oh God he has fallen down the stone steps. Oh God please please hold him- Baby! Look at Mommy! His forehead is bleeding- oh God he has a nasty cut! *Kiss his forehead. Hold our baby in My Loving Arms.* Oh God - I love this little guy so much - take away his pain and heal his wound. Heal him, for it is Your Will that he be healed! God? He's not even crying - look! Isaac! **The blood has disappeared from you, from my hand, from my lips; your cut is gone!** Oh God, my God, I praise Your Holy Name. Thank you. Thank you! I am shaking...from...laughter! God! You have given Isaac and me a giggle fest in place of a disaster...You are my Awesome God.

Lunch. Really. God, do I need food? *Not unless you want food.* I was just kidding. *I wasn't.* Food. I do want food. I don't want to think about what You just said, or what has happened, or <u>anything at all</u> for a while. I will wash my hands and prepare our lunch. Colby cheese, Parmesan for me, the lettuce, the chicken, an apple, butter, Caesar dressing...milk? Find the chopping board, a knife...God, must I occupy my mind with words and names and meaninglessness? Is this how I keep Your Thoughts out of my mind? *That is a way. It is tedious.* No kidding. Is there another way to look at this dilemma for me? I feel unable to function as You keep revealing stuff to me, but I don't want to think meaningless thoughts to keep You out, either. *How is it that you feel unable to accomplish anything as I occupy your mind? Have you not accomplished every human function throughout your day so far? Where have you failed in your job as Libby the human today?* Man, You do get right to the point. No, I have done everything I set out to do so far today. Now that I see the truth of my day, it has actually been easier with You right here, talking to me this way. So once again I need do nothing. That's Yours, from "A Course in Miracles". *I remember.* Sorry. *No, it's really a great thought. Just stay in that thought as we go on together. It is a sustaining thought, a refreshing thought, especially good for you today. I will make all things new.* That's Mine, too. From the book with the red letters, any translation. I remember! *Relax and breathe through this day. I have planned it as a picnic for you, my child.*

My body-mind has continued the lunch making tasks and we are now ready to sit down. The table is ready, Isaac. Let's bow our heads and talk to God. Thank you, Mother Father God, for our lunch, for our bodies, for our minds, for our hearts. Thank You for health, and family, and Nashville, and all the world. Amen. Good boy! You said Amen too! Let's eat this nice lunch, my baby boy. Look! A bluebird, sitting on the steps out the window... isn't he beautiful? Maybe we will see a hummingbird or two while we eat. It is late in the year to see hummers, but you know God, don't you little one? And so Isaac smiles at me with that beatific smile, a little cherub!

Listen! There's that new song on the radio. I'm going to turn up the stereo, Isaac. Sit still and I will be right back. Ah, that chorus, I love those words..."and I, I really want to know You. I want to make each day a different way that I can show You how...I really want to love You"...Oh Lord, God, YOU ARE SINGING TO ME! I feel immersed in a great pool of golden-pink Love energy. Thank You, Mother God. I don't remember anyone singing to me since I was a very little girl, and Mom sang to me in her sweet mommy voice. You have melted me once again. But God, those were words sung to you! *It is the same. You too are Holy; You are My Beloved Child. We are One in Spirit. Surely you have noted my great delight in showing you how much I love you?* Yes, yes, a thousand times yes. I have felt you winking at me, too. That's such fun.

Isaac, do you want more apple, or do you want some grapes? Grapes...grapes sound like a good idea for me, too. I think we still have some of those lovely red grapes. More milk? Okay. Look at that! There is my capiz-shell angel hanging in the window over the kitchen sink, and for a minute I thought she was moving her wings, as if truly alive! Gil bought her for me in Blowing Rock, North Carolina that Christmas, back before I even knew God. She looks like you, he said when he bought her... she is milky white shell, her gown and body outlined in gold wire. She has painted light brown shoulder length hair, a sweet little face with the hint of a smile... her white light is shattered into colored fragments with her movement - she **is** moving! It's like a special effect in a movie, like Tinker bell in the Robin Williams' version of Peter Pan. Now I'm close to her - she's just made of shell, like always! That was strange. God, please don't tell me that one of Your angels inhabits that bit of shell and paint and wire.

Oh, did I get your attention? In truth, angelic spirits (extensions of Myself, Thoughts of Goodness with wings) inhabit all things, just as I inhabit all things. So yes, an angel does inhabit that bit of shell and paint and wire, and no, no specific angel inhabits that angel figure. I was having a bit of fun with your perceptions, trying out your expanded Christ vision. My what? Does this have something to do with the colors outside, the light phenomena that I perceived? *Yes, as you have noticed, my precious one, your physical sight is more highly attuned now.* God, my God, just this moment I feel woefully inadequate to receive all this from You...how in the world will I be able to use this expanded vision if I can't stop crying? *Ahh, the tears will end, until they begin again. You are bless-ed, my child. You are My Blessing to the world. Open your eyes to see their need, and draw them to Me.* I'm closing my eyes, God, just for now. I'm closing my eyes and shaking my head

Libby Maxey

- please go! I need to be human right now. Please, please, go from my consciousness...*take the grapes and milk to the table, little one. Tend our baby boy.* Ohh! **God has kissed my forehead!** Here, Isaac. Let's eat these grapes. Let's look out the window and be silly...okay, I will tell you the Three Bears story...sure! That'll work. Then I will wash your hands and face, and you can watch Sesame Street while I unload the dishwasher, unload the dryer and re-load the dryer. Then naptime for you, meditation time for me. Hmmm....perhaps I will incorporate that MerKaBa Meditation I found on the web yesterday. That was from a very clear and beautiful source. *Thank you.* As I thought! You probably guided me directly to that website, too! *You've caught me again.* I love You, God. *Yes, you truly do. Ditto.* Ha! From "Ghost"! I suppose You were the "ghostwriter"! *There is a ghost of a chance.* You have a great time with our puny attempt at language, don't You? *There are so many opportunities for humor within human languages. I have fun with all of them.*

My watch says 12:15. Isaac, you have 15 more minutes of Sesame Street, and then it's naptime. Here is your fresh blanket, fresh as a daisy from the dryer. He loves his blankie so, calls it "boo", and yes, you can have one cookie. I think we have oatmeal raisin.

Did I turn around too fast? I'm dizzy; there are stars before my eyes. No, not stars. *They are tetrahedrons.* They are what? Sometimes, God...I don't know. Sometimes you challenge my ability to believe what You're saying! *Sometimes?? Yet you know they are tetrahedrons. The energy units; the tetrahedrons, travel in waves. They comprise all energetic creation. Remember Ernestine's drawing?* Yes. My blessed teacher Ernestine Madaleine, in Fort Myers. She drew a vision she had of me, dressed in a white robe, inside an iridescent tetrahedron. That drawing is one of my few earth treasures. *Now combine that image with the image from your Internet travels yesterday.* The MerKaBa! Yes, the standing tetrahedron, as in Ernestine's drawing, with another inverted tetrahedron interlinked. The points of the tetrahedrons intersected in such a way as to appear as a Star of David from the top view or from below. I had read about MerKaBa in "The Keys of Enoch" and other books, but this is by far the best illustration. I guess it resonates the most. *Precisely! You have been promoted. While before your true being was out of reach to your consciousness and remained "as above" now you are enabled to draw the*

26

"as above" into your purified field "so below". The symbolism of the Star of David made manifest. The Word made flesh.

You know, God, it's one thing to pray for such wholeness, such grace; to make affirmations and to read about being "the Word made flesh" but to have You say it; well, if it didn't feel so natural and so right, I would probably be *in denial. That's where you would be. Your ego mind still screams NO! But you have reached beyond; you have agreed with Me that YOU ARE THE CHRIST IN EXPRESSION. In you I AM well pleased, my daughter.*

Ohhh! *Describe what you are feeling, My Daughter.* You are flooding my energy fields with such an intensity; my body feels as if singing tones are vibrating from my cells to You and from You into the very atoms of my physical vehicle. I feel somehow as if I am being electrocuted; my entire body is engulfed in this electrical vibratory current. I feel as if I must be shaking all over my physical body. It's kind of a rabbit-hole experience, too. My consciousness feels immense, while at the same time feeling only a minuscule part of the All. There is a tingling numbness all over my physical vehicle and my ego mind has absolutely no control over my body. My hands are upraised, receiving; my palms and the soles of my feet are especially warm and tingling. I feel as if I cannot possibly live through this, somehow, but I have never felt more alive. In this Your Presence, I know I know myself to be the Christ. I FEEL YOU, GOD, AND I SEE THAT IT IS YOU. In this place, I feel satisfied, filled, whole, protected, free; yet I am unable to move my body except in worship to You, the Unmoved Mover, the King of Kings. I love You, My God. I love to be in Your Presence. Godfre Ray King described this field of energy as the "electronic Presence" and that is about as apt as English can get. I can't wait to find out how having sex feels in this field! *That figures. Looking for a better high already.* I am so happy in Your Presence. Thank you for leading me here.

Go get a Bible and read in Luke. Okay. I will check on Isaac and go back to the bedroom to *Isaac is playing with Me. We are playing kitty cat.* I just heard Isaac say "meow"! God you are so awesome! *I try. Thanks for noticing.* Okay. I have "The Living Bible" and here's Luke - what chapter? Something relevant to the millennium, something prophetic, what? Luke 19, no, that's not it. Oh Geez, knowing You - where is it? Luke 11:11 perhaps? *Not today, but that was pretty good.* Oh here - Luke 21 is the chapter with Jesus' prophecy about now...*just point to the spot*...okay, Luke 21:20, then "But when you see Jerusalem surrounded by armies, then you will know that the time of its destruction has arrived" God, does it have to be that way? And here I am, weeping rivers of tears again. God! I visualized this happening! Please! *No! It is My Will that this be prevented by the prayers of my children. Prophecy is a warning about what the law will bring upon My Earth by the denial of Me in you.* I pray, God, that the horror of this idea that armies surround Jerusalem is removed from the consciousness of the people of the Earth; that Jerusalem is restored to a City of Light in the Kingdom of Heaven. And so it is, in the name of Christ, the name all children share. *Well spoken. Your word is very powerful, you know. I stand behind it when your intention is pure, as it is now.* But my little prayer? You can't mean that this whole Jerusalem situation is fixed now! *Would you believe it if Jesus were the one to utter that prayer?* Well yeah, that would do it. *Consider it done. Jesus is in agreement with you; as is Yogananda, Francis, St. Germaine, - is that enough?* Yes. I am humble. I am humbled. I am overwhelmed. What will You do next?

Get the newspaper. You want to read the paper? I don't like to read it...it's so negative. I think today's paper is already in the recycling stack in the garage. *Go, then. Isaac is still playing with me. We are zooming cars.* When do I get to hug You? That's what I really want, to be held in Your Arms, cradled.... *I AM holding you now.* Here it is, The Tennessean. Everything on the front page is local news, mainly local sporting news, again. Unless there's a political scandal.... well, I guess I'm being judgmental. But world and national events, it seems to me, should have more prominence on the front page. There was probably a tidal wave that killed 250 people and they have that buried on page 4. *257 people, to be accurate.* What? There really was a tidal wave?? *Yes, look on page 4.* Yes! "Tsunami Strikes Terror in Japan" Oh God, please mend the minds and bodies of those who are injured, and hold tenderly those who have passed into Your Presence. Heal Your precious children in Japan. Amen. *Again you have been joined in your prayer. This is how the world is healed, my child. Tell my children, plainly, to speak words of love and mercy into situations that seem to horrify. Your spoken words are the vehicle my Love travels the world upon. Be of One Mind, the Mind of Love.*

Look again at page 4. There, that article about Zimbabwe. Oh, Father, it is about the AIDS epidemic in Africa, in Zimbabwe, Zaire, Rwanda - all those places so devastated by human atrocities. This reporter is telling about the idea that white governments planned the destruction of the African nations by using this virus on the population. Can that be true? *You have realized before that all thoughts are made manifest in Creation. My Holy Thoughts, your thoughts, the thoughts of those who have not purified their hearts and minds; all thoughts create. It is the Law.* So you are saying "yes and no". *Exactly! Some have thought the destruction of the African nations (this is about resources, money and power here, of course) could be speeded up by the application of disease to the population. Others have used economic methods. Many others have prayed for peace, for healing and for the nations to turn to Me..........so all these thoughts are made manifest in Creation. My Will is for all my beloved children to be whole.* Then that is my prayer. God, please make your children whole, in all the nations of Africa. Turn their minds and hearts to Your Glorious Love. Amen.

It's got to be Isaac's naptime. Hey God, want to read Isaac a story? *"Guess How Much I Love You" is my choice. He remembers.* That is a wonderful story. Big Nutbrown Hare and Little Nutbrown Hare, trying to demonstrate their love for each other. *Kind of like you and Me.* Ah, God, there You go again with that feeling!

Isaac, sweetie, let's get you ready for your nap. You are such a cooperative little guy about naps, and about alone time in general. *He comes to Me.* Yes. He is Yours, God. I remember when I was the only one who knew about him, growing inside me. His spirit came to me several times in my meditations. He was so beautiful, such a golden glowing light. And his power! *This spirit that you have called Isaac required a Mom such as you. You I trust to raise him up, listening to My Spirit within. I trust in you because you trust in Me.*

Meditation

Isaac is quiet. *Come to Me now, my child.* Yes. Meditative music, a candle, my pillows, water, You, and me. *Yes. Breathe Me in, breathe Me out. Fall into Me. Be still, and listen to me now.* I feel myself falling, falling; like Alice down the rabbit hole, but I don't care...

Notice the patterns of Creation; the mountains, the stones, the soil, the waters; all that which grows upon and within the Earth Creation. The trees, the grasses, the glorious flowers, the foods that nourish. See the beauty of Earth's Creation. You are part of it. You are all of Creation. Breathe. Breathe. Breathe. This magnificent Earth Creation is you, and yours. It is but a small part of God. Be one with Earth Creation. Breathe.

Images rush into my consciousness, like slides, only multi-dimensional. Beautiful earth images; jungles, mountains, the sky, oceans, lakes, waterfalls; some look like the wonderful, lush paintings of the movie "What Dreams May Come", some appear as straight from National Geographic! Now more and more images are of trees, and lovely plants, flowers, growing foods: all radiant with Life, glowing with the Love of God. For the beauty of the earth, for the beauty of the sky, for the Love which from our birth, over and around us lies. Lord of all, to Thee we raise this our hymn of grateful praise! I weep with the majesty of Your beauty, Eternal God. **I AM** part of it, and all of it, clothed here in the total appreciation and awe of Earth Creation!

Notice the animal kingdom in all its' diversity. Beauty, fierceness, and passion: life given animation, matter infused with Spirit. From amoeba to worm to squirrel to bird to chimpanzee to elephant to whale. Remember the dinosaurs? You were there, too. Be one with it. All of it is you, and yours. This animal creation is but a small part of God. Breathe. Breathe. Breathe.

Now images of animals flood my senses. I feel the lion's breath and the dusty breeze created from the shaking of his great head...see the elephant families, the families of cows, grazing free! We have not been kind to cows; I feel their immense sorrow. The animals cry out for human kindness and compassion. Truly they are our four-legged brothers. I see the earth teeming with wild creatures, happy and free, bringers of beauty and joy and boundless energy.

I hear all the animal sounds, as a symphony of raucous abandon. I feel the thundering of the herd of dinosaurs - Geez! It looks like I've stepped right into the scene from "Jurassic Park" Now time is telescoping and all the animals are blended into the One Spirit that created them...I am caught up, merged with that One Spirit, wild and free...

Look at your body. Feel you heart, beating with the beat of My Own Heart. Think with your mind. Breathe! Be in gratitude for consciousness, that we may be partners in the Creation. Be in gratitude for all human creation, for brothers and sisters, mothers and fathers and children, aunts and uncles and grands and greats, cousins and friends and everyone seen. All those who have crossed your path, all those seen on television, in books and magazines; all those you have imagined. All are gifts of my Love to you, gifts of learning. Human creation is you, and yours. Be one with all human creation. Be one with all humanity, be love for all humanity. Be Love. Breathe. Breathe. Breathe. Human creation is to be One, in full consciousness. Be fully conscious. Be One. Grow. Expand. Breathe. Breathe. Breathe.

The miracle of my body, given as a gift for my use. Thank You! Oh, and I do so **thank You** for my consciousness, this fabulous, expanding, Divine knowing that You share with me. And now images of people, all the people I know, who have passed by me on this journey...they are all so beautiful. I can gaze into their eyes here in my consciousness, something that most will not allow in their human-ness. Magazine covers, television screens; these images whiz by my consciousness...OH! There is an Image, and another! THERE IS THE IMAGE OF JESUS THAT I CUT FROM A MAGAZINE, and all the people I have ever known or seen are now blending into that Face, that Likeness. We are truly all One: the Christ Spirit.

Notice the patterns of Spirit made flesh. Thought creates. Human thought, purified, creates perfectly. Human thought, at-one in God-Thought. At-one-ment. Breathe. Breathe. Breathe.

Mother Mary, it is You! *Welcome, little one.* And Yogananda, so beautiful, so serene; and here is Francis, Saint Francis, so humble; such Holiness. Why are all of you standing? *We honor you.* Saint Germaine stands before me, looking into my eyes. He gently grasps both my hands, never dropping my gaze. Violet rays, faceted

31

rays in glorious, myriad shades of violet colors pierce my being, cleansing away all that is not God.... I feel so refreshed, so new. I am clothed in Light.

Yes! You are clothed in Light. Look around you. There is an elliptical light surrounding you, an egg of Light, the Essenes would say. You have created it, and it is you. It is prana, life. It is the perfection of whiteness, it is golden light. It is the Limitless Light, which comprises Me. It is the Limitless Light, which comprises you. Today the assembly honors you, because You are Holy. My Child, You are the Christ, in Who I AM well pleased!

Of all the wonderful images I have seen - Oh Father! Thank You for eyes to see and ears to hear! Saints and Mighty Ascended Masters are surrounded by their individual "eggs of Light", marvelous colors, mingling iridescences flowing within...no, the light has an organic look to it, somehow...like the images I have seen of neurological activity in the brain...and also the patterns are intricate mandalas around each Divine Being...now I see the patterns and lights between and among the Beings and with me! It is happening in my own Light! The Light rings and sings - it is Divine Thought! Oh, how Glorious!

Feel the cocoon of Light surrounding You. Your cells, filled with Light. Your DNA expanded. The DNA; that is the neurological connection you share with your brothers and sisters. That patterning, the mandala is strengthened when your mind is aligned with Mine and with your brothers and sisters, just as You have seen. **Why are you capitalizing "you" when You refer to me?** *Because You are Holy. Because I honor You. This is what I want to do for ALL MY CHILDREN - DRAW THEM TO DIVINITY. HAVE I NOT SAID, YE ARE GODS?* But we don't capitalize pronouns for any humans, except Jesus...OH! You are saying I AM now a Christ? *Yes, for a while now I have been saying that...*

A beautiful Being comes toward me. He is dressed in a creamy white robe, with a hooded cowl covering His face. White-gold light streams from His face nevertheless. He bows His head toward me, with a coy and courtly manner, and places in my cupped hands a red stone, warm and smooth. The stone fills my hands with warmth and weight. As I look at the stone, it becomes a marvelous ruby of uncountable facets, indescribably beautiful. Watching, the ruby becomes a rose, while remaining a ruby! The rose is soft and the petals velvety, but still it is a crystalline faceted ruby! Again it changes before my gaze, and the rose opens to reveal an **eye**, deep and compassionate, filled with Love....Who gives me this rose? I ask, but the Being is walking away, shoulders quaking gently as He laughs, silent.

This beautiful treasure, this ruby-rose, has again become a warm, smooth stone. I place it in the pocket of my garment. Thank you, God, for this treasure. What has this prepared me to see?

Lord Christ stands before me in an immense and glorious cloud of versa-colored Fire. He is at once a magnificent Angel; a Dove of Light; a Lion roaring with Power and Might; Jesus, the Lamb; and Christ, the Love of God. HE HAS COME in Power and Glory. His voice thunders like a shout in my soul, yet whispers *Many times you have come, Blessed One, offering to God your heart, your mind, your soul. You have endeavored to live by the One Law, to love God, neighbor, and self as One. Now all is added unto You, Beloved Child of God. This is where you say "Beam me up, Scottie!" or "Energize!" and You become the Ascension in the Light, as You have so often affirmed. Still, You can choose to return to your human state...*No! This is the perfection of my one goal! *That's what We thought! So again, Child of Light, is it Your Will to surrender to the One Will?* Mercy flows from Him, pouring from every cell of His Divine Body. I am kneeling before His Presence, cleansed, emptied and naked. Light flows from Him like a warm wind. I answer Him. I give You all that I am; use me. Without You I am not. I want to know God as You know God. I give You everything...Energize!

In that thought I am propelled into His Being. He clasps me to Him, our entire Being-ness merging, yet I can feel the weave of His garment next to my cheek. He wears a woven coat of every color, like a tapestry woven entirely of souls! We are moving in an open vehicle at extreme speed, traveling down a roadway that is lined with marvelous buildings constructed of soft, prana pink living stone. There are marvelous flowers cascading from windows, the sounds of people talking and laughing, tinkling glass. All sounds blend together in a perfect, seamless harmony, a song of joy. The energy of Oneness coordinates all the sights and sounds in a symphony of expanding wonder...this is Divine Order! The trees sway in this intent of Love. The architecture reminds me of a

Libby Maxey

street in Israel, Jerusalem maybe...this is the New Jerusalem! Lord
Christ chuckles with delight at my discovery, His happiness for
me bubbling from His Holy face. I glance down at the roadway
we travel upon. It looks like a golden mirror...gold! *Very good for
magnetic conductivity, We find.* He is laughing with Divine Joy, mirth
spilling from His beautiful eyes.

We come to a gate and smoothly click through it, traveling now
in rolling hills and green meadows, flowering trees all around. I see
orange trees, figs and date palms, almond trees, all blossoming and
bearing fruit at the same time. The sky is deeply indigo night, yet it
is clear and pristine day simultaneously. The sky is singing a song
like laughter, and all creation joins in. We pass a beautiful valley
that is littered with crosses of every description: rough wood, silver
and gold, iron and steel, many dark with bloodstains. Lord Christ
speaks: *I said to you once, take up your cross and follow Me! I say to you
now - Give up your belief in the cross of time and space. There is no death.
The Love of God is free!*

In that moment I stand alone, it seems, in a grand hallway, or so
it appears. There are gigantic marble columns all along both "sides",
although the columns are attached to nothing. This hallway goes
on and on, stretching beyond my imagination. I look left, between
two columns, and as I look the columns become jungle trees and
the expanse between the trees a vast and gorgeous rain forest, lush
and alive with creatures and plant life. The sounds of the jungle
are magnificent, earthy and wild. The colors are more intense than
I have seen with my eyes, the aroma of flowers overwhelming
in diversity and sweetness. This jungle seems infinite in itself! I
glance between two columns on my right, and the columns become
majestic fir trees, the scene becoming a vision of mountains and
sky, swirling snow drifting from the blueness of the pristine sky.
It is breathtaking and awesome; the Glory of God in mountain
form. I feel cold tears flowing from my eyes...I look again to the
left, and a vast desert scene commands my vision. I had no idea so
many plants and animals could thrive in such an arid place. This
is most beautiful; the colors muted yet subtly glowing. The sky is
very intensely blue, almost severe in its blueness. There are wispy
clouds that appear as angel wings. My mouth is dry. *This is Beauty.
I have preserved all Beauty for You, and for all my Beloveds.* It goes on,
and on, forever.

I feel myself moving forward along the hallway, and look left again. In this place are clouds, only clouds and sky, but the clouds are all clouds, all shapes, all types, all colors. Right again, and I see a solar system with two suns. That is not the solar system to which I am accustomed! It is magnificent, the symmetry and the song of Love created by the spinning planets. Onward I move again, faster now. In earth terms I know I have traveled many light years. There is a "rise" of sorts, and I rise up and up, into a glorious, dazzling whiteness. Closer and closer, I realize that there is an altar before me, immense beyond my ability to comprehend. I look and realize now that this altar is made up of Beings of Light, all in their positions of devotion to God. I look up as far as my vision (or is it my consciousness?) will allow. There is music; I turn my attention now toward the heavenly sound of singing. There are angelic voices surrounding me; the music is the beating of my heart. The sound soothes and nurtures me. Now there is One Being of Light before me; and I stand before this Being of Light. I know this although all I can see are beams of Light emanating from this Being from every cell. Each light beam is coming from an eye! I realize that each "eye" cell that I see is a representation for my own perceptive level or ability. Each cell represents a wholly receptive, fully sensate, totally knowing division within the Unity that is this Great Being of Light. *Look and see the Truth, Child!* My God! My God! How I love Thee! This Being is my God-self! *Yes! You see truly, Beloved.*

~~~

Whoa! Stop right there! I'm going to shake myself back to human awareness right now. I need to look around with my physical eyes. God, that could not be my own Self. That looked like what John the Beloved might have seen in his visions, or Ezekiel, or Isaiah. Not like something Libby would see. Not like something that You would reveal to me as being my own Self! *Yet it is so, my Beloved. It is so.* I need to get some water. I will be dehydrated from crying. And here's another thing, God. This is a wonderful, spectacular technicolor high that I'm on. I'm so very grateful, so filled with wonder. You are so exceedingly Great and Glorious. *Here comes the "but"!* Yes. Here comes the "but". Each time I've been filled with Your Glory, with the Holy Spirit; each time I've had a wondrous vision or a fabulous, mind-expanding experience – every time there has been a period of depression, of downtime following on

35

the heels of the experience. It seems the greater the experience, the deeper the pit. The last time I was filled with the Holy Spirit during the communion service at church, I had a period of depression and doubt and separation that just tore me up! Feeling separate after being One with You is the worst.... and now today. After today, after these visions and experiences and feelings...well, what will follow all this? And do I even want to know?

You do indeed want to know. You desire Divine Knowledge of ETERNAL ONENESS. Yes! I do. But the duality part; that has to go. And You have promised that if I seek Divine Oneness that duality will be no more. I want that to be Truth **in my experience.** *And so it is. My Beloved Libby, Your ego consciousness still exists and resists, therefore duality persists in Your consciousness. Believe Me now. You are the Ascended Master You have desired to be for so long. Some perception of duality remains to be cleansed from what some call Your "aura", or the cloud of thought around your physical body, but that is all. What You have called Your "dream" was the gentle cleansing of the remaining duality from your consciousness and the last million or so cells of your physical body. The duality thoughts you now present to Me are from thought habits that you do not even believe! Go ahead. Check this out!*

You know, I **don't** believe these thoughts any more! They seem foreign to me, as if someone else planted them in my mind. It's like what "A Course in Miracles" did to me. After a while, I couldn't even remember **how** to worry or fret over a situation; or I would remember how I "used to" react in a given situation, but not remember what thoughts would lead me to that reaction. So You are telling me now that I will not experience separation any more? *AHHH! Finally She gets it! Yes, and Yes, and Yes forever! Lay down all the perceptions of opposites, Little One; they are only tricks of the mind. You have occupied Your Holy Self with these long enough, have You not? You have given Your Holy Self to My Teaching, and are now prepare to realize fully that OUR CONSCIOUSNESS IS ALL THERE IS. In human consciousness, left and right make perfect sense. Red and green are recognizable as separate colors. Up is up and down is down. All of these opposites rely, however, on space and time, which are also constructs of human consciousness. Without "space" between, left and right have no meaning. Without edges, red and green do not exist as separate colors. Up means nothing without down. God cannot be "out there" if there is not an "in here". There is only One of Us, Indivisible.*

We choose to "individuate" to expand OUR CONSCIOUSNESS. Give up your belief in time and space as reality, for they are but constructs of the race consciousness of humanity. They are but rules of a game We are folding up and putting away. Live now, My Child, by the One Law. I AM THAT I AM. The beginning is the ending. There is only One. There is only Love. Now when you feel the thought "I love You" You can know in Your Experience immediately, in the now-point, that You have given and received. It is finished.

If I had a cigarette, I would smoke it. *Manifest a cigarette, if you wish.* God, why do I even want a cigarette? *It is comical, isn't it? Perhaps it's the "it is finished" line.* Now You've got me laughing so hard I'm crying! I want to go outside and look at the daytime here in Nashville. *Good. I will enjoy it.* You are getting a real kick out of my day today, aren't You? *Yes, and Yes again! We've been waiting lifetimes, centuries, for this day. You know that, too.* Yes. In this lifetime alone, it has seemed a very long time coming. I am really getting used to having You this close to me in my consciousness. It is great. Please, please don't ever go away again. *Please, please don't ever go away again, my own Beloved Libby.* Here comes that great rush of Your Immense Love again. It is orgasmic in a total body/mind/spirit sort of way, but there must be a better way of saying it! *Orgasmic is good. You arouse My Love for You; I arouse Your Love for Me. It is orgasmic.* Perhaps We can coin a new phrase, just the same, because the feeling is more than orgasmic in so many ways...hmmmm...

When I was thirteen...

I don't know about you, but I need a break from all the God-stuff. It's hard to take in sometimes. When I was a teenager I had a hard time taking most everything in. I tried hard not to think. I tried hard not to cry. I kept my distance. After Dad's transition our family moved to a little town in southwestern Michigan. Mom took a part-time job as a church secretary, and I had a new best friend. She was just about as strange as me, and we were both new kids in a small town. She was the preacher's kid. That pretty much says it all.

We attended religion classes from the pastor, and both of us joined the church. We sang in the junior choir. That was good. But the class - well, I realized the futility of getting a straight answer to my questions the first night. I guess the thing that got to me most was the notion that any person who was not baptized according to the rules **of that church** would go to hell. But God, how can that be? I thought You said You are Love! Since everyone else was looking at me like I had sprouted another head, I just shut up.

When I was alone, I would spend time down the street and up the hill by the town cemetery. It was a rolling hill, covered with meadow grasses, sandy soil and tons of sand spurs. There was a straggly oak tree at the top of the hill. Many clouds rolled by while I watched; many sunsets passed while I leaned against the tree. Not too many kids hung around there because of the cemetery, but that didn't bother me. I loved the light that came to the top of that hill. This was the place I could be truly me. But the rest of the time, I was numb.

We studied other religions, other traditions in our Sunday school class. We went to church services at Lutheran and Baptist churches. We attended Greek Orthodox and Catholic churches. I thought it was all absolutely fascinating and the ceremonies were beautiful. But the lesson taught was that these other religious ideas were wrong. The doctrine of our religion was the Only True Method of eventually, maybe reaching God. I knew it was bullshit. But we got to have breakfast out after every church visit. I kept quiet. Religion got colder and colder to me.

I was a teenager in a tiny little town with little to do. This was the 70's. You guessed it! We all partied, and partied, and partied. Summers went by in a purple haze. My friend the preacher's kid was out of control. She went off the deep end, quaaludes and seconal her drugs of choice. She was dating an older guy whom her father the pastor deeply distrusted, and with good reason. The boyfriend was her dealer. It was an anxious time, and I feared for her. I went to her dad the pastor and expressed my fear that she was going to **die.** Her dad, God's representative, was far more concerned that the boyfriend might be in her pants! I felt mighty betrayed, so I can only imagine how she felt.

But she didn't die. She became one of those strange Jesus freaks. That was even more baffling! I stayed away.

Due to my most fortunate ability to learn almost by osmosis, I graduated high school with honors and then attended a "hippie" college. That's how Grand Valley State College (now a major university in Michigan) was know then, because it was a cluster of five experimental colleges. I enrolled in William James College, basically centered on business and enterprise themes, computers and technology. I didn't really have a plan. But there, I met the challenge of my lifetime, my husband Gil. My initial reaction was to hate him. We both elected a course about labor relations and collective bargaining, and the class was in the dead of winter at 8 a.m. I lived in student housing, about a mile walk across campus. It was **damn cold.** Gil lived off campus and drove to class. I was one of two females in the class and had the biggest mouth, so I was a shoe-in to lead one of the collective bargaining teams. Gil led the other. WAR! He pissed me off right away by being warm and toasty, but then I found out he had Jack Daniel's and coffee in his thermos!

The following term we had another class together. It was spring now, and by some miracle we advanced from hate to love. I could tell him anything. We spent that spring in a warm fuzzy haze, our eyes clouded by real vision. One sunny day we went to a beautiful little nature park close to campus and hiked around. It was a sparkling day, little wildflowers pushing up through the sodden leaves, buds and leaflets all around in brilliant early greens. The air was so clean and fresh and full of life, we felt we could live on air alone. That day was the first time I touched heaven in full consciousness. But I

Libby Maxey

didn't know it. I had encountered Love, but I didn't recognize Him. I thought it was all Gil.

We took another class together in the fall. It was a kind of self-help psychology class in which we were to explore our pasts to determine why we were the way we were. Each person took a turn exposing his or her life story to the questioning of the professor and the class. Thank You God that this professor was a truly kind man! On my day, I lost it completely. I wailed about my dad, I cried over every guilty thought I had ever had. This release lasted well after class was over. The professor suggested that I write letters to my parents, telling them how I felt about all my stuff. To my astonishment I found I had no anger toward my mom, although I had directed plenty her way. I was hugely angry with my dad for abandoning me. And although this release was very helpful to me at the time, it did nothing to repair the anger I had with God. The professor made no suggestion that I write to God.

2:15

I will open my eyes and try out my legs. The dryer has stopped so I will gather the clean clothes and take them to my bed for folding later. Laura and I can fold while Isaac jumps on the bed to knock over the stacks! My legs are sleeping soundly, it seems. I feel as if I am walking on a cloud! Hey, maybe I'm just that buoyant now - God? *Yes, You do have the power to defy the "law" of gravity. You accelerate Your atomic structure to ascend, decelerate to descend. You remember the lessons, don't You?* That capitalizing You do; it's disconcerting. Arrogant, somehow. *Let go of that perception. In Your ascended state, mortal humans will revere you as Holy. Retain humility; remember Your function in My Plan. You have been fully prepared, Beloved. Be Love. Amen.*

There. Dry clothes, no wrinkles. I will go outside and sit on the front steps for a little while. I wonder if Aaron left any Coke in the refrigerator? Yes! Thank You, God, for the icemaker invention. *My pleasure.* Mmmmm, the sunshine is glorious. October in Tennessee is wonderful. Thank You, Father God, Mother Earth, Holy Sun. What is that? About halfway between the horizon and the ceiling of sky - God? That isn't an airplane, because for the light to be that bright, I would hear it. It's almost like a small sun, traveling north to south, quite slowly. *A comet. One of the signs and wonders described in that Book and many others.* Oh! Thank You! I don't recall hearing about a comet becoming visible to earth just now. There are others coming around...*There are more dimensions than are visible with instruments humans currently have in use. This "comet" is an Emissary of Light, visible to My children born of the Spirit. Watch. Another comes.* Yes! It's following the same path, circling the Earth from north to south. What is the purpose of this Emissary? *Creating and maintaining communications, sending and receiving divine ideas, divine intentions, healing tones.* Wait a minute! James Twyman wrote about "Emissaries of Light". I have that book in the bedroom! In his book the Emissaries that had been living in bodies, building Your Peace energetically, ascended and now *You have seen their energies, a manifestation visible to You as a like mind.* I love it when You answer my thoughts like that! *When You ask, I will answer.* But I didn't even ask! *No matter. We are of Like Minds! Asking and answering are opposites, Child of Mine. In the infinite, eternal, Light-filled, all knowing Mind we share there are no opposites.*

I'm walking now, God. Back to my meditation pillow. What can happen next? You call me, I come. *Yes. I love it when You answer My thoughts like that.* Please! Overwhelm me after I sit down, okay? *Yes, then too.*

One more cleansing breath and ahhh, here is the Christ Consciousness. It is so wonderful to reach up and know this Peace. Thank You God, for this gift of rest in You. Oh! Here is my meditation group from when we lived in Fort Myers, Florida! We are joining together in meditation, listening to the being of Light who calls himself Bagwhan Kenobi. This being came to us several times and our beloved teacher Ernestine painted him. He is a being of beautiful wisdom, and came to us at a time of many changes for all of us in the group.

Ah! Now I am joined by the group at Unity Church here in Nashville and again, Bagwhan Kenobi is with us. Our combined consciousness has formed a glorious geometric shape, a jewel of marvelous shimmering facets with Bagwhan Kenobi's energetic assistance. This being has not left the side of God in all eternity. Is he following me? He projects laughter, peachy-gold energy, and I feel the energy penetrating my heart. Rather, it seems, I have been following him! Oh God, it is my fervent prayer that the changes that follow Bagwhan Kenobi's time are spiritual in nature, rather than the hurricanes and earthquakes of human experience that came last time! *You have asked, therefore it is so. Prayer works because what You ask, You ask of Your Self to give to Your Self. There is only One Self. Your Holy Self simply asks for the true inheritance; the abundance that is God. Christ asks of the Father, who is One with Him. I'm paraphrasing Me from "A Course in Miracles" here.* Yes. I recognize the lessons.

I am alone with God again. I feel another energetic geometric shape surrounding me. It is like a pyramid, except it has three triangular sides and rests also on a triangle. A tetrahedron, shaped perfectly to fit over my physical being. Oh! The merkabah exercises! I touch the flat triangular side facing me, and feel a pulsing energy not unlike an electric shock, but pleasant and reassuring like a heartbeat. It is made of a gel-like material that is curiously powdery as well, while feeling also like nothing at all! The other triangles follow the angles of my legs as I sit crossed-legged. The edges shimmer with a white fire, and the faces are smooth and clear; I am reminded of how Star Trek depicts a force field. And here is another tetrahedron descending, although there is no up or down. This one is turned the opposite direction and is point-down, with the flat face to my back and the joint of the other triangles to my front. This one has an electric blueness about it. Oh! The tetrahedrons have connected and where they connect they form the six-pointed Star of David, the symbol of "as above, so below". God, this is intense!

This feeling in my body - I am observing, aware of my body's reaction to this Mighty Presence within and surrounding me. I am sitting rigidly, my hands at an odd angle. My body is trembling all over and there is an electric numbness. My eyes are open wide and oh, God! My appearance is the appearance of a person in spiritual ecstasy, seeing glorious visions! My breath is shallow and rhythmic, machine-like. The consciousness personality of Libby is not home, she is Home. My body is in God's hands. I will leave it and Trust.

In consciousness I lift my hands over my head as a symbol of letting go. I am aware that my physical hands follow. I feel my consciousness-self tumbling over and over in waves of Consciousness; that same gel-like shimmering powder that I now see is composed entirely of tetrahedrons! I AM AT ONE with this Mighty Current. *The tetrahedrons are energy units.* I see my DNA strand, and it is also composed entirely of tetrahedrons. I do not have any concept of big or small in this moment. Somehow I am enabled to see all things including the light of the sun, as composed of tetrahedrons. These marvelous units of energy can form any other geometric shape, any curving surface, any flat surface: anything at all. I remember a line from a book about Jesus' life where He stated that "God can form anything from His Light; it is the most marvelous clay of all." I love Jesus. He is the Bridge between the two worlds we perceive, until the Bridge is needed not and the illusion of "between" leaves our Holy Minds. Ahhh! I feel Jesus' Light Body super-imposing over my physical body! My face is soft and round, yet I feel the angularity of His jaw. His softly curling hair touches my shoulders. His Presence is such sweetness...

I cannot tell if this is a dream, if I am still meditating, or if it is real. *Yes!* All lines of consciousness are blurred.... I am in a whirling cone of light - no, I am the cone of light. Oh! **I Am the cone of**

light! I AM the Limitless Light...slowly descending.... now I am in a different perspective - I am seeing with the eyes of my body, watching the cone of light descend. Where am I? The cone looks like a whirlwind, descending from the light of a window - oh! It is the window above the altar at Unity Center! There is Patricia, and Eileen. Patricia has stopped talking and is watching the light descend. She was talking about "the true inheritance of Christ life" but she is watching, watching. It seems like forever, like time is suspended, all words hanging in midair, expectantly hushed. The light has stopped whirling, and now I see my Body of Light step out, as if a tear in the light was created by my desire to appear in body. Tears stream down Patricia's lovely face. Eileen is beaming joy. I glance toward the piano, and Denise. "Come", I whisper, and she smiles "Yes!" with her eyes.

Ever practical Patricia cries out "Breathe!" to the assembly of souls. How she was able to speak, I don't know. The grace and majesty in the room, the magnificent Presence these wonderful Christ Spirits have drawn to them, are overwhelming. All eyes shine with the Light of God. I am so honored and humbled to be in their collective presence. Thank You, God, for this Privilege. I accept my role in Your Plan for Salvation. Thank You...there is another light descending - no! This light is flying! It is a dove! Oh God, what a wonderful surprise!

In my bliss, I am one with the Holy Dove! I am feathered wingedness, gloriously free. I am seeing with the eyes of the Dove of Peace; I see only Love. *Mount up with wings like eagles!* And I stretch my wings, glancing left to see that they are now eagle wings! I lift my regal head and leap into the air; only now I am leaping with the mighty strength of a lion. Somehow I am simultaneously all three animal manifestations! *Peace, Wisdom and Strength; such You are. You are Holy.* Again I am one with the dove, now flying over the main street in my hometown in Michigan. Such a lovely little town. Ah! I remember last summer when I visited here for my high school reunion. I felt very strongly as I drove away for the last time that I would not see this place again. Then later I realized that I would not see the little town again with the same consciousness. *And truly, Your consciousness is now Christ Consciousness, never again to be infected or affected by race consciousness, the consciousness of those who have not remembered. Your body is also changed; transmuted. Look!*

I look like a wisp of light, flying above the treetops. What am I saying? There is Harold's old house, now a bed and breakfast. We had a séance there once. Oh! My curiosity has taken me right inside on a ray of sunlight, right through the window! The window glass just gave way to the light I am. Now I am back over the main street...You know, this is not as interesting as I thought it might be, God. I still feel as I have felt since we moved to this tiny town - that I don't belong. This was a place of confusion for me. It is not my home. You are my Home. *I want to heal that old feeling for You, Beloved, for wherever I AM, You too are Home. And I AM here, as I AM all places.* Now I am flying through the window of the Presbyterian Church. It looks the same! What is this, God, 1973? There is the pastor. He hurt me, God. *Choose once again.* Now I am seventeen, sitting in a chair in his office - oh God, not this! His daughter and I are close friends, and I am here to tell him that she is about to overdose on seconal. He will ignore what I am saying to him, choosing instead to question me about her boyfriend's sexual interest in her! *Choose once again, Beloved Child.* Oh God, the wave of compassion and forgiveness that has washed over my being.... Yes! I choose to thank pastor for teaching me about You! And truly, he did teach me a great lesson that day. I learned that what I want in a True Parent is uncompromising, unconditional Love, not the small pettiness of grasping human love, even from someone who calls himself Your own representative! I send you God's Blessings, pastor. Thank you, Brother. Oh my! His Spirit Self has risen up from the chair, and is merging with my Spirit Self! Forgiveness has made us One...I feel myself falling backwards; the images of this scene are shattering like glass, and fading into Light.

What is that smell? Oh God, I don't like that smell, or this sickly green color. Where am I? I feel small and alone; my shoes are new and tight on my feet. My collar is scratchy and I want to fidget. Where am I? I am going up - oh! This is an old elevator. No! No! No! Not this place, please, God...I thought I was finished with this place...I have forgiven my Dad, and my Mom. *Choose once again, Sweet Little Child, look with the eyes of Christ. Lift Your Vision from the little girl's perspective and choose once again.* There is Mom, sitting by his hospital bed. That can't be my Daddy. My Daddy doesn't cry like that. Mom is motioning me to walk to her. Little Libby, nine years old; so very innocent. So very curious. She has realized that her Daddy does indeed lie in that bed. Those are his eyes. He is so thin. He has both his arms strapped to wooden boards, with an IV drip in each arm. His hair is longer than I have ever seen it. I didn't know it curled like that! What is wrong with my Daddy? They told us he has cancer, but no one told me he was sick like this; but how could they? I don't know anything about sickness. I'm a little girl. This is so strange, to be truly here in this room; to feel myself as the little girl, to now know the whole situation, and to also have this expansive compassion for the whole scene. *Look at your father.* My vision is now over his bed and I look down upon - **My God! He is crucified! He died that I might come into Your Consciousness! He is looking back at me...he knows that I know!** Why did he do this, God? *He came to show you there is no death.* But he died! He left me! I felt so betrayed by him, by You, by everyone in my family, by my neighbors - everyone! Not one person told me that he was dying!

Choose once again. What? That is what happened to me! *Choose to see differently.* Whoa! Now my consciousness is inside my Mom's eyes! Oh God, she is a mountain of confusion, of sadness, of despair. She doesn't have any idea what to do or to say to me. All she knows is that Dad wanted to see me one last time, so she brought me here. I had to be sneaked in, because the hospital doesn't allow anyone under 14 to visit. My beautiful, compassionate mother...she didn't have any intention that I would be betrayed. Oh God! Betrayal is my perception, not reality. *The idea of "to leave" is also perception, Beloved.* But God, Daddy was gone to me. His image even left my mind; he didn't visit my dreams. That was truly death, to me.

Here comes another major rush of Your Divine Energy. What are You showing me now? What is this darkness? Why are You silent? Where are You? God? God! Oh my God! This is a rush of fear! God? Where have you gone? Oh God, Oh God, **don't leave me!!**

I will never leave You, nor forsake You, nor betray You. Just where would I go, my Daughter? I Am all things, I Am everywhere present. I Am You, I Am all persons. I Am the earth, the moon, the stars. The Image of Me will not fade from Your mind, for I Am You. When You look upon the autumn trees, I Am there. When the sunlight kisses Your face, know that I Am there. This one fear; that I would leave You as Your earthly father did; is the last veil before Your eyes. It is also the reason You have so passionately sought My Face. For if You see Me, I cannot be gone from You. If You see Me, I cannot be gone from You.

46

My Daddy is rising from the bed! He is shaking off the IV tubes and ripping out the needles; he is laughing and crying; his face is flushed with happiness! I can see him! I see his face! He is not gone from me any more...Mom is incredulous; now she is laughing hilariously! Oh Thank You, God! My little child Libby is healed, she is whole. The whole story makes sense now. *And a little child shall lead them....*

Our innocence shall lead each of us to You! *It is touching the innocence, awakening the little child's imagination; that is Your Task, Beloved Mine.* Oh Wonderful God, I accept! In this fullness of Your Spirit, I accept. God, is this how I, if I be lifted up, will draw all souls to You? I have said this prayer; spoken this affirmation so many times without really knowing what I meant. This is it, isn't it?

So? When do I see Your Holy Face? *You have seen Me, Child. When You are fully prepared, You will remember. Soon.*

I think I have brain freeze...

Gil and I graduated and got married. We had a double wedding with our dear friends Bill and Marcia. Gil and Bill had been friends for years and had made bets against each other about who would get married first. To cancel the bets we all got married at the same time! The day was lovely, the setting charming. A butterfly landed on the minister's shoulder during the vows and stayed for the rest of the ceremony.

Newly married college graduates, we had good jobs, money. We lived the material life, buying furniture and cars and vacations and parties and fun. We got a puppy. We had lots of friends and freedom. We went to Florida one February, and there, Gil told me he wanted to start a business in Florida. He hated the Midwest and the cold winters. I was 23 and it never occurred to me that we might fail; that we might not be able to continue the lifestyle to which I had become accustomed...nor did the cost of flying seem high from the position of having the money to take the trip!

It was 1980. Jimmy Carter was President. Gilbert's business, an infant and children's clothing outlet store (these were the pre-outlet mall days) was well received at first. We had invited our friends Bill and Marcia to come to Florida and share in the business. We all stayed together in a three-bedroom house. We had some great times there, but as the business floundered, so did relationships. I fell back into the mode of trying not to think, trying not to care; distancing myself from those around me and wanting desperately to go "home", but realizing vaguely that mom's house in Michigan wasn't it.

The business closed; lives separated. Gil and I moved into a very strange apartment complex, the people living around us reflecting starkly back to us how far we had fallen. I hated my job in the insurance agency. I felt trapped. We were financially strapped...but God was at work. Gil kept the computer from the store and soon had a thriving business helping other small business owners with the new technology, selling, installing and maintaining mini-computers. There was almost no competition. We hired college computer programmers and had a great time with it.

Baby boy Aaron was my second glimpse of God. I was one of the five new mothers in an over-crowded maternity ward, babies and visitors, monitors and nurses and all the other noises. But that first morning they brought him to me, I was nowhere but in the heart of God. I can say that now, looking back, because I have been there consciously since. At the time, the rush of Love that ran through me was a current, a torrent. I was changed. I didn't know it, but He had given me a small dose of how He feels for me, perfectly content with my notion that this was the love I had for Aaron!

Our little computer business was killed by overwhelming, overnight competition very soon after Aaron was born. Three computer giants opened retail stores in our area and suddenly we couldn't compete. Gil moved into managing one of the new computer stores, but our financial burdens were severe. I tried to be happy, and I was truly delighted being Aaron's mom. He was sweet and adorable. Life seemed hard, though. Gilbert and I had little time together. He was working long hours, maybe to make up for what he considered "his" failures. But he is a natural optimist, and tried to help me see the positives. I tried to be positive, but always there was a lack. I presumed the lack was my own failure. He tried to get me to set goals, but for all my supposed intelligence I had no idea how to set a goal. I had no clue what was missing that I could therefore be wanting from my life. I knew I was not happy in Florida. I held on to that.

Our Laura was born on the last full moon of December 1985. I so wanted that rush of love, but instead got a jolt of recognition. I felt guilty that I didn't have the overwhelming rush of love, as if I could somehow manufacture it. God was making me hunger for Him.

Aaron was 6 and Laura 3 when I went back to work full-time. One of Gil's good friends was an attorney and he suggested that I look into the paralegal business. He suggested two law firms and I wrote two letters, deciding in my mind which law firm I really preferred in advance. I got the exact job I wanted, at the right firm. I felt powerful. Perhaps I could set goals, even though what I had done seemed more a plan than a goal. Whatever.

The lawyers liked my sponge-like mind and my quick, sarcastic wit. The kids were doing well in school and day care. Gil still worked the long hours. Gradually I began to feel as if I was working 'round the clock, dreaming of lists and tasks undone after I collapsed in bed. I had less time to be unhappy with Florida, but I still allowed it to consume a great deal of my thought. Gilbert would ask me, totally frustrated, where do you want to go? I couldn't answer, because I didn't know. I didn't know anything anymore, even though at work my ability to solve complex problems was prized by everyone around me. Meanwhile, my frustrations, my anxiety, the rootlessness, the meaninglessness - these all grew like a jungle around my consciousness. I was being choked off. I didn't want to live like this another day.

That was the day God got my attention, catching me with my sarcastic guard down, using words in that little paperback, " A Return to Love", to save my life. Thank God.

Time to look at a clock

Three-thirty. Time to make a snack for the older kids. They will be home shortly...hmm...little pizzas and some fruit. Isaac is stirring around in his little bed, too. Here are some English muffins, some pizza sauce, and the mozzarella...hmm...an apple and a banana. Assemble these pizzas, pop them in the microwave...by the way, God, the microwave thing was an awesome idea. Thanks for that. *My pleasure.* While I'm standing here, what will we have for dinner tonight? A spinach salad, yes, and the broccoli. Better steam some carrots with the broccoli for Laura. I will bake the chicken breasts and some potatoes. Yes, there is some sour cream for the potatoes, and some shredded cheddar for Aaron. That was easy! Isaac will do pretty well with that dinner, too.

Hello, Laura! Hi, Aaron - please close the door behind you, son. Snacks will be ready when the microwave buzzer sounds, okay? How was school? Laura is telling me about a girl who rides their bus that gets teased constantly by the older boys. No one seems to like her. Laura is very upset about this. I feel myself listening intently to Laura, gently answering her questions and guiding her to understanding. I observe myself looking at Laura, looking into her eyes. I observe my consciousness merging with her consciousness; I can see the girl on the bus. I am inside Laura's mind! Laura wants very much to help, but is not capable of inserting herself into the situation because she feels powerless to defend herself against the boys' teasing. Laura has just let this thought go! She released the problem to God! The thought is leaving her mind in a golden-pink bubble of light! This is awesome. *When You joined with her in compassion and love, Your consciousness raised hers to understanding. This is another form of "agreeing in prayer".* Cool!

There's the microwave buzzer. Here is your pizza, Aaron. Get some fruit, too. How was your day? Any homework? None tonight? Good. You can play with Isaac tonight and help Laura and Dad with him while I am at my Unity class. Thank you. Yes, you can get on the computer for now. Geez! I'm kind of dizzy - that was wild! My consciousness went zooming into a black hole thing and now I am within Aaron's consciousness. Oh! He's thinking about nanotechnology again, and that is what he wants to research on the web. *Aaron has a marvelous grasp of energy movement, of ebb and flow, of transference, of transcendence, too.* Yes! His consciousness is vastly different from the consciousness I am accustomed to, but it is beautiful. It is as if I am observing a mandala of fantastic intricacy, merged here with him. *The "black hole" You observed, Child of Mine, is Your shared connection, One to the Other.* As if I traveled along a nerve. *More like the movement of energy between brain cells, actually. I have caused You to view this energy transfer on "Nova"* Yes! Fascinating! So You're saying that we, as individuations of You, are as brain cells to Your Mind? *Indeed! And I desire to use **All My Brain Cells**, not just the 10% many of you are satisfied with!* Use me! *I AM, I AM, I AM, now that You are fully willing.* Sitting down! My knees are buckling again. I feel my consciousness separating from Aaron's. He acknowledges my departure with a wink!

And Isaac is wide-awake. Hello, baby boy! Time for a hug and a diaper change...the big kids are home. Do you want to have a snack with them too? How about a slice of cheese...there you are. Then we are going to fold clothes in Mommy's room. You can play tent on the bed when we're done, okay? Hey Laura, will you please help me with the folding? Come talk to me. The light in the bedroom is beautiful. I love the light at this time of day, about an hour before twilight. Laura is standing in the corner where my bookshelf is, with all my sacred pictures hanging above. The light on her is beautiful...she stands just under the picture of Jesus, the one I cut out from an old "Association for Research and Enlightenment" magazine from the Edgar Cayce foundation. I held that picture in an open-eye meditation once, and saw in that face all the faces of the people I have ever known, many of whom I had not remembered for years until that moment. It was an awesome experience. *That experience will turn inside out for You. Look.*

Laura glances my way and smiles sweetly - oh! The image of Jesus has stepped away from the wall and stands behind her, fully manifested, even His feet! God, I have never seen His feet before...Laura's eyes shift upward, and He merges His Being with hers, and His face looks out from her lovely little face! It is still her face, but His face also...Steven Spielberg could learn a lot from You, God. *Oh, he has. He is quite aware of the Source of all special effects.* Laura has her eyes closed in what must be a wonderful experience for her. How is it that a picture cut from a magazine could have this power? *I inspired the drawing of the image.* How is this not a "graven image"? *My Child, You do not worship the image itself, but what the image represents to You. Because I in-spired (breathed My Spirit in) every circumstance surrounding the drawing of the image, the intentions of all souls involved in the production of the drawing and the production of the magazine have co-created with Me a field of energy that accompanies every copy. I breathed it forth, through My Beloveds. To a person not in touch with these holy intentions, the sight of the image would be distasteful. But You receive, amplify and give away this same intention when You gaze upon the image. It is an image that is therefore also a similitude.*

What? Do you mean that it is an image because of the way it looks and a similitude because of the way it makes me feel? *Yes, that, but more than that, too. When you look at the picture of Jesus the Christ and you see not only that one image, but also many others; that is truly the image of Christ. An image that is ever changing but changelessly eternal. It is a similitude because to see the images merged as one image propels the consciousness into assimilating Divine Mind, to being truly similar to the image.*

Telephone. Laura, get it, will you? She hands the phone to me anyway. Hello, Virginia! She wants to talk about the chaplain program she's heading up at Unity Church. The program is in the planning stages, created to help the church grow while maintaining a familial atmosphere. We're also attending a class there together about the creation story and its' metaphysical meanings. And we pray together. That's the best part. *I agree.* Virginia has had so many horrendous, defeating experiences in her life. She is like a porcelain doll, shattered and repaired with glue. She has nourished Your Light within, and now she shines best from all her wounded places. *Lovely metaphor. Seems somehow familiar...*Oh, You. You know that I know it's all You!

Laura has taken Isaac to play in her room, now that the clothes are all folded. Next I need to prepare dinner, but I will sit here on the bed for a moment and breathe with You again. Loving Abba, guide my thoughts to Your Presence. Break the seals that keep me from You. Lift all the veils. Shatter the glass so that I see You face to face...

~~~

53

Libby Maxey

It is Jesus, my Yeshua! He is on the cross; His holy head hangs down. My consciousness is filled entirely with the view of His head. The cross, the surroundings of Golgotha and the crowd are implied, somehow. I love you so, my Brother. I am face to face with Him! He is pale, He is trembling. His body is in shock. His hair is matted, bloody and sweaty. Thorns have scratched His forehead deeply and there are bruises on His face. He glances at me. His eyes, His wonderful eyes, so soft, so liquid with compassion...our consciousness becomes one vision and I look out at the scene below the cross with Him...together we see the faces, some laughing, many weeping, some stone cold, some numb with the pain of this moment. *Father, forgive them, for they know not what they do...* we have spoken these words together, as one consciousness! He looks deeply into my being - and laughs! His form, released, rushes toward me and He enfolds me in His arms. I feel the body of Jesus touching me, as our minds and hearts merge as the Christ. Glory to God in the highest!

Can you listen to the truth of that day, Beloved? You ought to know - am I prepared for it? *Just checking. Actually, "they know not what they do" was my mantra throughout that terrible time. As the whip cracked, as they jeered and taunted me, as the wood bruised and tore my shoulder, as the sun burned my ripped flesh, as I trudged along, knees buckling, as the thorns jabbed into my throbbing head, as the ropes were lashed 'round my wrists and ankles, as the spikes bit through my flesh, over and over, when the cross was lifted and dropped agonizingly into place, as my muscles and tendons stretched and snapped, as the blood dripped from my wounds, as I trembled with cold and shock...*I am sobbing, gasping; pained beyond my wildest imaginings, Yeshua! Please stop!

He looks deeply into my eyes, compassion filling me entirely...*My lovely child, my sister, do you not see?* **I allowed all of it!** *I came to fulfill scripture. Our God keeps His Word. I agreed to all of it. Every moment. Have You not realized that I was able to de-materialize (ascend) my body at any time? I know that You have had this realization. When You read of me on the mountain, with Moses and Elijah, You knew. I could have left the scene when they came for me in the garden, or at any time after that. Had I willed it, I could have discarded my body (died) at any time as well. You also know that I had the capacity to block all of the pain of the crucifixion from my consciousness. As I was hanging there, some of the time I did that, I admit. But the crucifixion was the highest* *and best special effect Our God could use at the time. It was intended to heal the minds of the earth children so that they could see the power of their own beings and the grace of forgiveness. Instead, Jesus has been held up as unreachable, as something You are not. But again I declare in full truth that I AM Your elder brother in spirit, just as Jake is Your elder brother in the physical. If We are siblings, We are equals. Your inheritance is the same as mine. You are all that I AM.*

I have another task for You, Beloved. Will You accept? Yes, Jesus, I accept. But please, don't capitalize references to me anymore. I feel unworthy of that kind of honor; even though you say I am worthy. Do you know what I mean? *I truly do, indeed. You are familiar with the passages in the Bible when I ask, even plead, that humanity not deify me as Jesus. You cannot become that which you deify. Separation thoughts come from deification. There is duality. Becoming Christ means accepting the Christ self as unified consciousness. There is no "other" to worship. So here's the deal. You stop capitalizing references to me, as an individual, and I will stop capitalizing references to you as an individual. For the purpose of clarity, we will continue to capitalize the references to our Creator, and of course proper names. We agree that these references are from our shared state of awe; from our vast respect and honor and praise for the Eternal One. So truly we are now brother and sister! You have accepted our sameness, finally. Haven't you? Do we have a deal?*

Yes! Deal! Oh my God, Jesus, you are squeezing my hands! *Well, yeah! I have my little sister back, fully conscious! Praise God! I'm feeling very happy about that, okay?* Sure! I feel what I am feeling, and also what you are feeling, too. *Isn't it cool?* Cool doesn't begin to describe this high, though! *Yes, it's time language expanded to include how it feels to be in the unified consciousness. That's another lesson, though. We need to talk about the task at hand.* Oh yeah, the task I already accepted. What is it? *Return with me to the crucifixion scene. Look again upon the faces.* The faces, the people. I feel such compassion for all of them, the unawakened. *Remember the words I spoke then as the Christ I am.* Which words? You only spoke Truth as Christ. *Exactly. So what the unawakened souls attempted to do in crucifying the body of Jesus was to silence Truth, which is Eternal.* Yes, I see that. *One residual effect of the crucifixion was to implant this thought in race consciousness: I will be crucified for speaking Truth. As an example, think of the many times you have heard someone say "He will kill me if I tell him how I really feel!" Or how about "It would kill her to know the truth" How many times have*

55

you felt that strangled feeling when you held back truth? I couldn't begin to count! *Pray, my beloved, pray and believe for yourself and for all your selves that this core belief be eradicated from race consciousness. Being truthful (filled with Truth) brings freedom, not death! Interestingly, this core belief combined with personal identification with Jesus rather than with Christ self also manifests as the stigmata wounds.* Wow! I can see how that happens! Actually, the idea of crucifixion as even possible - that the eradication of the body could in any way eradicate the Life that resided for a time in that body - is a perception. *So true, Liberty. Actually death in any form is then a perception. Death is perceived as being "separated" from life, but that is not possible. You understand the depth of my request for your service. Your prayer becomes a prayer for the obliteration of death as a perception. Beloved John wrote about this "And I saw the holy city, new Jerusalem, coming out of heaven from God, prepared as a bride adorned for her husband; and I heard a loud voice from the throne saying "Behold, the dwelling of God is with men. He will dwell with them, and they shall be his people, and God himself will be with them; he will wipe away every tear from their eyes, **and** death shall be no more, neither shall there be mourning nor crying nor pain any more, for the former things have passed away."*

Okay, that'll be enough. Overload! There must be something I need to be doing...

I'll go make dinner

Yeah, dinner. I'll do that. I feel like I need to keep shaking my head to keep those last thoughts out. This can't be for me. How can I possibly be of any help in removing thoughts from <u>race consciousness</u> ? It just seems ridiculous. Now here I am standing over the sink, sobbing uncontrollably. What is this about? *All that is within your consciousness which conflicts with the great truths you are now internalizing is bubbling up to be healed, Liberty mine. You know how this process works. Your consciousness is now Christ consciousness and increases to include each soul you touch. You are now piercing veils of negativity that have been held in race consciousness for two thousand years. There is turbulence.* Yeah, turbulence. I must remember to stop asking questions for a while. What is that Liberty stuff about, anyway? Oh Geez, I've done it again.... cancel! Tell me later, okay God? *My pleasure.*

Chicken breasts, seasonings, olive oil, the potatoes. I think that's all I need to get started now. Oven 350. This is boring. I could do this without engaging my mind at all. I just don't want to go there right now. I feel like I will not exist somehow, like there is something huge lurking between me and the total freedom that would come if I really went there, all the way, with Him. Not just to the door, but opening the door and stepping all the way through, in faith. God, I am trusting. God, I am trusting. I know that I am coming up against things held in my consciousness from past lives, from pre-consciousness in this life, from negative imprinting in the consciousnesses of those around me. Oh Loving God, lift from my mind the unreal perceptions in race consciousness. Be Thou my vision in all things. Eliminate all pre-conscious and previous lifetime negative imprinting on the fabric of my consciousness. Fill me with your Grace. Remove fear of the unknown and unseen. Release your Divine Courage into my energy field. I let go; I surrender all that I am to the depths of my being. I am the fulfillment of my creation. I am the ascension in the Light. Amen.

Potatoes scrubbed, chicken seasoned, into the oven. I still need to chop the broccoli and the carrots and the salad stuff. Laura has taken Isaac over to the neighbor's house to see her girlfriend. She is such a sweet nurturing sister. It's now 4:45, so an hour for the baking stuff puts dinner at 6:00. The chaplain meeting is at 7:00. I'll call Gil to remind him of the meeting.

Voice mail again! Thank You God, I guess, for voice mail. It's not as easy to be thankful for voice mail as it is for icemakers and microwaves. I think now I'll get some iced tea and go outside and sit in the swing chair. God, are you with me? *Ah, here's my chance! What are you up to now, Yeshua? This is you, the non-capitalized you, isn't it? Very discerning of you, Liberty.* Oh yeah, that! The Liberty thing. Is that my new name, or something? Like Simon became Peter? *Actually more like Saul became Paul, but yes. Upon those to whom I give a new name, a new name written on a white stone, I will build my church. Peter is symbolic of the foundation stone.* Hold up now. Just what do you mean by "liberty"? *Look it up.* Okay! The dictionary is on the shelf by the computer.

Okay - here it is, the Merriam-Webster says: the quality or state of being free; the power to do as one pleases; freedom from physical restraint; freedom from arbitrary or despotic control; the positive enjoyment of various social, political or economic rights and privileges; the power of choice. Also, a right or immunity enjoyed by prescription or by grant, a privilege; permission to go freely within specified limits. The third definition is an action going beyond normal limits, as a breach of etiquette or propriety; risk or chance; a violation of rules or a deviation from standard practice; a distortion of fact. Finally, the fourth definition is a short authorized absence from naval duties. So, Yeshua, where do I fit in here? Which definition am I? *How do you define liberty?*

Well, I think it's freedom with maturity. It's when the ability to choose wisely accompanies the freedom to choose. *Lovely! Very well said. In spiritual terms, liberty is also a great privilege, granted by God our Father. It is His permission to go freely without limit of any kind. In God, liberty requires action beyond normal limits, breaching the boundaries, reaching beyond the distortion of human vision to see with the eyes of Christ. It is choosing to take a chance. It is about evolution. It is God's authorized Presence in all that you do and in who you are.* You have twisted Merriam-Webster. I love how you do that in the New York Times commercials. *Yes! That is I, too. I am surprised at your discerning, Liberty. But not to change the subject. You. The subject is you. You are now Liberty. You are at liberty to be Liberty.*

Are we finished with the dictionary? My body is weak in the knees again. The swing chair in the pine trees beckons. *Come with me again.* Where are we going? *Come with me to the New Jerusalem.* I see Laura and Isaac playing next door. The sunlight is at that perfect point in the day, when everything is sharp and focused. The sky is so perfectly blue. The breeze is whispering in the trees around me, and the chair feels as if it is a cloud. Ahhh, I breathe You in, God. I see You all around me. I see only You. I hear You all around me. I hear only You. I feel only You. There is only You, and You are all. I am one with God. I am one with God.

~~~

Over there - what is that? What is that I am seeing? Just there, beyond the focus of my eyes, I can see.... it's like I see the edge of time, a tear in visible space filled with a sparkling light. Our everyday reality superimposed over the True Reality - oh! Awesome! And what the...that's the pink bicycle I wanted for Christmas the year I turned six! And the stuffed koala I wanted.... and there is my royal blue Toyota Celica! There is a table dressed as for a great feast - there is an opulent abundance of everything I could possibly imagine! The stuff looks like a hologram; it's shimmery.... this is like the storehouse of everything I ever needed or wanted, waiting for me to ask for it; yet it is all implied, not manifested. In this moment I know that I know that this abundance is true for all beings. It is beautiful, glistening Light, waiting to be formed into whatever we desire.... oh my God, this is what You mean! This is the abundance of things hoped for! This is our good, heaped up, pressed down, shaken together and running over! And it exists, RIGHT HERE, AT MY FINGERTIPS!

Keep looking, keep your eyes open, child. I'm staring. I'm rigid with bliss again. I glance at my clothing to find that I am clothed in a white garment. I am not in Nashville anymore, and yet I see all the ordinary backyard surroundings. I also see <u>through</u> all the backyard surroundings. I am walking with Yeshua. He wears a garment similar to mine. Our feet are bare, and the grass caresses our feet. We approach a stone gate, with massive green and gold-veined marble stones. This is one of several gateways to the city we will enter - oh yes! Twelve gates.... Yeshua is sitting on the stone wall, beckoning me to rest with him. I settle beside him, my hands touching the stone...oh God! The stones! I can see the surging Life within them, the veins of green and gold pulsing with the heartbeat of God. The sparkling gem-like green looks like it is winking at us in the Light here. I can sense the intention of the stones - they live to serve God, and Yeshua, and me, in this moment. They support me, surrounding me with strength and purpose. Here, they separate one sacred space from another. The breeze lifts my hair, and I look around me. The trees, the grasses, and the flowers - all are vibrating with the same Life, the same intention to serve. The very stones will cry out, and their cry is "Holy, Holy, Holy is the Lord God of Hosts". This must be heaven, though I still see the backyard surroundings. Somehow the surroundings have all seamlessly come together in my consciousness. The gate is here, right in my own backyard!

What do you remember about the New Jerusalem? Suddenly a beautiful scene appears in my consciousness, an image of a fabulous banquet celebration. I recall hundreds, thousands of souls, gathered in a great hall. My dad, grandparents, all my spiritual heroes. Beings of Light from other civilizations attend, also. The room has walls of a sort, but is also open to the breezes. There is a wonderful tree surrounded by pools and fountains in the center of the hall. Beautiful gemstone tables in concentric circles ring the great tree. As I glance about, the tiniest thought of recognition or the smallest eye-to-eye connection brings about immediate joining with the other, until in one panoramic sweep I am joined in consciousness with everyone, and we all dwell together in Christ mind.

I must have been ready, for the teacher appeared

Whew. Together in Christ mind. But it had to happen, because that is the Law and the Promise. With guidance, I began to seek, earnestly. My soft-cover copy of "A Course in Miracles" grew worn; the places where my thumbs rested became smooth. I began to be aware of the Presence of God, and would often hear His "voice" in my mind with real recognition. Every time I went to the library or the bookstore God showed up. God showed up on billboards, in music, in casual conversation. I began to live.

Around that time, I found a "Mighty Companion" in the form of my wonderful teacher, Ernestine Madaleine. A truly great teacher, Ernestine consistently required that we seek our answers from within; that the truths of our own inner Christ were far greater than any truths she might speak. The first night of her beginning meditation class I apparently freaked out some of her students with what I experienced, so she moved me to the advanced class after that one incident. Then the expansive depths of meditation began to open to me, and in the unconditional love and acceptance of Ernestine's class, God began to reveal Truth in brilliant colors. Ernestine talked of the greater works, and I learned of universal ascension. I was entranced. I was enthralled. This was me.

Being located in Florida began to be a blessed time to learn of God. I even loved my break with meaning in this place I once hated, because I had returned to Truth...but I knew this place on the earth was not to be my earth home. Gilbert got a job offer in May 1995. It was with a for-profit hospice and home health care corporation with several locations in New England. There was a great title and a great salary and promises galore. It sounded too good to be true. God let me know that I was the observer in the situation, and I began to be aware that I was entering into a darkness, a testing phase in my spirit life. Gil took the job. The house went on the market. The kids went back to school. The house sold in October, but Gil's company, who had been renting an apartment for him and flying him home every other weekend, hadn't decided where they wanted him to locate. The area served by the corporation was quite large, and they were reorganizing as well. I rented a house in Florida, not wanting to move Aaron and Laura until we actually knew where we were moving!

Thanksgiving came around. I had been feeling weary, run-down. I thought it was stress. But I was pregnant. Gil and I had been very glad to see each other every other weekend! And now the promises of the new company began to collapse, one by one. First, no insurance for me, the baby, our older children. Things began to deteriorate rapidly upon his return to New England. His boss, the woman who had hired him, "resigned" in humiliation over some serious mental health issues. Gil was scrutinized. He was assigned to "puff up" some financial documents for a bank loan, but he refused. On December 31, 1995, Gil flew home to our rented house in Florida. He was without a job. I had to tell him that the rental on the house was ending too, as of January 31. Our landlady's aging parents were moving in so she could help them.

Now what? We had a month to figure things out. I felt curiously un-concerned, still mostly in the observer mode. I rested, basically. During this time, baby Isaac's spirit-self came to me several times. He has a strong and beautifully witty spirit; God told me he was a "Joshua" spirit, whatever that meant. The end of January came, and with no job prospects in the area, my dear Mom accepted our whole family into her small home in my Michigan high school town.

Aaron and Laura absolutely loved small town life. They thought it extremely cool to be able to walk around town at will! They were accepted immediately into their new schools. Having never seen snow, they were enthralled with the Michigan winter. Mom was still working full time, so I would have a good dinner ready when she got home. She loved that. We all got along extremely well for such small quarters. Mom and Gil have long been great pals, so that was a tremendous blessing. I kept house, read and rested, walked around town, visited old friends, visited with the neighbors, drove kids here and there. Gil scoured newspapers from Indianapolis to Atlanta and kept in contact with his many friends in the hospice movement. The savings were rapidly dwindling. Isaac was coming soon, too.

In March, Aunt Betty and Uncle Max sent the classified ads from their copy of the Nashville Tennessean with one ad circled. It was a regional type hospice management job based in Chattanooga, Tennessee. After a month of interviews and committee decisions,

Gilbert got the job. He moved to Chattanooga in April of 1996. The doctor said it was too late for me to move. Again, I stayed behind with the children. Isaac was born on May 28, 1996. His doctor, a born-again Christian, blessed him beautifully when he said, upon seeing his birth weight "Oh thank Heaven, he's 7-11!" It was awesome.

Isaac came to live with us, and the first weekend of July we drove to our rented home in Chattanooga. I felt fresh, kind of raw, as if I too were a newborn. Chattanooga is a wonderful small city. I had never met such charming, open people. It had never been my experience to have a long conversation with nearly everyone I met, but in Chattanooga, you need to be prepared to stop and visit with people. And be ready to eat frequently, because people will offer to feed you. The people here, in the "buckle of the Bible Belt" were alive in a way I had not experienced before, though I soon learned to keep my mouth shut about things metaphysical! I recognized that many of the people living here realized the truth of their own beings, whether they had put words to it or not. We really enjoyed Chattanooga.

But Chattanooga was to be a stepping-stone. Isaac was 15 months old when we moved to Nashville. Gil had been offered and accepted a wonderful opportunity at a hospice planning to build a residential facility. He had worked on a similar project in Florida. He was back into the true work of hospice, working again in a heart-based organization. He was delighted. The family was supportive. We would have relatives nearby!

Aaron and Laura continued to bless us with their flexibility, and soon settled nicely in their schools. They very much enjoyed family gatherings with aunts and uncles and cousins, something they had not known in Florida. Mom retired, and moved in with her sister and brother-in-law, the same Aunt Betty and Uncle Max who had sent us their newspaper. Mom's younger sister Kay and her husband Jim retired to the area. God guided me to Unity Church for Positive Living and my openhearted spiritual family. Thank you, blessed Mother. This book began, innocently enough, as a personal dialogue with God. We bought a big old neglected brick house, renovated it, and moved in. We are blessed beyond measure. And the book continued, building the truth of its' words in my being. And then what I was imaging-in came true.

Some time later

I stopped writing right here in late May 2000. It had taken a year and a half to image-in this far. Aaron now a senior, Laura a lovely freshman in high school, the "baby" is now four. I am a chaplain at my Unity Church and my prayer life has exploded. During a chaplain retreat this spring, for the first time I experienced the Holy Spirit so completely that I had no conscious ability to control "my" voice or "my" body as the Holy Spirit spoke through me to the chaplains. Then later in spring I had a kind of spiritual breakdown, I guess, soon after I saw what Annalee Skarin calls the "treasure house of God" in her work "The Book of Books". I quoted scripture and called it "the abundance of things hoped for" or maybe that wasn't my voice calling it that.... I don't really know anymore. It seems, quite often, that the Christ mind is very truly my own mind, and I cannot differentiate the God or Jesus voice from my own mind-voice.

Anyway, one Sunday near the end of April I walked outside to offer the lawn mowing brigade (Gil, Aaron and Isaac) cold drinks. It was late afternoon, with the sun at that particular angle that bathes everything in a golden light. I was not feeling particularly spirit-filled in the moment, but rather about my human business, when I glanced out at the small valley and the trees between houses. There it was - with open eyes I could see the tear in the fabric of reality. The door to all things. The brilliant sparkling Light of the abundance of God. That place in consciousness (and in true reality) that Jesus could also see and confidently use according to his true desiring to serve. I saw my pink bicycle, the one I wanted when I was a little girl of almost 6; the dance-with-me life size doll I wanted when I was 4. Things I had wanted or asked for but long ago forgot. There was the stuffed unicorn I asked for when I was about 10; there was the blue Toyota I wanted at 24. And there were nebulous things, future things that are only just forming in my mind. I saw a huge table, loaded with every conceivable food and drink I could possibly desire; beautiful, perfect ripe fruits and vegetables, steaming casseroles and plump warm loaves of bread, bottles and casks of drink - an absolutely marvelous feast. I saw, with open eyes, the possibility of everything. The experience lasted about a nanosecond. At the time, I shook my head and blocked it out, and went on to take drink orders!

The next day I went outside to look again, in the same place. Nothing. Just trees and grass and squirrels. Then I cried. I sobbed with the enormity of what I had seen. There was nothing my ego mind could refute. The bicycle, the things long forgotten, the future plans that only God knows.... only God could have shown me this abundance, and it was truly by Grace. I have asked, sought, and knocked on the door, but when God answers the door in such a marvelous way...it feels overwhelming in ways I didn't even know existed. Perhaps you have realized that what I imagine or describe in these words I have actually experienced, with some happening prior to the description being written, some soon thereafter, as with this experience. The writing of the words somehow prepared my mind for the experience to occur, I guess. This experience, however, was particularly shattering because it was my first open-eyed, fully conscious vision, fully registering on all levels of my being as it happened. I was unprepared for the naked, totally vulnerable, completely out of control feeling that accompanied this massive blessing.

Something else happened around the same time. I took Isaac to the dentist and after his examination; he chose a prize from the dentist's goody box. It was a clear plastic top with a colored paper insert for spinning effect. The paper insert was surprisingly beautiful, a mosaic pattern of colors. It was quite entrancing when spinning. During our good-night rituals that evening, Isaac asked "What color is God?" and I responded, as if he were referring to skin color, with the idea that God appears to each person in their own skin color, so that God is not black or white or red or yellow. Isaac, impatient with my stupidity, said "No! God isn't just all colors like that! God looks like my top, when it is spinning!" When he said that, I had an immediate rush of recognition and remembrance.

What I then remembered was another nanosecond experience that I had forgotten, unable at the time to process. It was a glimpse that was given to drive me relentlessly onward, seeking God. It happened in September 1995, as I was "returning" from a meditation. I had been very deeply relaxed and was out of body for some time. Upon opening my eyes, I perceived a great white-gold Light both with my physical eyes and with my spiritual vision. I looked deeply at the Light, my consciousness drawn irresistibly toward it. I saw bands of energy, waves and bands of pulsating, undulating, spiraling Light beaming from a central Light core of immensity beyond description. Each pulsation of energy was brought about by a tone, a deep all encompassing sound that is a thought from the mind of God. Each thought contained universes and worlds, eons and forevers, completed. Each tone was a song of new creation. I then perceived that God gazed upon the entirety of Her Creation, and Divine Love flowed in an amazing cascade of Light, igniting all the other thoughts as they cavorted and pulsated, responding in kind to this grandest vibration. I watched as this tone of Love moved out further, birthing new colors in the waves of Light, new resonance in the undulations, heading directly to the minds and hearts of God's beloveds of earth, circling the planet in spiraling tendrils of God's own Love Thought. I remembered that I have seen the Limitless Light...the very Light that is God.

It seems strange to have to remind myself that seeing and knowing this stuff is a good thing, because it often feels undeserved and challenging. It feels like a huge responsibility. It's difficult finding someone to talk to, and then it's tough being able to coherently discuss what is indescribable! So to process "my" thoughts, I require a good bit of quiet and meditation. My life is very blessed and calm, generally. But it was late May and school was out. My teens were home for the summer, hogging the computer all day, surfing the web, fighting, and teasing the little one. Quiet it was not!

Pentecost happened. The day of Pentecost was June 11. That day I sat in a blazing fire during the 9:30 church service, completely engulfed in the Holy Spirit. I have a conscious remembering of very little of that experience, except a feeling of complete broken abandon, an emptying-out, and then a glorious filling-up, with fire. A heat that did not burn yet burns still. Holy Light tingling in every cell and fiber. I feel it now, typing these words.

Human life continued without pause, as it does. Soon I was one of the driver/counselors for Laura's youth group as we headed to "Summer Connection", the annual youth retreat held just outside Asheville, North Carolina, at Warren Wilson College. A more picturesque and beautiful campus I could not imagine. But the kids, the kids - after a few awkward moments, they shined their

Christ-selves non-stop. They were so filled with Divine Love it was amazing. And they were completely natural about it...natural Christs! It was something I had only read about as a possibility, prayed for in faith, and tried to raise up in my home. But among these teens, it is their way. It is their truth. It is their life! *I am raising them up, you see. These are my little children, set to lead the world to righteousness. What parent can resist the zeal of her teenage child? These young Christs will lead the world to the greatest wave of awakening ever known in Earth history. You have heard the evangelist Benny Hinn say, and it is truth, that more people will be "saved" during this time than since the first Pentecost after Jesus' ascension.* Oh yes! That must be why Benny Hinn has shown all those thousands of young people in his crusades, completely on fire with the Holy Spirit. *Yeah, it's a little plan I've cooked up.... and it's well underway!* I know I could not resist one of these young people!

I had become satisfied that summer 2000 was going to be filled with Experiences. I wanted very much to write more, image-in more; because I felt that was the way God was giving me to actualize my dream. But I knew that God had some other good for me; something new to reveal...I just couldn't seem to get it. More than once I had pleaded with God, wanting to move on, feeling constrained, wanting more.... so in love with God that I felt that only the expansion of being an ascended being could possibly give me the capacity for God that I desired. I looked for the book, the song, and the thought...a few phrases of wisdom. Enter Andrew Harvey.

Rev. Patricia heard him speak at a Unity conference, and the very first Sunday after she returned, we were all tuned in to Andrew. I read his work titled "Son of Man" and thank You God, Andrew's understanding and relationship with Jesus bowled me over. More and more often I experienced Jesus, momentary times with his presence, and longer times enveloped in him. In one section of "Son of Man" Andrew describes the phases of spiritual life as exemplified by Jesus. Carnal man, awake man, spirit man, resurrected man, ascended man, and then as the agent of the Holy Spirit, breathing the fire of God to fully awaken minds made ready to awaken. Andrew said that God was calling all of us to this plan.

In "Son of Man" Andrew Harvey included a discourse direct from Christ Jesus' mind. The first time I read it did not register on my personal mind at all. Only upon stumbling back upon it did I read it with full consciousness. I read Christ's words once, kind of numbly, and then again, coming to the part wherein Jesus, in his beautifully compelling way, calls us to breathe the fire of God as he did at Pentecost and continues to do even now…. Jesus' presence was instantly, majestically at my right side, and then with a whooshing feeling, his face zoomed around from my right side and came to rest about three inches from my face, eye-to-eye *I dare you*… Dare me to what? And I knew… *I dare you, beloved, to breathe my fire on the nations.* **Breathe my fire on the nations!** But I haven't even mastered being human! I haven't ascended - doesn't that have to come first? Are you just stringing me along? Why don't **you** breathe the fire of the Holy Spirit on me, **as continuous experience**, before you ask any more of me? Sometimes I just can't get it anymore! You want more from me and I haven't a clue how to do any of it! You know, sometimes more than a nanosecond glimpse of what you're talking about is in order, don't you think?

This upsets you. **Yes it does!** *Beloved Liberty, I call you even higher! You cannot believe that ascension is the end of spirit-life!* No, of course not. *Then now, upon your impending beingness as an evolved, ascending and descending Liberty spirit, do you not see my timing? Your new goal, to keep you reaching. Your new blessing, to cover you with never ending Love.* Thank you. But if I'm all these things you say, why is it so difficult to be this, and to see it? *My difficulty is in seeing when you are **not** in your Christ mind. From where I am, which is also within you, I seldom perceive times when you are not within range of our One Voice. **See your ascending and descending as consciousness first.** The body-mind will respond. Let go of what you think you need to do and simply be that which you are.*

Jesus, that sounds so lovely. Let go and let God and thy will be done and I surrender all and all the rest. Human life makes all that hoo-ha extremely difficult. Like, for example, how am I to let go and let God if I haven't one moment alone to be with God? *I see your point and I know the difficulty. In time, which is where human consciousness reigns, one cannot see the connectedness of experiences. This period of busy-ness in these summer months has been, as you have accepted, a time of experiencing. But always, and you know this, periods of wisdom flow from periods of experience. You are entering a period of Grace and Wisdom beyond your image-ining.*

I know. I know! This is so beyond my little personal control that fear overwhelms me. I didn't know there was still such fear in me! This life, this Christing, is such a razor's edge existence. In consciousness I know the pinnacle feelings of God's marvelous bliss and peace; and then I fear that I will fall. Sometimes when I pray with someone I feel so powerful, because His Power is surging through me. I feel pride in that, but I want to be humble! Dear God, help me know in that it is Your Strength, Your Power, not mine, but Thy will be done! Oh Jesus, please help me.... I know my complete and utter dependence on God, but I need to know that as a constant state of consciousness, don't I? How can I be worthy if I feel self-righteous in any way?

Ahh, Beloved, that is what the Grace is for. It is a balm to soothe these turbulent feelings. This narrow way is a razor's edge. Child, be grateful to God for these fears. These are cleansing fears and anxieties; something like God's electric fence along the sides of the narrow way! Think ye that I did not have these feelings as Jesus, or in one of my other incarnations? When people wanted to praise me instead of our God, there were times when those prideful thoughts came into my mind, as well. They are part of the race consciousness, which says that anyone who has these kinds of powers must be a God. That is a truth, in a cosmic sense. But as we have discussed, separation comes from this kind of deification. I have experienced a kind of deification with some members of my church. When I pray with them and they see my naked passion for You and think...well, I don't know what they think. But they look at me as if I am set apart, when I really want them to know that they can also experience God in this way. And they are beginning to experience the Holy Spirit more and more deeply. It is really very beautiful to watch. *Yes, it is delicious.* Yeah! Delicious. Delectable! *It is my prayer also, Beloved Liberty, that these precious ones come to understanding, and bliss and peace. So we agree.* Amen!

Jesus, I feel so weak and powerless to become what you are asking. *How about trusting God and me? I think we can handle this quickening and bestowal of Holy Spirit power. I think we can manage to cleanse and purify every energy field, every cell, every thought, word and action. I believe we are capable of lifting precious Earth and all her brave souls to planetary awakening and evolution. You and many other beloveds have heard my call and are right with you in this process. From every spiritual practice I have called, speaking in the Christ name familiar to each person's practice. Your very cells answer back: Yes! Yes! Yes! I AM COMING, AND I AM YOU. Your evolution is at hand. I AM with you all ways, always, forever. I AM you. So how about this affirmation for a few days: I AM that which I desire to be.*

Oooh, I like that one. I AM that which I desire to be. Wow! That opens a door or two. *She gets it!* Huh? What do you mean by that? *I have opened the door wide for you, my child. Enter.* I AM trusting. I AM trusting.

As above, so below

Last night I went to a class on forgiveness offered by Rev. Patricia at Unity Center. We were each assigned to write a letter from God to us. Finally, the God letter! But God gets to write to me? God, do you want to write a letter to me?

Indeed, yes! So long I have waited to write a letter to you, my own Liberty. I have longed to tell you of the depth of my love for you. I tell you each day, but so seldom do you notice the breeze as I caress your skin. I sing to you in the song of birds and the wind whistles at your beauty. I wink at you when I peek from behind the clouds as the sunlight I AM. I tingle in your palms and rush up your spine as the Holy Spirit cascades through your energy fields. Ah! Here I AM! I AM all you perceive, and more, and more. Forever I AM more. I Am that which you desire to be. Dare to think it not robbery to be equal with me, as Jesus did. I have given you this great desire, this overwhelming devotion to the evolution of humankind. You have perceived ascension as your goal; that was an intermediate step. I have so much more in store for you! But first, a proper letter.

YHVH

Heaven

September 28, 2000

Beloved Liberty,

When I think of the magnificent spirit of Liberty you are, joy rings out from my heart, causing the saints and angels to sing in praise of your creation. Liberty is the spirit that frees the imprisoned. You are Liberty. Just as Jesus is the word love made flesh, you are the word liberty made flesh. From my idea of true freedom you have grown. In you I AM well pleased.

I AM your Abba, your Daddy. I love you with sweet and gentle love, wanting only goodness for you, only peace and tranquility. I love you with mighty and powerful love, as your forever protector, guardian and watcher. You have never left my sight, and you never will. You have never left my side, and you never will. You are my own precious daughter. I do know how many hairs are on your golden brown head. I know the innocence of your heart.

I AM your Mother God as well, tenderly supporting and nurturing, ever filling your mind with wisdom, forever holding you in my arms, showering you with abundant joy, keeping you in health and wholeness, warm and well and fed and clothed and prosperous.

I AM your Brother God, too, manifested to you as Jesus. Jesus is the first-born natural Christ, born without the idea of separation imbedded in his cellular makeup and raised without the idea being implanted in his mind. Mary saw to that. Joseph protected his young mind too. And you perform the greater works of which he spoke every day by overcoming thoughts of separation, and by teaching your children their inherent oneness with all that is.

Life in the body is our experiment in co-creation that you playfully, joyously and courageously embrace over and over; each time you accept a new body, a new time, a new set of circumstances to overcome. Precious planet Earth is your playground, the most fabulous theme park in the history of the universe. The theme? ENJOY! Be in joy! I AM ever holding your hand, lifting you over the hurdles, balancing your bicycle as you learn to ride, speaking encouragement to your being, leading - so that together we have some good fun! Unlimited loving laughing singing dancing outrageously hilarious fun!

There is a hymn sung by saints and angels that you know and love, because it begins to describe my Love for you in a way that the human mind can grasp. The verse goes like this: "Could we with ink the oceans fill, and were the skies of parchment made; were ev'ry stalk on earth a quill, and ev'ry man a scribe by trade...to write the Love of God above would drain the oceans dry! Nor could the scroll contain the whole, tho stretched from sky to sky!"

My beloved, everything I have is yours. Everything I AM you are. Claim your inheritance! Claim your at-one-ment!

Forever in service to you,

God

Awesome. That is truly awesome. Perhaps my musings should end here, but then again, how could they? Because You have brought up some stuff that is just about impossible to fathom, and definitely seems impossible to put into practice. For example, you have painted a lovely picture of me as expanded and unlimited beyond my current capability to "see". In my own home, I have extremely limited "liberty" to do or say what I truly want to say. My throat often hurts due to all the words I choke back. I know that most people, my husband and adult family members in particular, consider it "preaching" when I speak my truth, even casually! They attack me with their own wounds and I shrink away, because I feel in those moments absolutely crucified! I want to protect this Christ child within me, just as I want to protect my physical children from harm. So I keep my mouth shut, and pray.

Most of the time I keep my mouth shut at church, too, because I don't want to blow anyone's mind, or sabotage anyone's fragile faith with greater truths than they can handle at the moment. I have in fact been "restricted" to being chaplain for only those who others feel capable of "handling" me. And that is because of You, and the way Holy Spirit manifested through me at the chaplain's retreat. Then there are times, during church services, when I feel Your Presence with such overwhelming strength that I want more than anything to fall to my knees and praise You. But that would be too Pentecostal, or something. "We don't want to turn anyone off" is the refrain I hear. Well yeah, I don't want that, but what about me? **I want to be turned on! When is it going to be my turn?** And even as I ask that, fear grips me, because I know that when I actually claim my "turn", there is no turning back, and I am one with You forever.

Part Two – Application

We're in this together now

This dialogue has become a day-to-day journal, now. It is present moment, and you are with me. As I type away I experience. What happens next I truly cannot imagine with my own mind, but can only remember. The "Daily Word" yesterday was so very comforting to me, especially these words: "By thinking that I have to be in control of a situation, I may be thinking myself into a dilemma. I rescue myself by acknowledging that my quest in life is not about being in control, but about letting God express life, love and understanding through me." God is in control. Thank God.

I know that I know God is calling me ever closer, and the experience I have sought is so near, so near...I know that I know that the "end" of this story will burst forth shortly, and I will be changed, though not necessarily in that order. I give up all control of what, or when, and especially of how. Sometimes I feel anxious, wondering about effects, about how those around me will react. But God is in control. Of everything. And God has already planned all effects to be the highest and best for everyone. So together, let's take a deep breath or several and just let go. Be still, and know.

Today is October 1, 2000: World Peace Day. The chaplains held an all-day meditation at Unity Church today. Last Sunday, Virginia called me to discuss my part; the meditation hour I was to lead at 2:00 on Saturday, October 21. We agreed to a sort of "creativity" session, first a guided meditation and then the meditators would draw or otherwise create something; then we would share our experiences. Sounded rather ho-hum to me (and to her, she later told me), kind of a been-there done-that idea. But I was willing to work with it.

The following day I received an e-mail about a worldwide peace meditation for peace in the Middle East, a live web-cast hosted by James Twyman and others. It was scheduled for 2:00 on Saturday, October 21. Ta-da! That was what my hour was for and about, I just knew it! To continue the synchronicity, Virginia called me. She was delighted right along with me! The prayer for peace flowed from God through me in minutes, and many other ideas came into my mind. Instead of ho-hum, the fire of God, the zeal of Spirit was my companion.

So today was the day. Our first hour this morning was spent in breathing exercises, led by our wonderful chaplain sister Denise. At one point in the first exercise, Denise described the breath of God traveling over our foreheads to the back of our head and neck area. In that moment I felt the hand of God traveling over my forehead, gliding to the back of my head and then cupping my head and neck as I cupped my own newborn childrens' precious heads. Then God drew me to Him/Her (there was no distinction) and I was, in that moment, complete Trust, nestled there in the arms of God Almighty, maker of heaven and earth. Many images and memories of my earthly baby-hood came flooding into my mind, such as the smell of my mother's milk, and the soft sweetness of her gaze; the gasoline and oil smell of Dad from his job at the gas station where he worked while he was going to college. I had always wondered why I liked those smells! Then a more conscious memory, one of being placed in a basket or bassinet, sometime in early May of my first year of life. I was about four months old. The sun was shining on me but not directly, and the windows were open wide. I was supposed to be sleeping, but the smell of springtime was too captivating, the song of the birds and honeybees too engrossing. I saw whiteness flapping and fluttering overhead. I remembered thinking that I must be back with God, because of the whiteness and brightness of the light, and the angel wings. I remembered my confusion when Mom picked me up and I saw the room from an upright posture, realizing then that I was human and the fluttering whiteness just a covering for the windows.

Denise moved our attention from the back of the neck on down to the shoulders and chest area, and we were instructed to allow the breath of God to fill our heart centers. The Love of God was all over me then, surrounding me, enfolding me, singing to me...I was vibrating all over, awash in God's Magnificent Presence. My cells were ringing and tingling everywhere in my body like never before. Angels and saints and ascended masters spoke heavenly music in my ears, speaking and singing of God's great love for me, telling me they were witnessing my birth in Spirit. After that I have little conscious recollection, but "returned" to find my body curled up in the fetal position, weeping with joy, vibrating madly all over. Silent, I prayed my hope that witnessing my experience didn't scare anyone else in the room, but no one said a word.

The next hour we were assigned to meditate on an affirmation of our own choosing; something that resonated deeply in our souls. I had been pondering on the affirmation I would choose, but had no certainty about it. I knew I wanted to affirm my highest truth, the most expanded word-picture about myself that I could imagine. At last, I settled on "I Am Liberty the Christ" but wrote " I Am Christ Liberty". I realized then that the second version was much more desirable, actually, because then my identity was primarily with the Christ, before my identification with my own personality, Liberty. With my second or third breath into the meditation, I realized with great wonder that "I Am Christ Liberty" in reality places my identity first with **God** (I Am), then with Christ, and finally with self, and truly, all identities are of equal necessity in this realm, as Love, Wisdom and Power; as mind, body, spirit; as subconscious, conscious and superconscious. The trinity; our threefold beingness, is balanced in the Christ; and each interpenetrates the other when that balance is in place in consciousness. Balance must be chosen.

October 31

Halloween! Spooks and goblins and all that. I listened this morning as the talk show deejays stumbled around about Paganism and Christianity, about the devil and demons and all that. It is so comical. Just have fun with Halloween as a tradition, or don't! Some of us like a little more drama than others in their ride back toward God; some of us choose to look close at evil to make looking at God that much more delicious! When we don't want the contrast anymore, we will all abandon evil as an idea. And there I go again! This is just what I am afraid of, God! *What, exactly? What are you afraid of here?* That I am taking on Your Voice! That I cannot differentiate You from me anymore, in what I think or write or anything! I have such a hard time trusting that, and it feels so arrogant to trust that, too! But then You reward me in such beautiful ways for listening and acting on Your Voice.... like sending me to listen to Neale Donald Walsch last week. And Gil, too. Thank You for him going too. He seems to be awakening a bit more and I was able to see that and be comforted because of it. Very sweet You are, God.

A bunch of us from Unity Church drove to see Walsch in Atlanta. He was awesomely normal and holy, at the same time. I felt such longing to hang around him, especially when he spoke of being great friends with Marianne Williamson, with James Redfield and others, and the marvelous conversations and prayers they must have together! I so ache to be able to speak freely, while at the same time I feel such angst about what might come out of my mouth! We bought his newest book, "Communion with God". On the drive back to Nashville, the group was talking about writing as therapy, and someone asked how my book (these very pages) was coming. I replied, very softly, lump in throat, that I was feeling a lot of anguish about it, because so much of what was coming to me was in One Voice, and that it was very difficult to "own" that Voice as my own.

And wouldn't You just know it, the <u>very first subject</u> God discusses in "Communion with God" is those souls who have heard, written down and acted upon the One Voice! People whose names you surely recognize, like Jesus, Paramahansa Yogananda, Guatama Buddha; you get the picture. So if you'll excuse me, I'm overwhelmed again. And because of my declaration of sorts, when I actually said the words "I hear in One Voice", I **am** hearing You in this wonderful way more and more, seeing connectedness more. The edges are becoming so blurred, not because the edges are physically going, but because I can see the flow. I am a witness to the dance, Your Dance.

So what does this mean to you, Daughter? What do you want it to mean? I want it to mean that I am gaining power, gaining wisdom in You. I know that I am Love, Your beloved. I want it to mean that I am trusting You in a surrendered, abandoned, totally wild and free way. I want it to mean that I am so clear, so transparent that You show up through me in exactly the way those You would touch need You in that moment. For this writing, I want it to mean that the beloveds who read this realize the greatness and grandness and oneness of their own beings, if only for one Holy Instant. I want it to mean that I am lifted up, drawing Your beloveds to You. I want it to mean that Your Word, written and spoken through me is Your Truth and Our Truth. I want it to mean that I am filled with confidence, with faith, with courage. I want it to mean that I AM CHRIST LIBERTY!

Your Voice, as it comes through Neale, is different than how I "get" You, though, and I get the feeling that the way You speak as me is a more comfortable, intimate, "touchy-feely" way. *That is so. Neale's books, though deeply personal in effect, are for ecumenical use because they present broad concepts; as reference tools. The way I speak through you is on a daily life level, a "how, then, shall we live?" place, very descriptive of feeling. You have become emotionally unclouded, so your "feelings" are quite pure. You have a marvelous capacity for visioning, together with an abundant vocabulary for My use. Quite helpful.* Glad to be of service. I love all the ways You have spoken through Your people. So many different personalities, sometimes coloring Your words with their personality "stuff". I think one of the clearest (besides Neale Donald Walsch) would be Helen Schuchman *Yes, A Course in Miracles, yes* and another would be Barbara Marx Hubbard *and your personal favorite "Revelation: Our Crisis is a Birth"* oh yeah, that is a groundbreaker *Universe shaker!* I'm praying right now that Andrew Harvey lets Jesus and his own Christ self speak from the One Voice. Forget the research and trust.... **that** would be his book of books. *That could be arranged. I will suggest it.* That's it? That's how simple prayer is? *But of course. You ask, I answer. We've had this discussion.* But it's never actually **seemed** simple. *Live and learn.* You are a scamp! I <u>love</u> these conversations! *As do I, my beloved friend. As do I.*

11/1/00

What a meditation. I am amazed, astounded, overcome. Dear God, only Our One Voice can portray what You have shown me. Thank You! Here goes...

~~~

A wonderful way to describe your individual natures is to call you "life streams" of the One Life. Image-in a fiber-optic thread, emanating from a light source. You have seen lamps made from this kind of material, and the fibers shimmer and dance, lighted by a central core. If the light source is pink, the fibers shimmer pink, with a brighter pinkness at the termination of the fiber. Your life stream is much the same, except that your "fiber" is the Light itself, and is infinitely more flexible and pliable. You emanate from the Great Central Sun, God, Source: the origin of the thought that is now manifesting as you, living in a physical body on the planetary body, Earth. Your body is as the terminal "ending" of the fiber of Light. Your body is meant to be the beginning of worlds without end, and it returns to that meaning when you begin to hear in truth our one voice. As you listen and hear our voice, you lay claim to the power of beingness contained therein. You lay claim to fullness of being. You lay claim to fullness of joy. You are illumined, enlightened, redeemed: your light beams directly from the Great Central Sun, unimpeded. What was the "terminal" end explodes into a new sun. Have I not said, Ye are Gods?

Your life stream has meandered through the galaxies and universes, and does still. You have consciousness all along your life stream, not just at the "terminal" end, the body. Your life stream is interwoven with the life streams of every other being you have ever (in eternity, that is) seen, touched, thought of, known intuitively, recognized, related to or shared with in any way. Your thoughts, expressed, become as life streams expended from your own engine of creation, mind. Do you see how this could be very entangling?

God, could I interrupt here? Seems crazy to ask to interrupt my own Self, but geez, I'm still dazed and confused. *No problem. What's the trouble?* Could we perhaps be a bit more descriptive here? When You were showing me these concepts it was all with thought-pictures, and the images were so beautiful. *What I showed to you was your own life stream's meander. If you wish to reveal the beauty you are, go ahead. Take over.* Like I can do that. Sure. But again, here goes...

In the "beginning" of me-ness I recall the light wave, or tone, vibration - I was propelled outward from the Great Light, from Source. In the beginning I merely observed, as if I were composed of eyes, just eyes, seeing everything, focused on nothing. I began to observe space, space between the light waves, or tones. Further on, I began to notice variations in the Light - colors. Still, the Great Light was primarily visible, but it was beginning to divide. I was noticing "other" beings form, but the Light was still the only component of everything. Soon I began to realize that the experience of the "other" was differing from "my" experience - I could discern happenings in the other's life stream that were not the same as my own. I thought I would like to "share" the "other's" experience. Immediately I became one with the other, as I desired it! "We" merged, blended; new colors were born, new life streams (thoughts) darted joyously from the melding. For a very long "time" this was my experience: melding, blending, expanding. Life streams joining, intertwining, departing. So very beautiful....

Eventually this must have gotten boring, because I became involved with a Creation project - the Terra. This is a truly blessed place, this earth. Many life streams came to implant the Light, and we wove a blanket of protection around the beautiful Terra. Our thoughts and experiences of Divine Life, Unity, are implanted in the very fabric of Creation; seeded throughout. The life streams here today are the same who seeded Creation. We have forgotten the purity of our Origin. But it is the same, still; we are still those same life streams, propelled from Source...wait a minute, God! This sounds like the creation story You gave me a few months ago, when we studied Genesis at Unity Church. But that was a story about how **You** created the heavens and the earth, not about me *but child of Light - do you not see? It is Our story! Do you remember how it goes?* How about if I just "merge" the experiences through the wonder of computing?

Beginning

The Ancient Lord of Omniverses calls out to our God, saying "Come, Beautiful Oneness. You have reached the understanding

of Universal Creator. You are God of a new universe. Go, create."
The Ancient Lord of Omniverses opens a panorama, a never-ending sea of no-thing. Blackness so deep and dense, our God feels a suffocating sense completely new to His experience. "Yes, Beloved Oneness, this is your new challenge. You are ready. Create freshness, newness. Be."

There is a sweeping sensation, and the Ancient One recedes from our God. Our God surveys the chaos of the deep no-thing, and says "Let there be Light" because all the Gods know that this is the first step in creating a new universe. This is the only instruction given, though, in the Book of the Gods. From there, Creator Gods pretty much have free rein. You can't go wrong if you call in Light first, though. It's omniversal insurance.

Great and glorious shafts of shimmering Light burst forth from our God's consciousness, shards of glittering clear whiteness scatter from the center of our God-mind, traveling out and out, billowing, glowing Light flowing into the universal forever. God is in awe of this, His own creation. He had no idea the Ancient Lord of Omniverses had gifted him so lavishly! Our God watches the Light cavort, rolling over upon itself, great globs of glory gathering here, dispersing there. Mandalas of Light in intricate designs spiral and dance. Our God ponders the next step in this creation. He is aware of what other Creator Gods have done in their universes. Some have created vast gem and mineral universes, planets appearing as glorious gemstones, perfect mirrors for looking back upon Godself. Others created fabulous greenhouse planets; with such diversity of plant life even Our God's imagination was expanded! Our God makes the decision. I will re-create my Self, in an endless mirror...I will know Myself in my Entirety.

God gazes upon His Light, Her great and marvelous gift. God declares: with Light I build my Creation, and Light is the stuff of all that I am. With Light is my consciousness expanded into the chaos of no-thing. Our God breathes...noticing the planets now cooling, billions of planets circling the great globs of Light. The colors of cooling Light catch Our God's breath with their beauty. Our God was not so aware of the varieties of color contained in Light, from the palest milky white to deepest indigo.

Our God ponders what next to create; how to create the highest and best creation yet imagined by a Creator God. Our God loves the mineral and gem creations, finds creeping and crawling creations most interesting. The ideas of octaves of dimensionality, all inter-reacting, intrigue our God's mind. Our God is partial to lush vegetation and wild scenery. Water-based planets work well with mineral, plant and animal creations. I will combine all these on my planets, our God decides. Oh, the beauty! As Our God blissfully ponders on, tendrils of God-Thought-Light weave reality.

How to best enjoy the creation, too - Our God wants to be involved in everything in Creation. Micro-manage, even! Hmmm....Aha! Individuations of Me! I will send my God-selves forth on waves of Light to do the work of Creation, to the furthest reaches of my universe. In this way I will know my beloved creation, and my Beloved Creation will know Me.

The Light reaches further into the universe, and our sun is born. Planets encircle the newborn sun, and God watches. The third planet is particularly beautiful, and God names her Terra. Upon this rock I will build my church, God decides, and it is so. Upon this planet will the beings be given a freedom unknown in any universal creation. The blessed ones to inhabit this Terra will learn to know me, but they will choose to know me. To these my Beloved Children I give true freedom. The liberty I know is for these children. The power I know is for these My Beloveds. I give to these Holy Ones my whole beingness. But all this will they have by their own choice. Each being will have the seed of my Entirety, and be created for Eternity.

Our God smiles upon the Terra, and our Creation is. Life began for all of us. The Ancient Lord of Omniverses smiles too, knowing. In this new Creator God, our God, She is well pleased.

~~~

Wow. That's a wonderful word-picture of what is indescribable. *So is Genesis. So is Darwinian evolution. It is all the same picture, written as many ways as the idea of "beginning" can be written. It seems I repeat Myself endlessly.* You do! *And every repetition is different, yet the same. The Mystery of God.* I didn't realize that You used the term "liberty" in the "Beginning" discourse. The writing came before I

Libby Maxey

received my "new name" *Your I Am identity.* Yes. I guess You'll let me know what that means in due time...*there is only now.* Okay, You'll let me know now! *The liberty I know is a vast concept. It is total freedom of beingness. Romans 8:21 says "the creation itself will be set free from its bondage to decay and will obtain the freedom of the glory of the children of God" This freedom is the freedom from the very idea of death, of decay. It is the Truth of Life Eternal. You, as one who has self-chosen to evolve, will prove my point. That there is no death, and that Life Eternal is attainable and* **desirable** *while in the body!*

Welcome, holy child I am...

It's a gorgeous late November day. Thanksgiving is over, and the Christmas season is upon us. Nashville's Christian radio stations are playing Christmas songs 24/7. Hearing these has taken me to Bethlehem, and to being more and more okay with and present in my own birth into Spirit. I am truly being born again. Accepting Christ as your Lord and Savior cannot take you all the way to this beingness - but it does open the door. Accepting your own being as Christ is the true healing. But most of us have so far just stood around the door, peering inside once in a while, but mostly surviving outside the consciousness that truly sets us free. Step inside! Open up to the Christ consciousness; begin the walk of faith that is the greatest adventure.

There is a great man of spirit and truth called Neville. He wrote a book called "Resurrection" that God uses as a reference tool with me. You know what I mean - it's like the Bible or "A Course in Miracles" or "The Aquarian Gospel of Jesus the Christ" or many others I could name - books that God can guide you to and use to guide you to Him. A book you can open and there it is! Exactly the answer to your question. Just before my meditation this morning God led me to this book and I opened it to read this:

"How would you feel if you were that which you desire to be? Wear this mood, this feeling that would be yours if you were *already* that which you desire to be; and in a little while you will be sealed in the belief that you *are*."

And so I meditated on the state of *feeling* how it feels to know myself as the ascended Christ I am. And I expanded upon the feeling aspects by meditating on seeing and hearing and tasting and smelling and *being* the ascended Christ I am. I was tingling all over, feeling myself rising up... but it must not be time for fully manifesting because the phone rang and Uncle Jim came over with a load of bricks for an outdoor building project.... but this, this guidance.... this is it. All the knowings, all the words, all the Power - I am being born.

Manifestation has become easier, because now I have more understanding. For example, several years ago I surprised my dear friend Elizabeth (and myself) with an answer to a simple question. She asked me "What do you want most in your life?" and I answered, amazed in the truth of my words, "I want God to lift me up to Him and hold me there, in Her arms." As I spoke those words, a powerful image came into my mind of myself, childlike, being lifted to the Face of a magnificent Light, held under my arms by the gentlest of hands. This image has stayed in my mind.

Lately I began having a wandering "pain" under my arms; nothing I could touch and find, but there just the same. I asked God what this was about. Instantly the image of being lifted up came into my mind and God spoke: *I lift you constantly, Beloved. Know this now.* I thought about changing that thought in my mind, to alleviate the "pain". But it hurts so good! The intention behind the thought is so pure, and the knowing that God lifts me up so much it hurts is greatly comforting.

And then the thought came, that to truly *feel* the fullness of anything, I have to embrace the totality of that which I want to feel. And there is my difficulty, and my challenge. With my human mind I cannot hold all the thoughts that comprise the totality of my desire. I must be out of my mind to have these thoughts! It seems that this is where; according to "A Course in Miracles" that God must take the final step. My mind has expanded exponentially, and I have held magnificent thoughts in mind, but my desiring is beyond my imagining. This is God territory. Please help me, Great God of Wonder, and lead me. I am blind, except to Your Glory.

The Melchizedek experience

The first week of June 1995 our family still lived in Fort Myers, Florida. I was Ernestine's devoted student at the time, and was just a few days away from receiving my ordination as a Universal Brotherhood minister. God and I were in the honeymoon phase, the time just before the great temptations and the wilderness. It was the last week the kids were still in school so I took advantage and went out to Sanibel Island to visit a good friend for a swim and lunch at the resort where she was staying. The day was perfect; the breezes warm; no humidity, the water of the Gulf of Mexico still cool and refreshing. Maureen and I sat in cabana chairs and looked out at the sparkling water, talking and laughing. There were some clouds on the western horizon but the rest of the sky was cloudless. But *those clouds!* There was something about them that mesmerized me.

At first glance the cloudbank looked like a thunderhead, but there were circular cloud-shapes within and behind the greater bank. I watched and the shape of the formation gradually changed before my eyes, and I saw that layers of circular and elliptical "clouds" formed the greater part of the formation, and numerous smaller "clouds" disappeared in to and emerged from the great clouds. I glanced over to Maureen to exclaim about what I was seeing, but Maureen was asleep! That was my cue, apparently, because I leaped up and raced into the water, running and splashing out into the water, heading for the sand bar way out there, my eyes trained on the clouds, but now my consciousness was calling these clouds a ship. Somehow, I knew what I was feeling was an overwhelming recognition.

Beyond that, I had little remembrance of this experience at that time. In my mind I referred to it as my "Melchizedek experience" even though I had no knowledge then what that could mean. While in the water, I *thought* I remembered several beings standing around me. There was a tremendous luminescence and I *thought* one of them said to me something like "Be thou baptized after the Order of Melchizedek" but the memories were so vague and so foreign to my own thoughts that I dared not reflect too much on what it might signify. At the time I had only two references to Melchizedek, one the mention in the Old Testament of the priest-king Melchizedek and the other seemingly useless knowledge that in the children's book "A Little Princess" Sarah named her pet rat Melchizedek. But the experience was extremely powerful; I knew that much. In retrospect, it was probably the first time I felt the tingling, ringing Presence of God in my body. I was unable to write about the experience except in vague, ineffective terms, until right now. Now I remember.

As I ran out into the water, laughing and splashing like a child, a small vessel like a bubble of the greater cloud emerged and came down, sliding on a beam of light from the centralized intelligence of the great ship. The bubble vessel met me exactly where I stopped, gasping wildly and out of breath, overwhelmed with excitement. I touched the bubble, gently caressing it as if it were a friend. The surface was warm, pulsing: a gel-like elastic light with intelligence and intent. It fell away or withdrew and three beings were revealed standing there before me. I remember feeling my heart pounding madly; I remember wondering how crazy my hair must look. The three beings looked into me, through me: I felt their thoughts of Peace envelope me, and I was peaceful. These were my spiritual heroes. Saint Francis as Kuthumi; Saint Germaine of the violet flame, and Sananda, Lord Jesus. Sananda was in the center of the three. All was silence, except for the quiet roar of the gulf water. The beings spoke to me in thought waves and in thought pictures. Their thoughts and intentions were directed to my mind as one thought - there was no opposition to the central will of the great thought, no posturing for attention or personal recognition. I could feel their combined thoughts rebuilding the bubble vessel and now I was within the vessel. We lifted off together, again using a beam of light from the central intelligence of the great ship; gliding soundlessly toward the cloud of light.

As the light of our vessel merged with the great ship's light, we were deposited within a vast round "room". The transfer was seamless, as with thought. I perceived a rosy pink light, very comforting and warm. I was completely at ease, as if this were a normal experience for me. My personal mind marveled at that (still does). I am given to know that this ship is a way-station for evolved beings of the Great White Brotherhood and the hierarchies, all who are working diligently to raise the vibration of God's beloveds on earth and the Terra herself. I also understand that I am one of those working diligently, and the ship is familiar because I am often here in spirit. This is the first time my body has been purified adequately for the lifting experience. I realize that this experience is a great blessing and gift to me. With that realization, I am again aware of the three great beings surrounding me with their glowing white robes shining, and there are others, many others, present. In a sweeping gaze I recognize members of my earthly family, earthly friends - shining brilliantly in their Christ Presences. I realize that everyone I know, past, present and future, is here in Christ formation. They are all here to bless me. They are all gathered around me. My mind asks, "what is this gathering about?" and I am wrapped, cocooned, in twelve spiraling light ribbons. The light streams weave themselves together, forming a tubular column around my body. Somehow I understand that my DNA is now rewoven and completed. Being within the light tube of completion is very comforting, very soft and peaceful; like a returning. I rest in this space for a time.

As one breath the three great beings make their presence known to me again, and we stand together waist deep in the waters of the Gulf of Mexico, while simultaneously within the great ship hovering above. The faces of the three look like fire, burning clear. Their robes gleam whiter than whiteness, with tiny sparkling flames of every imaginable color dancing all around them. It seems Sananda's fires are more pinkish, like compassionate love, sometimes more golden. Saint Germaine's little fires are, as expected, more violets and purples. The energy around him is charged with violet tetrahedron energy. Kuthumi's little fires contain many shades of healing green; many tones of earthen color, and there is great understanding with him. The three are filled with joy, their faces full of mirth, crinkly with laughter. From somewhere in my being I ask, "What's so funny?" The three nod and smile in one accord.

From deep within and from far beyond me, from a time before time, there arises a vibrating tone with a suddenness like the cracking of a whip, and a flame begins to burn from the center of the earth, entering the light tube surrounding me from beneath the water. The flame burns clear, yet all colors are visible; when it reaches my physical feet it begins to burn violet, until from the soles of my feet to about one foot above my head I am engulfed in violet flames. All that is within me in resistance to God burns away. My physical eyes observe the ashes falling gently on the waters of the Gulf. As I become aware of the flame, at the very same instant, the three beings lift their hands and water pours over me. So water is pouring down, fire is burning up; all within and around me "opposing" energies mingle and dance. In one voice, like thunder, the three great beings say, "Be ye baptized after the Order of Melchizedek; with fire and water we baptize thee. Put on the garment of immortality and rise up, holy child of God." Beams of pure joy and delight stream from the great three into my being, lifting my physical self higher and higher in the spiral light tube still surrounding me. Hands upraised, the three great beings send forth rays of energy, pulsating energy, from palms and hearts, energy that lifts me still higher and holds me there, suspended between the Gulf of Mexico and the cloud ship. The woven tube of completion has become a clear, faceted column of Light, like a pillar. *In you I Am well pleased. Remember your self now, beloved child I Am.* There is a gasp, like an expectation fulfilled at last, and I open my "eyes" to see all the Christ Presences surrounding me again, thoughts of grateful congratulations filling the consciousness atmosphere of the great ship, perceptible to my senses once more.

My body is sitting rigidly in the sand when I open my physical eyes again; I am vibrating all over (I called it shivering then, even though it was 90 degrees). I watch the water covering my legs and then falling away, waves undulating. My mind is numb. The great cloud ship hangs there, gradually becoming more and more cloud like, and then I watch as parts of it move away and the rest simply dissipates. I feel small and bereft and bewildered, sitting there on the sand. It took a long while before I regained physical presence enough to arise and walk back to the cabana chair, even longer to be able to speak, and several years to have the capacity to remember. .

And still the question: What does it mean?

It means, my beloved Liberty, that I mean what I say. Do you remember from Revelation "I will come in the clouds" and is that not what you experienced?

Oh, my God...*Exactly. And when I said, "I go to sit at the right hand of God".* But it seems like you're always at **my** right hand....

Precisely. It means you, if you choose to experience ALL THAT IS, can be all of everything, as you. As a creator god myself, part of my function is to open you, my creation, to fully desire your god-ness. To have no further opposition to your god-ness. To rise above duality while still experiencing its' effects as I did in the personality of Jesus and, by the way, as Melchizedek. To see beyond. To see me. And I Am at your right hand, and his right hand, at the President's right hand, and at the poorest child's right hand. Have I not said, YE ARE GODS? And Ye are God's. And Ye are God. Because we are One Life, ever expanding. Heaven is where we are. Call heaven forth, my child. The children are crying.

I am crying. *You cry a lot.*

I can't help but feel that it means something else, too. *Wonderful! Still, you want more! Then I ask you, Liberty mine: do you really want to be one with the One? Can you want to be Sacred Unity, declare, "I Am One with God" and know Truth? Do you really desire to know what your Melchizedek experience means, totally? Are you willing to expand to include ALL THAT IS? It is a big bang experience, beloved...*

Yes! I want all of it, to the extent that I can even know what I am wanting...there is fear, it seems just when I want to declare how much I ache for Oneness I am shaken and drawn away but some fear from out of no where...*sweet child, you walk **through** the valley*...and I know that my consciousness has expanded to include race consciousness thoughts, and they sometimes pop up and I am momentarily convinced that these thoughts are mine, somehow...

Are you finished with your acceptance/denial? Liberty comes from freely giving up limiting yourself by thoughts not of Oneness. These thoughts will come, until they do not. Return to Neville's thought - how would you feel if you were that which you desire to be? For you, in this moment, this question has four faces:

Y   That which I desire to be, I Am.

H   I Am that which I desire to be.

V   I Am all that I desire to be.

H   I Am All. I desire to be.

I have used the first two affirmations. What is the deal with the Tetragrammaton at the beginning of the affirmations? This feels like we're still talking about creation, about the creative principles. The first thought "that which I desire to be, I AM" is a beginning, really, a declaration of wholeness, of entirety. The second affirmation, "I Am that which I desire to be" is to me the sending forth, or the decision to define desires, to separate or categorize desires. For example, to identify me as liberty and Virginia as courage or Jesus as love. What about the third affirmation? "I Am all that I desire to be" what does God desire to be? God wants us to consciously know our holy selves in the completeness of the originating thought that created us whole, and in that way God is all that God desires to be - is that it? "I Am All. I desire to be." This affirmation closes the circle, doesn't it? It is the omega. Claim allness. Be. Ernestine used to marvel at the "isness" of God. I get it. God's goal is to be purely God in us, to dance freely in us, to flow in our veins and sing with our voices and laugh.... *and be All that God can be. God wants to be known, beloved. God wants the spontaneous hugs of her children, returned to wholeness. Beings be-ing. Lights lighting. Lovers loving. Writers writing. All players playing, laughing, splashing, en-joying.*

So what do I do to get there? There isn't another book to read; none of my old tricks are working well right now. It seems that everyone I know is currently confused, too. My meditation is fragmented, as if the mind I once meditated with is in shards, sparkling tiny shards of light that won't stay connected; my thoughts flit about, and these are God thoughts! It's like I'm on the biggest downhill roller coaster drop, about to come to God-knows-what! *Exactly. And all you can "do", beloved daughter, is trust. This is God territory. This is the great unknown. This is your birth. You don't have to know how. Just stay in the knowing of Who. It is a big bang experience.*

Back to the Tetragrammaton, the four faces of God, creating. God is, first. God is what? second. God becomes that, third. That which God has become, becomes God, fourth. The circle is complete. But you see, God was all that in being God is, or the first principle. This is true also for God's image and similitude - you. As above, so below: as within, so without. Humanity got lost with the God is what? part and forgot the simplicity of isness. You have to define what "is" is. Very funny. Defining "is" will be Bill Clinton's legacy. Truly, you are hilarious, and you choose the ridiculous to describe the sublime. *It's a hoot, don't you think? But back to our subject. To describe these four faces another way, you could say first, there is the thinker. Then there is the thought (word) expressed, so "the word becomes flesh". Then the thought, expanded, returns to the thinker. And then what do you suppose happens, beloved?* The thought, in expanded form, is again expressed by God? *Yes!!! Worlds without end, Amen! Do you see that liberty and courage are parts of the greater definition of love? Love is courageous, love is perfect freedom; love is the glue that holds everything together.* So are you saying that my being will expand to fully express love? *Stick with me, girl. I have this part figured out.* You know very well I'm stuck on you, my brother!

The Sermon on the Mount

It was March 1994 when I first became consciously aware of the concept of personal ascension. One of the members of Ernestine's meditation class excitedly told us about a book on ascension that she had been reading called "The Crystal Stair" by Eric Klein. This was also my introduction to the idea that the personality of Jesus is known in the beyond realms as Sananda. Now, in January 2001, it has been nearly seven years since those ideas were reawakened in my consciousness. According to medical science, our bodies become completely new every seven years, so a new cell has replaced each cell that existed in my body seven years ago. I am literally a new person, completely re-created. Ascension has been my one desire since the day I first realized the possibility. It is my belief that every cell in my body is now imprinted with that one desire. Now, the imprinting moves beyond personal ascension to assisting others in their own resurrection and ascension, to planetary healing and wholeness.

Recenty I was introduced to the Aramaic words of Jesus, whose name in Aramaic is Yeshua ben Alaha (Jesus son of God) through the ground breaking works of Neil Douglas-Klotz in his books "Prayers of the Cosmos" and 'The Hidden Gospel". Our church family was blessed by sharing these fresh and wonderful interpretations of the Lord's Prayer and the Sermon on the Mount. One Sunday Reverend Patricia graced us all with a talk about Douglas-Klotz' ideas surrounding the Sermon on the Mount, during which I was transported to realms of Light beyond any I had experienced prior to that time. Every word she spoke was alive, on fire with the Presence of Alaha (God as Sacred Unity). My body underwent wave after wave of Divine energy vibrations; I vibrated with such intensity that even an hour later I found it difficult to focus my eyes and drive home. During Patricia's talk, as each word Jesus really **meant** impacted my mind, I was also receiving revelations and visions; some of which I remember, others still awaiting my mind's comprehension. I remember feeling very certain that each of the "beatitudes" was a threshold; a gate of consciousness; and that spiritual understanding of one beatitude led to understanding of the next, and so on.

Midway in her talk, Patricia got to the beatitude commonly read as "Blessed are the pure in heart, for they shall see God" and then read Douglas-Klotz interpretation "Aligned with the One are those whose lives radiate from a core of love; they shall see God everywhere" my heart was filled to near bursting, and I beheld the image of Christ, standing in a stone doorway. The doorway, or gateway, was an oval shape, perfectly framing the Lighted image. I knew what "clothed in Light," meant, in that instant. I stood on one side of the doorway, heart pounding, squinting even with my spirit eyes at the brilliant Light pouring from His beautiful image. I say "His" even though I was completely unaware of gender at the time. He sent me calming, peace-filling thoughts to ease me, and I was at peace. He held out his arms to me, stepped forward and greeted me as His equal! I felt completely, totally equal to Him, truly like a long-awaited friend being greeted after a journey to a distant land. We then stepped through the open door together, hand in hand, heart to heart. The experience continued, though all that I consciously remember are the crashing waves of Love vibrating within and around me. During the entire experience, I marveled that I was still able to physically hear and understand every word - even the whispers and sobs of the people near me!

Aramaic was the language spoken by Jesus: a lovely and lyrical language completely unlike English. Each word or word fragment has numerous, interrelated meanings and nuances of meanings, so that to interpret a word from Aramaic to English stifles much of the possible meaning of that word. It is my belief that Jesus said nothing without knowing exactly what he meant to say, and that he meant each possible meaning contained in each word, as well. Additionally, in my visions the "pictographs" or "ideographs" that comprise the writing of Aramaic hold meanings discernable to the higher mind intelligences we are just beginning to remember how to access. So Aramaic (and other ancient languages) may be not only a form of communication for the human mind, but for spiritual mind as well.

I don't know about you, but the beatitudes as translated in the King James Version of my childhood seemed cold and difficult, insurmountable. They didn't seem like blessings at all, but rather more of a curse! I didn't like the idea of being poor in spirit, or meek; I didn't have a clue how to hunger or thirst after something called righteousness; I hadn't any idea how to be pure in heart. Being reviled and persecuted didn't seem like stuff to look forward to, either! Why would I want any of that, I wondered. But Yeshua ben Alaha meant more, much more, than is found in the small English interpretation.

Contained in the nine beatitudes (as interpreted by Douglas-Klotz) are the bases for realizing that you are "on your way" to complete Knowingness, to the Isness that is Alaha as Sacred Unity. They are the signposts, the markers on the path. The human mind begs to know "Am I going the right way? How do I know?" and these are the answers. Douglas-Klotz presents the following as "one possible new translation from the Aramaic":

Tuned to the Source are those who live by breathing Unity; their "I can!" is included in God's.

Blessed are those in emotional turmoil; they shall be united inside by love.

Healthy are those who have softened what is rigid within; they shall receive physical vigor and strength from the universe.

Blessed are those who hunger and thirst for physical justice; they shall be surrounded by what is needed to sustain their bodies.

Blessed are those who, from their inner wombs, birth mercy; they shall feel its warm arms embrace them.

Aligned with the One are those whose lives radiate from a core of love; they shall see God everywhere.

Blessed are those who plant peace each season; they shall be named the children of God.

Blessings to those who are dislocated for the cause of justice; their new home is the province of the universe.

Renewal when you are reproached and driven away by the clamor of evil on all sides, for my sake... Then, do everything extreme, including letting your ego disappear, for this is the secret of claiming your expanded home in the universe.

For so they shamed those before you:

All who are enraptured, saying inspired things - who produce on the outside what the spirit has given them within.

Ahhh. Doesn't this interpretation of the beatitudes make you feel much better about being in the human state? Everyone who is on the path in any way can relate to one or two of these comforting sayings, and feel okay in the process! That is more of what the Jesus I have come to know and love with all my heart would say to us.

Back to the opening paragraph of this chapter. I followed the One Voice in writing it, though I had no clue where it was going, but now I get it. It seems that although personal ascension is a lofty and admirable goal, I have been missing the essential point, at least part of the time. "Seek ye first the Kingdom of Heaven, and all else will be added unto you" he said, and I realized: ascension is a **result** of seeking. It is a manifestation, an outcome "added unto me". Knowing the nature of my personality, it is the ultimate carrot God could dangle, but I realize what I truly desire is the Source of all manifestation, the presence of God. The creator of carrots, not the carrot. But all of it is okay - all of it is Divine Order. God is supremely understanding of our needs, all the time.

Yeah, but...

I so blithely typed the concluding paragraph of that last chapter and have been angry and frustrated since. I've been blocked and in bondage to my questioning for a week! Maybe the bondage is part of the process. At least it's part of mine! This is what has been circling in my mind, God: Why would You give me such a goal, and then another even grander goal, if You want me to give them up? I agree that I cannot possibly understand with my finite mind how such goals could come to pass. I agree that I do not understand the process, any more than I understood the process of puberty or how I am currently understanding the process of menopause (what do You say to menoSTOP?) Am I just to allow it to happen, just like those physical processes? Why would You provide me so many fabulous experiences of how ascension feels if You don't want me to know what's going on? Why the big mystery?

Sweet child, peace be to you. It is difficult, I realize. You will understand, but presently there are no words, no explanation.... but maybe this will help. You do not know the mechanism of menopause, correct? Does anyone? *No, not fully, not yet. Your scientists know that menopause is, the hormonal triggers, the symptoms, the eventual outcome...but not the complex design, nor the mechanism, nor the timing. Such is true also of resurrection and ascension, your next evolutionary step. This process is, however, far more complex. The entire body mind system, the emotional body, the spiritual body; all have roles. All subsystems and supersystems have roles as well; all in concert with Divine Timing. It is not possible to explain in finite terms. What I want you to do, child, is allow it to happen, just as you know intuitively to allow menopause to happen.* It doesn't seem that I have much choice with menopause; it's going to happen whether I am allowing it or not. *And so it is with evolution.*

*The real choice is this: will you allow it to happen gently, or will you be kicking and screaming throughout the process? You have chosen to be one of the first to evolve; you have volunteered to be a guide to others who will follow after you. Worldwide ascension will look something like water coming to a boil. The heat is turned on and the water molecules begin to vibrate. The molecules nearest the heat source vibrate faster, expanding, and soon the molecules on the bottom form bubbles. Meantime, all the molecules are warming, vibrating; motion begins to occur throughout the water. Then suddenly one bubble rises to the top, explodes, **and seems to*** *disappear! Soon more bubbles rise to the top, exactly as the first bubble. Time passes and eventually **all the bubbles rise to the top and seem to disappear.** Complete evaporation has occurred. So it will be with the evolution of the world; do you see? The personality Jesus was the first bubble to evaporate; his physical body was the first to complete the evolutionary process. I was lifted up, and all humankind will follow this example. If not in the earthly "pot", then in another; but all will evolve.*

That helps. Thank You. Now, with menopause, I am taking conscious steps to lessen the effects, to make this transition easier for me to handle. For example, I use soy to alleviate menopause symptoms. Is there anything I can do to consciously make the transition to evolution easier? Is there anything I can do to make the transition more conscious? *Still going for the massive experience, the big feeling, eh? Will you be tremendously disappointed if the process is so gradual that it is unnoticeable, like the transition from puberty to young adulthood? You realize there was not a "big day" when you became, suddenly, adult.* To be very honest, yes, I will be disappointed, because that's not the example Jesus showed to the world. Rising to the top, like a bubble of expanded consciousness, exploding into new form - that's what Jesus did. *That is one outcome. It is one result. There are others - that is the reason for asking you to give up all your ideas surrounding ascension. Is it possible, do you think, for God to have many other ideas? There are many individuals waiting, waiting, waiting as you are; and all have ideas of how and when. I am asking all to give it up. Let go and let God. She is full of surprises. For some the transition will be gradual, for some sudden, for some in private, for some in public. More than that I cannot describe. God knows your need in this regard, beloved. God knows the highest and best "way" to do this evolution thing. You cannot know because it is indescribable. But this I promise - it is indescribably delicious.*

Was there an answer to my question in there? What can I do to help the process? *Let go of the outcome and relax. You can be more lovingly connected to your body temple - perhaps ask yourself "what would Jesus eat?" and "how would Jesus exercise?" and "what supplements would Jesus take?" and "would Jesus fast?" I will tell you this: time is short. Time is indeed very short. Loving preparation of the body will ease the transition. There is no magic formula since each human body has differing requirements, but there is plenty of guidance available.* I am aware of that. I had a knowing about a year ago that there was some supplement on the market that would be excellent for my body, especially at this menopausal transition. I went to the local health food store and stood there, and heard "Look for Me. When you see Me, you will know it" and there it was, on the shelf - a supplement called "Source of Life" and it's absolutely perfect for me. *Precisely. Excellent example. I remember our delight!* You are cool. This whole God experience is cool. I'm not angry any more. Thank you so much for patience with me. Fasting? *You'll know. It will be cool, too. Fasting, since it is a commitment, has a payoff.* I never thought of it that way!

Yeah, but.... phase 2

So much of what I have read and heard from spiritual teachers of late has been in conflict. In "Communion with God" Neale Donald Walsch's latest book, You say that all things are knowable. Others say that many things are beyond our knowing and we must simply trust. Which is it? Oh, never mind...that was a question that you most certainly would answer "Both" and I know that "both" is the true answer. But it seems there is no answer that is completely true from the dual mind, or that could be expressed in duality language, which is what we've got to work with. The co-founder of the Unity movement, Charles Fillmore, was certain that there were answers to all his questions. *Since you are asking the big questions, how would you like to be enabled to know the answers?* What a question! It would be wonderful! *Be careful, child. What you ask may cause people to "revile" you in ways only known to fully Christed beings. You have difficulties in being "different" as it is. Re-read some of your previous words.* I am humbled. I want to know more than I want to be understood. I accept the difficulties. I have you.

Beloved, all is knowable in the absolute. I withhold nothing from you. Have I not said, "All I have is yours"? Further, all I am you are. We are indeed One Spirit. However, in the realm of duality, where you now dwell, opposites exist and seem quite real, though in the realm of the absolute any idea that would negate is not known. For example, evil appears quite real in the realm of duality. In God mind evil is not, because the ideas or thoughts leading to such a manifestation cannot exist. Evil is a result. God is Love. Love cannot conceive of harm in any way, and "evil" is a result of harmful thought. It is not possible, because God Is. Anything that would compromise "isness" cannot be. That is why Neale Donald Walsch re-presented the Ten Commandments as the Ten Commitments. These are promises that explain how, once you re-connect to God mind, you are neither able to think such thoughts nor manifest such results. It is quite simple. To quote Charles Fillmore, "thoughts held in mind produce after their kind." Same idea. Hold to God thought and your daily consciousness, then your subconscious, your perceptions and your manifestations, are healed. This is why "A Course in Miracles" is so effective when followed to completion. The ideas presented erase duality thinking while simultaneously infilling the practitioner's mind with God thought.

Thank You for getting my attention with "A Course in Miracles". I am so grateful to You for that.... *and I to you, for listening. There is another "course" I would have you take, beloved Liberty, if you desire answers to your questions, the how's and whys that cannot be answered in the duality languages of the earth-mind. Do you recall the greater gifts described in "The Keys of Enoch"? The gifts beyond the gifts of the Holy Spirit given in the Bible and the Book of Mormon*...hmmm, the gifts of spiritual-scientific languages, the raising of the dead (!), something relating to angels, I think...I'll just go get the book. Here it is, Key 113, verse 44:

> The People of God will also receive five additional Gifts of the Holy Spirit when they are fully actualized. These will be the gifts of speaking in **spiritual-scientific tongues, resurrecting the dead; speaking angelic languages;** the ability to **see and work with the angelic teachers of Light** in this world and the co-existing worlds; and the **understanding of the mysteries of the Shekinah Kingdoms** whereby all embodiments of your Overself can be experienced by you in reference to other worlds which you occupy. [emphasis mine]

So what are you getting at, God? I don't feel like spiritual-scientific languages are my thing...*What would you say to seeing and working with angelic teachers and remembering angelic languages? These are beyond duality and would serve to answer your questioning. You continue to seek and knock, hunger and thirst. I keep My promises...what do you say?* Wow! And saying wow seems inadequate in the extreme - is there an angelic language equivalent that would more adequately express what I am feeling? *If indeed your "wow" implies agreement, then yes, there is an angelic expression for awed acceptance. But these languages are for understanding, for the knowings that you desire. The languages are not so much spoken words as telethought communications, as direct imaging in the form of pictographs. You will have new understandings, truly wonderful knowings, but most will not be transferrable to human language. Do you remember the experience with the obelisks?* The time when it seemed that stone tablets and obelisks, covered in letters and hieroglyphics rushed by in my consciousness? *Yes. Some of those pictographs represented angelic languages.* So I have been prepared. *Yes. Superconsciously, and now consciously.* Question. Is this preparation what my teacher Ernestine saw in the reading in

1994 when she said my mind was being continually "packed with information"? *Yes. She was able to observe the transfer of knowledge from superconscious to conscious realms, to be available for your use as needed. You have yourself noticed this in the dream state.*

Okay. So now I'm conversing with angels, working with them, all that stuff. I have these great and wonderful knowings; my mind is expanded beyond human imagining. Will I even be able to explain any of this stuff to myself? My mind operates in human language; my thoughts are in word form. How is this going to work? And another thing - what is being fully actualized? *Ah, Liberty - there you go again, asking the questions that require answers beyond duality. But you are not completely correct about your thoughts. That which you consider "God thought" often comes in the form of experience, usually in meditation, which you then transfer bit by bit into word thought as you explain the experience to yourself. With new commitments come new abilities, little one.* So I won't understand until I know. *That sums it up quite well.* Geez. And I thought I could come to You for answers! This opens up a whole realm of new questions. *So it does. Many mansions yet to explore, beloved. Wait until the conversation about resurrecting the dead!*

Hey wait a minute - what about being fully actualized? You didn't answer that - or did You?

Actuality

Shirley MacLaine, unknown to her, has blessed me greatly. Several years ago she really pissed me off. It was early in my own spiritual journey; before "A Course in Miracles" became my constant companion. In reading one of her many books, she talked about traveling to Sedona to visit with a visionary someone in her life had recommended. She spent several days in Sedona, sightseeing, visiting the visionary, talking with other spiritual types, and shopping. She mentioned casually the great monetary cost of her spiritual journeying. There was the blessing! I flushed in anger - at her, at God, because I did not believe that spirituality could be bought, even though it <u>appeared</u> that she was buying at least some of her spirituality.

In that moment I determined to find God simply by being myself, living my life. The only God I could love would be found in my own home, within my budget. I knew that finding my God did not require going to see "masters"; could not require attending certain retreats (or even church, for that matter); would not require baptism in a river; and did not require even reading certain books! Although I knew that any of these could be helpful, I also knew that the God of my being was there, within my being. The great confirmation of my determination came in "A Course in Miracles" in the lesson "You need do nothing". I cried and cried, profoundly relieved that anyone could find the God within by asking, seeking and knocking. That simple.

I have read numerous books, yes. I own quite a few books, but if I could only have one book, I would choose "A Course in Miracles" and it would be enough. Many feel that way about the Bible, or the Qu'ran, the Bhagavad Gita, the Vedas and Upanishads. I have listened to God-inspired music. I own quite a few CD's now, but there is plenty of God-inspired music traveling radio waves, too. I have attended meditation classes in my own town, and now attend a wonderful church in my own town. Only once have I traveled more than 20 miles to attend any spiritual gathering, and that was the retreat with my daughter's youth group. Mostly, I have learned to listen. I have learned to hear the One Voice within me and to respond. That is what God means when He asks us to obey - She wants us to listen and to hear, truly hear, and when we hear truly what God is saying we are joyfully compelled to respond Yes! Yes! Because what we hear, truly hear, is exactly what we <u>want</u> to do and to be.

I asked God about His meaning of "fully actualized" a few paragraphs ago. Usually the answer comes immediately (if not sooner, like even before the asking!) But this time I waited several days, listening. Just when I thought maybe I hadn't heard and began to look in books for the meaning, the answer came. God answered, and continues to answer. And this answer is heaped up, pressed down, shaken together and running over! It means resurrected, evolving toward ascension and beyond. He has confirmed that I am a resurrecting being, right now, as I type this page. It is really happening! Let me explain.

In January sometime, it was announced in our church that a "Holotropic Breathwork" seminar would be held on a Friday evening in March. I knew something about the subject, and had long wanted the experience. So I knew this was for me, as did many others in the congregation. Holotropic breathwork is a means (for most) of bringing up blockages within consciousness, and with the assistance of their own inner healer, to face them and move beyond. I thought that I knew there were no further blockages in my consciousness but it seemed arrogant to know that, even though it is true. I felt that God had another plan in Mind for me in using the breathwork. *Oh yes, and yes again, beloved. It is not arrogance to know Truth. The plan is continuing, as well.* No kidding! Usually I have to depress the "italics" icon when You want to take over typing, but not that time! May I continue? *Continue as "I Am".* Huh?

The session lasts for two hours. "Sitters" watch "breathers", since some of what comes up can be volatile. An altered state of consciousness is reached by rapidly breathing in and out without pause, for as long as it takes to reach the altered state. My body began the familiar tingling trembling and my consciousness exploded within just a few breaths. I was profoundly grateful to reach that state, the tingling trembling that heralds the Presence of God, because I had not been "there" for about six weeks. I was starving for the Presence! I realized that I would be able to stay in this expanded state, even grow in it, for two whole hours! I was overwhelmingly joyful at the prospect of being in the Presence of God for such a long period of time, feeling totally safe, completely abandoning my human-ness for such a period. I lay there quivering, weeping with joy, and discovered that my head was resting on none other than Jesus' lap, while he stroked my forehead and wiped away my tears. He was delighted to have this time with me! I chanted his name, Yeshua ben Alaha, over and over and over, weeping and tingling, vibrating so deep within my body-being that I knew that I was having and would have a sacred experience.

That image faded away, and I began the deep rapid breathing again. Deeper and wider my consciousness grew, while closer and more present Christ consciousness drew, merging, joining; jolts of electrical energy exploding through my body. My hands and arms, feet and legs were twitching and moving in circular patterns, trembling wildly. My body convulsed in a wave-like pattern, contorting with energy. In a cool, detached way I noticed how odd it was to have full observational power of my body but absolutely no control over these movements. It felt as if every cell was on fire, and I knew that this body was being cleansed and purified at a cellular level, completely and with some sort of finality. It occurred to me that I have been preparing for this enormous physical cleansing, listening and responding to God's guidance in diet, exercise, supplements and healing agents. I was aware that someone placed a pillow under my right hand. I was also aware that people were watching me. I knew that I was alternating between smiling blissfully and weeping madly, between flailing and rest. When this period of the breathwork was "finished", I was very thirsty and drank 16 ounces of water in two gulps. Then I resumed the breathing.

Peace, marvelous, comforting Peace washed over me and engulfed me. I felt cradled and held, while simultaneously suspended in gel-like "light". I was totally opened, trusting with certainty. The wave-like vibrational energies swirled around and within me, and angels surrounded my body. There was no way conflict of any kind could touch me in this sacred space. To my right, where he is always, was precious Jesus, holding my hand. Saint Germaine breathed violet fire over me, continuing my purification and transmutation in his position at my head. To my left sat beautiful Saint Francis. His beatific smiling understanding of my process enveloped him, blessing me with absolute comfort. My beloved Daddy and dear Granny were at my feet. And Mary, wonderful Mother Mary, was my heart. My arms were outstretched, cross fashion. Wave after wave of bliss poured through my body. Thought forms and thought pictures cascaded through my mind, like silvery liquid. I heard others in the room screaming in agony, and I could see what was happening for them in consciousness. My hands, of their own accord, opened and faced those who were screaming, and God's own living, life-giving Peace poured from my palms, as more and more Peace filled my being. Words of an origin unfamiliar to my consciousness came from my mouth, and I knew these were Divine prayers, bringing complete healing. I felt, truly, like an instrument of Peace.

There was a shift. The Light beings were no longer surrounding me. I resumed the deep rapid breathing, profoundly relaxed, body totally limp. A shield or protective force field of invisible yet incredibly blue Divine Light formed around my physical body. I knew this was the protection of the Archangel Michael, even though I didn't "see" his mighty presence. I felt intense exhilaration and excitement, while remaining totally relaxed. The electrical energy surrounding me made a crackling sound. I wondered if anyone in my vicinity could hear or see the energy. I knew that something extraordinary was coming. I recalled the latest guided meditations from the meditation class I have been leading, about chakra opening and balancing, transforming the primal energies into their Divine counterparts. The One Voice spoke "You are prepared". But the "you" was a melded sound, including "you" and "I" and "we" and "thee". "Are" also included "am" and "prepared" implied "ready" and "completed" and "purified". Each word an inclusive thought, rather than an exclusive description. It seemed totally natural.

There was a whirling, spiraling energy and I felt myself standing on a stone slab, a shining black-brown stone that somehow contained all of Earth's energy. I was totally in love with the energy. There was an aroma of rich, fertile soil, the reborn Earth of springtime. Every possible requirement for lavishly and abundantly fulfilling all forms of life was contained in the sensate energies swirling around me, and there was no question of survival, only the complete knowing that Life is eternal. The solid rock. I was standing on the solid rock of eternal Life! I knew myself to be Eternal Life, one with and part of all Life. My base chakra, grounded in earth energy and already opened wide, exponentially expanded to include the entire earth and all life forms in this eternal Life fire. A deep humming vibration began in the area of my base chakra, extending down through my legs and into the Earth. Or was it the other way around?

The vibration moved into my sexual center (yes, it felt great!) The energy became a rich, blood red pulsation. Sacred, prayerful images of sexual creation and childbirth flashed in my consciousness, followed by images of marvelous artistic creation, musical creation, scientific creation, architectural creation - like God's own version of Art History 101. In the melded, fluidly inclusive language, God talked to me of human creation. Every creation, done prayerfully and in conjunction with Divine Purpose was truly co-creation with God, and blessed. God opened me to see my own co-creations, this writing being one of those. I felt and knew my pro-creative chakra expanded and energized by God's own pleasure. God is pleased with me! A marvelous satisfying bliss came over me in waves of blood-red fire energy. A whole pack of cigarettes would not have been enough!

Feeling mighty good (and wondering what might have been coming out of my mouth) the energy moved to my solar plexus chakra. It was as if the light of the whole sun filled my energy field and I felt certain that the light must be visible to everyone in the room. The glorious golden yellow light left nothing in darkness. The light energy was a dancing, singing, bell-ringing playful music and I laughed aloud, feeling like I was about three years old without a care in the world. The air was perfumed with sunlight smells, lilacs and freesias and fresh grass, linens hung to dry and flapping in the summer breeze, salt water and sandy beach smells, coconut oil on warm skin. Despair could not exist here, I thought. And the Voice, my own and His combined, words melded into meanings laughed, "This is fullness of joy"! And every negative emotion I had **ever in any human life** on Earth experienced gathered in a dark whirlwind above my solar plexus chakra and vanished. I watched this in complete amazement, and while my attention was on the watching, my solar plexus chakra expanded, actually blossoming like a fabulous orange-yellow summer flower, larger and larger until I could perceive nothing else in my visual field. My focus went to my right cheek, because I felt a soft breeze on my face. I knew that I knew this was the breath of God, and the light became Divine Light. My emotional body was divinized, and I was quivering with Joy and astonishment.

I knew which chakra was next - the heart chakra. I wondered if my body could handle any more energy and actually felt fearful and anguished. Involuntarily the deep rapid breathing resumed, and I decided to trust, trust, trust the process. Very slowly, gradually, a vision opened in my consciousness. It was familiar - a white marble structure, intricately carved with symbols to allow the Light to breathe in and out. It has six sides - a hexagon. The "walls" are two layers of marble and the carving is such that if you were standing outside the structure you could not actually see inside, even though both layers of marble have the carvings all over. There is just enough space between the two layers of marble to make a walkway. There is no doorway and no roof.

Inside the structure, carved into the marble floor (which curiously does not touch the walls) is a six-pointed star, the Star of David. The thought of a landing-pad flits through my consciousness. The shape is very flower-like as well as definitely being a star. While I am noticing the star/flower union, I realize that the shape is the same as the point of intersection in the down-pointing tetrahedron and the up-pointing tetrahedron that is now visible there in the center of the marble temple. The intersecting tetrahedrons look as if they are made of clear, shimmering bubble-stuff, though I "know" this material is stronger than anything in human experience. As I am thinking the thought about the look of the material, a flame of intense, surreal beauty appears suspended in the exact center of the tetrahedron vehicle.

My desire is to touch, to hold, to gaze deeply at the flame, to be enveloped by the fire and to be immersed in it. The fire responds to my desire and burns brighter, clearer, and purer; finally I notice the color of the flames. As I look into the fire, it appears predominantly pink, a peachy-golden pink that has also a hint of yellow; like a vestige of sunlight yellow cast over the pinkness. Then realization floods my consciousness - this is my heart! This flame is the Holy of Holies in the temple of my heart! This is the center point of who I am, the balance point of my being...and I feel a surging, pulsing, throbbing torrent of Divine Love implode and explode from within and beyond my heart center - Divine Love erupting with a big bang, dissolving what had been my limited heart center while simultaneously creating in me a new heart...with great compassion I watched Libby lying on the mat, sobbing uncontrollably. In that moment of compassion I heard the melded Voice "when the inner becomes the outer" and "the inner has become the outer" and "the above is the below". The Voice held such a melting tenderness, almost tearfulness - I was weeping with joy in spirit as well as in body. I rested in Grace for a time.

The deep rapid breathing began again, while I was resting and unaware. The energy moved slowly, imperceptibly to my throat chakra area, like a covert maneuver. God knows this is a tough chakra for me - will and wisdom and speaking truth. This is the area of my greatest challenge in this lifetime...and I can be resistant. I often maintain silence. I am often asked to maintain silence. That being said, it is also the area that brings me my greatest joys, for when I do speak Truth, I feel balanced, whole, enthusiastic, joy filled. After the deep breathing tapered off, I remember nothing but a deep, rich blueness, very soft and velvety, yet also containing the sharpness of a faceted stone. From very far away I heard my own voice, childlike, crying out in bewilderment and anguish "How do I know it is Your Will?" and "how do I know it is Your Voice?" and "how do I know it is Your Wisdom?" and on and on, plaintive words and meanings floating there in the velvety atmosphere. Then nothing, nothing. It felt as if I stood on a pinnacle, all around me a void unimaginably vast. A tone sounded, from within and beyond me, growing, vibrating the blueness. The tone was Divine Assurance, and the Voice that is also my own voice spoke. "Beloved, how could your voice, your will, your wisdom, not also be Mine? I AM all in all, all in you, all in everyone. You have chosen to speak in our voice, follow our will, and rely on our wisdom. Speak with our voice, little one, speak! My children strangle on the little wills of the world."

I swallowed hard, and it was as if a knot in my throat dissolved. All the Truth I had ever choked back, words I had been unwilling or unready to speak out was released, dispersed to the soul made ready for that Truth. I wanted to shout my acceptance, but my human voice was choked with sobs. Realization of the depth of devotion to Divine Will within my Christ being flooded me. The simplicity of the revelation from the Voice of God-in-me was astounding. I wondered how I could have been so dense!

I don't remember a shift occurring, probably because I was dumbfounded with awe, but shift happened anyway. Pulsating, vibrating violet energy "descended" into my third eye chakra area, feeling as if a crystalline amethyst life force surrounded my head in a violet stone of immaculate perfection. Again I felt, as a human being, incapable of accepting what was occurring in my consciousness, so I "surrendered" my bodily consciousness altogether. From here on I remember nothing of what was happening in my body-mind; so absorbed in Christ-mind I could not maintain even observer consciousness of my body. I did not care at all. I was not the least attached.

Totally immersed in Spirit, voices both human and divine sang in wonderful harmony "Be Thou my vision". It seemed I could "hear" every version of that song ever sung in every voice who has ever (or will ever) sung it, all in glorious waves of the intent behind the words. Concentric desires to see as Christ, all the time, and to see, really envision Jesus, to see God with my own eyes welled up, and the violet energy throbbed, growing in intensity until there was a soft "poof", like a sound without sound and the energy shattered into shards of glittering, incredibly tiny amethyst crystalline tetrahedrons. Revelation dawned like sunrise in my consciousness, and the melded Word of the Living God spoke to me, the I am Liberty *"Be thou My Vision"*. I knew, I knew, I knew in this blinding violet light, that I was blind but now I see. I am Liberty, and I see with the vision of Christ. I am God's vision of Liberty. I am the eyes of Christ in manifestation. I am the Christ so many need to see, the ordinary made extraordinary. Visions beyond my ability to describe came then, glories beyond anything yet seen upon the earth. *To you, my beloved, I give the gift of revelation. Reveal, child. Reveal all of Me in you.* Returning somewhat to what we call reality, I knew that my third eye chakra was now the open door that no one can shut. I observed the room and the beloved souls there as if I were one eye, floating in space near the ceiling. On automatic pilot, the deep rhythmic breathing resumed. Body consciousness returned. I thought for an instant that I was "done", that my process was over.

Cosmic laughter rang out, like the bells of the Universe were ringing with merriment. What's so funny? I thought, and a tsunami of God-Presence swept over my body, deeply immersing me in

113

the laughing vibrational energy. Inside my skull I felt a whirling warmth that erased all the edges created by flesh and bone there. Washed away in God's amusement, again I lost all contact with my body-mind; but this time in a more instantaneous way, without deciding to surrender. The decision had already been made.

From beyond my newly expanded vision, a tiny pinpoint of beautiful singing clear light appeared, expanding as it came "toward" me. The Light encircled my consciousness; my consciousness was ringed by row after row of angelic beings, all part of the wondrous clear Light. I recalled for an instant a drawing of a white lotus flower on the cover of a "White Eagle" book in my possession. This lotus blossom was like a massive, majestic choir formation, and each petal the white robe of a member of a heavenly choir. What I was experiencing was very similar. I looked more closely at one of the angelic beings, and realized with a jolt that this is the image of one of my own incarnations! I looked around, carefully noting the faces of the beings - many seemed extremely familiar, like my own personalities; others were members of my many families, earthly and from other existences. All of "them" knew me; this I knew with certainty. Another great certainty came over me then; that all these minds were within my own mind! *You are crowned with many crowns, beloved of God.*

The Divine Light grew bright, brilliantly luminous; the choir I am sang to me about being crowned with Light; the Light became a flaming clear pillar surrounding everything in my consciousness; my mind **SCREAMED** HOW CAN I KNOW I AM THINKING THE THOUGHTS OF CHRIST? HOW CAN I KNOW IN MY EXPERIENCE THAT MY MIND IS CHRIST MIND? And at that very instant, I heard a keening wail, an agonized cry from someone in the room...and my consciousness went directly to the crying soul, praying passionately, fervently, devotedly, Oh God, dear God, heal your precious children! Heal your children! Over and over, hearing cries from around the room, hearing cries from around the world, I cried and sobbed, praying with everything I am that God heal us, all of us, body, mind, heart and soul. Exhausted, spent - all was darkness.

In the midst of glory, my beloved child, you have cried out for your brothers and sisters. This is how you know, my beloved Liberty. This is how you know.

114

Peace beyond understanding came over me in a profound vibrating rush. The arms of my sweet Jesus surrounded me, and I rested there. But then my humanity prevailed - I needed to pee! Somehow I managed to stand, and my sitter came from behind me to help me walk to the bathroom. Someone in the room laughed with a marvelous childlike laugh, and I felt the happiness of his laughter. I giggled, walking unsteadily toward the bathroom. As I sat down, I had the thought that the timing of this human need was pretty humorous, and simultaneous to that thought, heard *yeah, during my resurrection I had to pee down the pole!* I laughed so hard if I hadn't already been sitting down to pee I would have peed my pants!

I returned to the room, and the music denoting the end of the breathwork was playing. Two hours had passed! Before I had time to wonder about what Jesus just said to me breathers and sitters were moving about the room, being our human selves again.

We were asked to share our experiences later, after a break to draw a picture of what we had experienced. I drew my own eye, a single eye, with the flaming Yod symbol in the center. I didn't say much, but my dear friend Ruth knew. She asked me "Are you ready?" And my answer was immediately "yes". I said it smiling, calm, without any hesitation and with finality.

An hour and a half passed, and I was driving, almost home. It occurred to me that nothing had "come up" in me; no opposition to readiness had surfaced from my subconscious mind. Realization flooded into me, I felt the Presence of God strong in my body. If there is no opposition in me, this time I must really <u>be ready</u>! I was trembling with excitement, exhilaration, a trusting apprehension of the unknown and unseen - and glanced at the odometer. 11077 miles were registered. I glanced at the clock. Wouldn't you just know - 11:11! I glanced at the CD player - 2:22 seconds on the cd that was playing. The lyric was "...until all that lives in me is the Message" and I knew that I knew that I knew - all that lives in me <u>is</u> the Message, the true and pure message that Jesus came to deliver - that we are human and we are Divine, just as he is.

Resurrected

That's some chapter heading. Where is this going, God? *You wake in the middle of the night with insight and revelation and still you wonder?* Oh, the born again information? *Yes. And you thought it was just a lovely little explanation of a troubling concept!* I wondered what it was about. I wasn't questioning the idea of "born again", or at least I wasn't questioning consciously. *Then the information must be about you.* Is that how it goes? But I don't quite understand how this applies to "resurrected" *Just go with Me here.* Like I would make another choice? This is a One Voice revelation, too.

~~~

In springtime the trees put forth lovely little blossoms. Many would say that being born again is like this - springtime blossoming. And this new awakening, this delicate flower of renewal, is important and beautiful. It is the awakening to the Christ self. It is the realization of the possibility. But there is no birth here, because the delicate flower is purely possibility, subject to many outer hazards. Similarly, the awakening being. Will the awakening Christ be blown apart by the wind? Will the blossoming spirit get enough water? Will a squirrel eat the blossom? Will there be a hard freeze? Is the tree (the teacher, pastor, human guide) healthy? Circumstances of the outer world play a very strong role in the life of the newly awakened being.

When all goes well and bees and butterflies visit the blossom, a young fruit will appear. It is small and hard, bitter. It bears little resemblance to the ripe fruit. The embryonic Christ is much the same, hardness protecting the growing flame inside, still subject to outer influences, but not so delicate. Each summer rain fills the fruit with growth and potential; likewise, a drought will end the possibility of fullness. The merciful rain of Spirit during this time of growth has the same effect on the embryonic Christ; similarly, a lack of teaching and guidance will cause a withering death. When the embryonic Christ listens and hears, a process of expansion, of sweetening, of softening occurs. The Light shines each day on the growing fruit of Spirit.

Finally the fruit is fully grown, heavy, ripe and sweet. But even now the appearance of the fruit may be deceptive. Perhaps the fruit has grown from a rotting tree, and the core of the fruit is rotted. So it is with the young Christ. If the core beliefs of the young Christ are Truth, she is centered, healthy. However, if at the core the young Christ holds beliefs of unworthiness, of guilt and shame, the center cannot hold. But so often it is difficult to discern the difference by appearance alone.

Whether healthy or rotten at the core, the fruit has no preference if it is harvested and eaten by a person or if it drops to the ground as food for birds. The difference now is that whomever eats of the rotten fruit will spit it out and discard the core; the seeds will neither take root nor grow. The healthy fruit, on the other hand, whether eaten and enjoyed by a human body or dropped as food for nature, serves the purpose of the fruit and completes the design by its' use for nurturing and for re-creation.

This appearance of fullness, of ripeness, is where the human will can cause great trouble. Many Christing beings alive today are here, appearing fully ripe, **thinking** the self to be filled with the sweetness of Spirit. But at their core they hold thoughts and feelings of unworthiness, guilt, shame, anger, death and separation. Often the very religion they espouse teaches these thoughts. The center will not hold. All thoughts that negate Truth, that oppose Truth must be canceled, erased, eradicated. **Thinking** themselves full of Spirit, these Christing beings teach and preach, seeding others, feeding others, who listen because it is their will to listen. Much of what these Christing beings teach and preach is helpful, kind and true. But the center will not hold.

The Christing being who has fed on Truth, whose center is clarified, purified and filled with love of God, neighbor and self **knows** she is filled with Spirit. Fully ripened in Spirit, this Christ has no desires of her own, but only wants to feed others hungry for spiritual food, for Truth. And this, beloved, is the new birth, this dying to personal desires, this fully ripened sweet compassionate nature, this willingness to be consumed, this willingness to be implanted in the earth as the Tree of Life. The center will hold, because the center is the will of God. The heart is the Heart of God. The mind is the Mind of God. Oneness is remembered. One is born again, and the birth is the fullness of Spirit. Spirit is made flesh,

117

then flesh is made Divine in the process called resurrection, and then ascension. Look once again at Jesus on the cross, giving his body to seed the idea that Life is eternal; that death is illusion. He cared not that the body would die; his concern was to feed those hungry for spiritual food. Truly, he was the first fruit of the Spirit; the fully ripened sweetness implanted in the Christ consciousness now being fully born. *In you. In you, and in many others. This is the time.*

This is the time

Nearly Easter, 2001. I looked at the calendar today and noticed that there is a full moon on Palm Sunday. This Palm Sunday is also the first day of Passover, and Easter Sunday this year is the last day of Passover. I wonder how often that happens? No doubt it is significant. *This is the time.* I knew You would say that!

Now is the time to be. Be all that you are! Stretch your self-imposed boundaries - use your gifts! You mean I can now be omnipresent? That I can appear to be in two or more places, fully conscious, able to know simultaneously what is happening everywhere I am...that would be wonderfully effective in prayer *Oh my beloved child, you delight me* Is that a yes? *An emphatic, joyful, triumphant Yes!* Oh my God...what have I asked for this time? *You desire to manifest omnipresence, which entails teleportation and imaging and thought-transference and angelic languaging, clairvoyance and clairaudience, and by noting the effects such omnipresence would have on prayer, healing and the working of all miracles. Go and get the Keys of Enoch; there is a definition there for you to use.* Something about the gifts of spirit, I guess. *Yes. There.*

Keys of Enoch, Key 113: 41-43

Their (the aware) vibratory powers form the collective Messianic garment through: the *healing powers* of the Holy Spirit; the proper attunement of *spiritual instruction*; the spreading of *wisdom given by the Holy Spirit* so as to unite all wisdom traditions into the Living Light; the *discernment of spirits* that inhibit the people of the planet from knowing their true identity with God; the *prophetic preaching* as to the Key of Knowledge working within and beyond time; the manifestations of *speaking in tongues* that unite the body with other levels of intelligence (which can show patterns of previous spiritual teaching); the *interpretation of tongues* so as to understand how different levels of knowledge can be coordinated (irrespective of the genetic capacity); the power of *miracles* showing the interpenetration of life into the Infinite Way; and the gift of active *faith* which shows how we must progress beyond the "milk of being a new-born child of God" into the Messianic fiber which cultivates the Kingdom of God on earth - seeing invisible things becoming visible. [Emphasis mine]

In desiring omnipresence, my child, you have marked a completion. What do You mean? *You have requested that which will propel you, in an utterly captivating, breathless-with-anticipation rush; you know, that magnificent crescendo of beingness that you have sought as your heart's desire...and have known with total knowing that THIS IS FOR YOU, my beloved...the desire you have made flesh will quicken your very flesh.* Oh, my God, what have I asked for this time??

~~~

I had to go for a walk just then. I just got out of my chair and walked away from the computer screen, from the keyboard, from that damned italics key that is operated from Beyond. It didn't help. God is so present to me in everything I cannot get away, cannot tear my eyes off Sacred Unity even in sleep. I dream about people who go to my church; people who have physical challenges or desire healing in other ways; I'm with them, in the night, praying and doing healing work. *You do this work in many realms.* Enough. Let me become accustomed to teleporting in the dream state, please, before we advance to other realms. Am I really present with the persons I dream about? *Yes, beloved child. As usual, before you have asked, I have answered.* You know I just need to **shut up**.

Back to the walk. It is springtime, still early, here in Tennessee. The first wave of blooming stuff is over; the bigger second wave has begun. All the fruit trees are blossoming; the sight of one such tree so beautiful I nearly dropped to my knees, tears flowing. Only a few people have changed the oil in their lawnmowers and numerous blooming weeds still wander the lawns in patches of purple, white and yellow. The air is saturated with growth, with potential, with unrealized ripeness. I realized that I have this very same power of renewal and rebirth within my being. In rhythm to my walking I chanted, "I am the resurrection and the Life"; just spontaneously, no thinking required. And I knew it. I knew it surely, deeply, in certainty. **I am the resurrection and the Life.** All the power in the universe is mine to use. God has written to me, in my book of Life, that *I am completed.* And there, He just did it again - the italics just came on. *No thinking required.*

While I have your attention I will answer an unasked question. Great! What am I wondering about without knowing I'm wondering? *Your "clumsiness" and unfocused vision, the "corner of the eye" phenomena, the sounds within sounds; other sensory strangeness you have noticed without regarding.* I have noticed, but I figured it was yet another adjustment in my process. *And that is true.* The focusing thing is unusual, though. It seems as if my eyes are borrowed from someone else and I'm getting accustomed to them. Or like using binoculars at the beginning of a concert; at first the maneuvering is slow and lots of the images are blurred, but by the end of the concert the focusing is smooth. *Control of all your body senses has been transferred to your I Am presence. You are focusing from another octave of reality, from a different dimension. You are focusing from your evolution.*

This chapter will have to end there. I cannot respond to that.

Living death

Easter Sunday was two days ago. The traditions were, for me, complete emptiness this year, even though the music and presentations at Unity Church were incredibly inspired. In this moment the crucifixion/resurrection process is excruciating and exhausting. And I feel utterly alone. In know of no person on earth to whom I could express what I am feeling, and even if I could express it, I don't feel like talking. God is present, yes, but God is impersonal. Not detached, but not immediate, either. God is observing; allowing. Sometimes, when one of my children needs to learn a lesson on his own, I have observed myself behaving this way. Simply standing by, watching, ready to rescue, but not planning to step in except in disaster. *All that you have ever been is dying away.* Yes. I feel something like a zombie, like the walking dead. Between worlds, I guess. *And you are mourning, grieving for Libby.* How do You **do** that? The italics just come on and my fingers type a sentence, and before I notice You have done it, there it is! *And now you have realized how deep is your grief, my beloved child, for this self you have been...I am here. I am your Abba. Come, rest in Me.*

~~~

It took a long while to stop sobbing after **that**. He is mightily correct, though: I am grieving. Before He typed "and now you have realized how deep is your grief" I had no real idea where all the anger and depression of the past few days had been coming from. I didn't really seem to care, either. *All the experiences, all the life you have lived up to now in your body has served to polish the lens of who you really are. The lens is clear now and your I Am presence stands ready to shine in full brilliance. What you were is no longer. Who you are is beyond the time and space limitations of the physical and can no longer be contained. You are prepared, Liberty.* So why is it that I feel so damned inadequate? I can't even pray; it seems that the words are completely without meaning. Even thinking of Jesus seems horribly empty - but no, it isn't even that...it's the act of thinking that seems empty. I look in the mirror and see my same old face, and I know my name and who I am, but I am totally out of touch with my true identity as the Christ. My identification with Jesus or Yogananda is out of reach, too. Obviously this is a phase of my "becoming" but I want it to end. What is the purpose in this? Don't answer that!

The phases in Jesus' illumination took place in a linear, definable fashion; necessary for the living symbol he is. However, in the process of becoming Christ that the rest of us endure, there are fits and starts, and one phase gets tangled up in another; almost as if we could not manage to complete one phase from beginning to end if we knew we were actually "in" a particular phase. We would self-abort. I was not able to consciously know of the extraordinary significance of my spiritual baptism until recently; however, that period of unconsciousness did nothing to prevent the unfoldment of the next phase. In contrast, I was conscious of the revelation that began my resurrection phase but am now undergoing a deeper death, a more massive surrender to what I now know is the truth of my being. This must be the pain of knowing.

I feel an intensity of loneliness, an empty, tortured alone; a no-thing that I could not have believed existed. The garden of Gethsemane; that's where I am now. Everyone around me sleeps, unable or unwilling to accompany me or support me in this dark, suffocating density. I long for the Presence of God, yet I feel undeserving and incapable of even feeling that vibration because of the darkness. It is a beautiful bright spring day, but I feel undeserving of such splendor and incapable of truly appreciating such beauty. I am nothing and no-thing, a mass of confused thoughts in a tired mind. I am hungry but nothing satisfies; thirsty but drink cannot quench my thirst. Being surrounded by others leaves me feeling even more alone, bereft, isolated. All the sacred music I have loved leaves me feeling hollow; words of comfort in my books jumble together and fly apart, meanings gone to me. Prayer does not comfort; words will not come. I feel useless to the people who ask for me to pray with them, wondering, "why ask me? I am powerless, lost, nothing". And I know that I know that none of this is Truth, and yet for me in this moment all of it is supremely true and real. I know so surely that of myself I am absolutely nothing, so I want nothing of myself. There is nothing for me in being the self I have always known myself to be, but of myself I cannot separate this small self, what I am, from the greater self, who I am. I cannot seem to "be" at all.

Libby Maxey

I lay it all down. I don't want to seem, I don't want to pretend, and I don't want to be whatever I have been. My only desire is to nakedly be WHO I AM. I'm done with play-acting, pretending okayness when really I am broken into bits and soundlessly screaming to be ONE. I call for Jesus and he comes, sadly smiling that even he cannot console me now, that this dark chasm is mine to cross. My sobbing is even hollow and dead.

My body is heavy, weary, limbs weak, muscles tight with anxiety. Exhaustedly restless even in sleep, and nightmares, too - God, I haven't had a nightmare in years! Oh God, why have You brought me to this place? This awful, horrible grimness that I know isn't real, and yet it surrounds me, engulfs me, and worst of all, numbs me to You.... Oh my God, please lift me from this black hole. All I want is You, God, Oneness with You - without Oneness I don't want to be at all...I am emptied, deeply and profoundly empty, and indescribably hungry for Presence, for the Beingness I AM.

Here's my cup, fill it up!

If the degree of the emptiness I now feel is an indication of how much God will fill me (plus Grace) I am in for the greatest infilling of this lifetime, and possibly many lifetimes! In some moments there is tremendous hope in me because of this, but then I sink back into the abyss. It's an odd thing, this realization of boundless goodness in the midst of the dark. In "wilderness" periods I have previously experienced I was not so aware of the goodness, only despair. And even though I feel disconnected, there are moments when I wonder if perhaps I am more profoundly connected than ever before and am simply unused to the immediacy of the connection, and so I overlook it because it is too simple.

In meditation this morning I repeated the highest, best affirmative mantra I know: I Am that I Am. As I turned this over and over in my mind, speaking it aloud and in the silence of my heart, I was dissatisfied. It is not enough. To me, the best and highest way of explaining what this means is this: God as Creator, humanity (me) as created. It is a statement of balance, of Divine Beingness knowing Divine Beingness through created beingness. In the story of Moses, he asks "Who are You?" and God answers, "I Am that I Am". I was dissatisfied and embarrassed by the arrogance of being dissatisfied with such a mantra! But then I remembered: in some translations, the answer is given "I Am **who** I Am" And then AHA! There is a **big** difference in the two statements. This statement, "I Am who I Am" is more in line with Jesus and his teachings - more in line with "I and the Father are one" and the infamous "It is not robbery to be equal with God" If God can be contained in Jesus, then truly He can be contained in me! And it is not robbery; in today's world, it is necessity!

This also points to the basic dissatisfaction I currently feel with church: we are spending too much time creating and then looking at what we have created; meanwhile missing the Creator of All Things! I just want to be in the Presence of the Isness of God. I want church to simply be a gathering of souls, hungering and thirsting for the manifest Presence of God, creating the atmosphere for God to manifest. The normal church activities can occur, of course, but if all church is about is to present these scheduled activities, then where can God fit in? God is not invited in if the schedule must be met! We are running around doing rather than being still, being, even though on the marquee out front it says, "Be still and know". Perhaps we have gotten too close and some are fearful. It seems we have reverted to "Spirituality 101" in every lesson, too. Perhaps even Rev. Patricia feels this fear. I will wait and watch. I know this congregation is ready to break out of everything that binds us to "the human condition" and see Him face to face. I also know it would be pointless for me to try to "find" God elsewhere, in another congregation. I'd have to go Pentecostal to love God as freely as I do (in church, that is) but I think the Pentecostals might tear me limb from limb because of my expansive theology. I would have to keep my mouth firmly shut, even more so than now.

But I do know that I am forever ruined for normal, everyday church. Geez, I'm even ruined for normal, everyday days! All I want, all I can think about is my next encounter with the wonderful, all-encompassing Presence of God. It's an addiction; the holy aching desire for God to "come down" and for my own I am to rise up. That's the mystical marriage, the Sacred Unity. It is the holy, fiery passion that occurs when the I AM of God "comes down" to merge with the personal I am. All I want is to be filled with this passion. All the time. Always.

Go back to the roses, beloved

God has guided me to revisit some of my writing surrounding meditations and thoughts from the beginnings of my journey. For a reason I cannot yet understand the One Voice desires that my experience from January 8, 1996 be shared here.

~~~

There is a spiraling energy drifting before me, and I grab the energy with my right hand as if it were a rope, allowing the energy to lift me from my body. I observe that I am clothed now in shimmering pastel light and while making the observation, a magnificent golden being greets me and simultaneously draws me in to his presence, caressing my hair and filling me with peace as we travel with great speed to our destination. "All is well, little one" is the message the being conveys to me in a constant stream of thought, like a heartbeat.

I gaze to my right, aware of a hazy pink light there. The guiding being is gone from my consciousness. I travel toward the pink light, full of curiosity. As I approach, I realize that the light is actually formed by the reflection of white light on an amazing array of marvelous, ruby red roses. The roses are living beings, and as I come nearer they form an arbored pathway, drawing me toward my own living intention. The roses are intensely, pulsatingly red; with neither leaves nor thorns, though they seem to have intertwining stems that connect one to the other, like a nervous system of sorts. They love me and follow my progression down the path, forming and re-forming in a seamless dance of arbor-building. I notice an end to the path, an opening-out into a circular area. The roses surround the circular area, forming a spherical room. I feel completely at ease, totally protected by the rose-beings. In the center of the circle is a raised white marble pool, just large enough for one person. There is a bench of similar white marble encircling the pool. Some of the roses curl around the feet of the bench and some climb to the lip of the pool, almost in a curious manner.

With some trepidation, I walk up to the edge of the pool and look in. I know that once I look at the water I will be forever changed.

The water is deep, and draws my gaze into it as if it has consciousness. The water is countless shades of blue and green and turquoise; the colors seem for an instant to form the shape of a rose and in that observation, I am suddenly above the pool and simultaneously in the water as the water, *the living water*, spirals up and around me, lifting me up. The roses lift their heads and seem to smile their approval. The water is definitely water; it feels like water, yet I am not wet. As I think this thought the water becomes as fire also, flames spiraling around me as the water does the same, mingling in a dance of opposites that is cleansing, soothing, healing, renewing.

The roses hold me tenderly as I lay there weeping softly, providing the softest bed imaginable. The aroma they consciously project is restful, cleansing and healing. After a time the roses assist me in sitting, then standing. They draw my attention up toward the white light, and the canopy of roses withdraws, leaving only my self and the All That Is.

~~~

So God, where are we going with this? *Perhaps the symbols in this experience will give you some clues.* Ah, You're not going to just give it away this time, are You? *You will find the answer more delicious this time if I do not.* Okay. I'm ready for some more deliciousness. *As I have noticed.* Thank You, Wonderful Abba. I feel overwhelmed with gratitude that You have noticed...Thank You.

Now for the symbols. For some time I have used Ann Ree Colton's "Watch Your Dreams" to gain insight and understanding into not only my dreams but also my meditation experiences. The descriptions are sometimes obscure and strange, but amazingly on target for me. This book was a guide used frequently by my beloved teacher, Ernestine. I also use the "Keys of Enoch" which is highly symbolic from cover to cover, as is the Bible. Most nouns can be considered as symbols and also many descriptive words, such as colors. I have studied most of my meditations in this way.

Spiral - love; releasing from the lower bodies into the higher consciousness; a phoenix initiation; freedom from karma.

Rope - Symbol of the silver cord; also, in some instances can be revealing the processes of kundalini power. A rope can indicate a means and way of escape.

Gold - (the golden being) - Spiritual power, grace, enlightenment

Pink - Love and devotion; tenderness; reverence.

White - Spirit, perfection, purity; the transcending power of Spirit, union with the Supreme Being; the vibrationless state of light.

Ruby - (the Voice is saying to break the phrase "ruby red roses" into three separate yet united symbols) - The ruby is the arch-stone supporting all jewels. While the diamond is the crown of spirit, the ruby is the crown of the son-of- man power on earth. One perfect ruby condensed as a perfected jewel contains a velocity of ether equal to millions of heartbeats or blood particles of consciousness life. The ruby is a healing jewel...the ruby indicates access to miraculous powers of healing for humanity...a powerful meditation with the ruby or *red rose* in the heart center communicates healing life fire into the closed and unknowing hearts of the world.

Red - **rose red** - Communication with a saint, blessing from a most high saint, selfless healing, and highest personal love expression. **Ruby red** - integrity, respect, authority earned, a sign of approval from the Master.

Rose - the rose is the purest flower in the floral kingdom. It is a protective flower creating an atmosphere of purity. It also sanctifies the environment, as the powers of dark cannot come nigh a pure rose. The rose is a symbol of the human spirit.

Circle - the soul; protection, the eternal. Three circles relate to three phases of understanding coming into balance. (This was interesting because the bench, the outer rim of the pool and the inner surface of the water formed three concentric circles. Now to figure out if three phases of understanding have come into balance!)

Pool - a birth matrix or font of birth...an angelic healing pool in which angel vibrancies purify...to experience being immersed in a pool for baptism is a symbol of being received and penetrated by the Christ.

Water - pool of clear water signifies the First Heaven, a birth matrix, purification. A cascade of water means spiritual power; a stream of water indicates the conscious flow of life moving into the ocean of all life.

Blue - (particularly royal blue) blue in general represents emotional, mental and spiritual peace. Royal blue is a sign of blessing and a promise of substance and expansion.

Green - peace, vitality, healing.

Turquoise - a remembrance or protection from Atlantean times; initiation into the world's akasic records to add to the consciousness a memory necessary for the present state of evolvement.

Blue rose - grace

Fire - Purification, initiation. If the fire is controlled, one is being protected during the cleansing. Also, Melchizedek initiates through fire to bring about manifestation and de-manifestation telepathies. Tongues of fire represent a demonstration of Spirit's presence and power.

Scent or aroma of the rose - healing, used to open the heart center.

The evening after I looked up all these symbols I had an extremely vivid dream, and I know that I know that the dream expands upon the roses meditation, adding even more meaning (and more symbols!). This dream was a vision, really - that is what a highly symbolic, vivid dream often is - and it unfolded like this.

My daughter Laura and I were at a place that I initially thought was a resort. It was a very beautiful location, surrounded with water like an island, lovely trees and green visible out of the many windows. But then I realized this was a "birthing place", where many were giving birth and others were assisting. Though it seemed totally ordinary at the time, there was no gender identification with the idea of birthing, though there were more women giving birth than men. The assistants (and everyone else, for that matter) were serene, calm; the atmosphere was of complete peace, even though there was a sense of swift activity. This was not a clinical setting; there was neither fear nor pain. Some wept softly, but only with joy.

Laura was the one giving birth, but there was no idea of a "father" of the child, no feeling of a man of any kind involved. In fact, she did not appear pregnant, "filled up" but not with weight. She was giving birth to this child with the sole intent of giving the child away. In an odd sense I felt as if I were one with her in the experience yet also the observer. While I looked out at the water from a room shaped like a giant window-faceted jewel, I simultaneously watched Laura effortlessly, easily and joyfully give birth to a baby girl. The tiny child looked exactly as Laura had looked as a newborn. Laura stood up, totally unaffected, wearing a peachy-gold colored gown, smiling blissfully with the joy of giving. The assistant, a beautiful androgynous being dressed in a glowing white lab-coat, reverently handed me the newborn child, wrapped in a shimmering clear blanket. I unwrapped her and gazed at her naked perfection; she looked not only like Laura but also like every other child I have ever seen, including myself. She yawned and stretched and looked directly into my eyes, and the entirety of Christ consciousness passed between us in a mighty rush of Love. In that same instant I realized that Laura was also holding the baby, that Laura and I shared the same body as melded beings.

I/we held her tiny back and cradled the crown of her head, lifting her to kiss her third eye as one being, sharing one thought. The vibrating energetic wholeness of our three-in-one Christedness was awesome. As our lips touched the baby's third eye, a sky blue light opened as if the pureness of a new day had just dawned. Visions of life perfected appeared in the sky blue light, scene after scene of wonder and glory. It was an immaculate experience, holding this Christ child while also holding my child of flesh, the three of us one consciousness in that moment that held eternity.

The assistant reappeared, smiling, arms outstretched. Laura and I, as one being, put the baby in the assistant's waiting arms. And in the instant of looking at the assistant's outstretched arms, we noticed that her outstretched arms also held the entire earth and every soul living on earth. The earth and all her occupants accepted this Christ Child.

Whew. Only slightly cosmic. Symbols in the dream are:

Water - First Heaven, purification, birth matrix. See previous entry.

Trees - progression and evolvement in this earth; trees in summer (fully leafed) indicate harvest time and its rewards and/or a dramatic ending of a situation.

Green - Vitality, health, generosity, abundance; forest green also means peace and healing.

Windows (also glass) - insulation or protection; also witnessing and receiving knowledge; numerous windows indicate opened vision.

Giving birth - to birth, hold, see or cuddle a baby symbolizes birth to the higher self; to be born anew. Delivery of a baby means that the dreamer is a midwife to the birth of the higher self of another.

Jewel-shaped room (I have used the diamond reference here) correlates to spiritual initiation; represents the higher self; the eternal treasure of the superconscious.

Prana (peach-gold) harmlessness; restoration; rejuvenation.

White (assistant's clothing) spirit, perfection, and purity.

Third eye - remembrance of manifestation powers; Divine Mother principle; Holy Spirit wisdom, prophecy and revelation.

Lips, kissing the forehead - symbolic of an anointing blessing bringing peace; a touch of the Holy Spirit.

Sky blue - alignment with the pure spheres of cosmic music; hope; divine assurance to the one seeking higher mind; clarity of mind; a blessing from heaven.

Trinity - this concept has many meanings, but a particular phrase from "Watch Your Dreams" jumped out at me: All beings, *when blended,* work in triad action to accomplish a particular task for God.

Outstretched arms - symbolic of surrender to sacrifice of the small (ego) self for the sake of others.

God, You're going to have to help me out here. This is information overload. *Shift your thinking. Step outside the box; lift your consciousness to the consciousness of your desiring. Think with the Mind you seek.* Do you mean to think with the full potential of my own mind? To contemplate these experiences from the Christ perspective? *That would be stepping outside the box, yes.* I keep hearing references to "stepping outside the box" - in popular culture, business circles, even Rev. Patricia used the phrase - does that mean something too? Some sacred geometry reference, or something? *Absolutely, yes, and absolutely.*

Stepping outside the box

The ancient mystery schools of Egypt, Kabbalists *and every other wisdom tradition* (there, She's done it again) have known and practiced in various forms the ideas of sacred geometry; that every created thing is based on geometric forms; the very templates of creation. In studies of the atom, geometries are clearly visible; in cellular growth and structure science has shown the basis in geometric forms. *In the study of platonic solids is the explanation for the phrase "step outside the box" found.* Okay, if the cube is representative of the earth *then I Am saying step outside of earthbound thinking* (He just will not quit it!) OKAY! *Have I not said, over and over ad infinitum YE ARE GODS? Think with the Mind that is your inheritance! Please!* Well alrighty then! I have been trying to do that...*yes, trying, but no you have not! You have danced around it, dabbled, played with it, peeked in, resisted, pushed it away, but you* **have not accepted the full truth of who you are!** But I don't know how to do that! I don't have a clue how to do more than I am doing! This knowledge has to come from outside my own thinking! *Well, duh, my beloved child.* You are a Master of chastisement. *Not my favorite aspect, I assure you, little one. Just allow your mind to open, expand, become. Your Self does know. All things are knowable, but we have already covered that. You have done all of this before. Allow the full remembrance to flood into your body-mind...just allow. The rest is already done.*

The roses, then. I allow the full truth of this experience to come through me now. *Yes.* Okay - the rope and the spiral are saying that the centers of my physical body have been united, empowered, fully activated; I am now the phoenix, arising from earthiness to claim my true reality. *Yes!* With Your Grace (the golden being) and my devotion (pink) I am One with the Light of Being (white). *Go on.* The ruby - this is a recurring symbol for me, as is the rose. Two phrases from the symbol definitions are especially meaningful to me in this experience - one is "crown of son-of-man power" and the other is "access to miraculous powers of healing for humanity" *Precisely. You are crowned with such power and such powers, beloved Liberty.* And the red colors mean to me the same selfless healing as an expression of Love manifested, the humility of such healing being a sign of the authority *of Christ-as-you.* You just take over sometimes. I love that about You. I was going to type "authority of Christ" *Yes, I know, still keeping the identity outside yourself.* The roses felt like the entirety of the human spirit, acting with one intent, pure and sweet. The idea of all humanity, acting as One, miraculously healed healers all, crowned with Christ spirit...*now that's outside the box!* Yeah!

The circle and the pool symbols are combined, and the trinity of circles is important, too. So in the balance of the human trinity; body, mind and spirit; is the Christ-self born to eternity. *My idea of you, complete.* You keep telling me that I am this wonderful, completed being. How come I feel like such a slug? *It's that acceptance thing, little one. You do resist your chosen purpose. And you will continue to feel this way until you do not. Accept. Allow.* It seems that there are powerful forces keeping me "away", holding me captive in the sticky muck of *race consciousness* (!!!!!) *This is where you must rise up, consciously. Ask for help, and more help. You do not ask for such help.* Because I feel like it's all me. *Even if it were, do you not realize that you have Mighty Help?* Well, yeah...but not in the moment, I guess *more resistance - do you see? You are the one pushing away! You peek in and run away! My child, my sweet innocent, what you have accepted as your purpose is a heroic task. You have accepted a purpose that is scorned, rebuked and reviled as impossible, ridiculous, laughable...need I go on? You have a Mighty cheering section, ready and willing to slay all your dragons, transmute all the thoughts that are anti-Christ.*

Anti-Christ? Oh no, not now. That's a whole 'nuther can of worms. Where was I? *Blues and greens - the water and fire are seen together, therefore interpret them together.* Okay. The colors of the water and the marvelous image of the rose in the water together mean peace and healing, of course, but more specifically for me is the expansion aspect, the initiation requisite for evolvement. And Grace. Amazing Grace. The water now, the living water forming a spiral around me. Water in general is the flow of Spirit, so this that I saw as living water means Divine Life flowing, removing all that is not Divine Life from my bodies, releasing me from the wheel of human life into Christ consciousness. *Lovely. Now the fire, beloved.* These were tongues of fire, also spiraling, mingling with the water and demonstrating Your Presence and Power protecting and purifying, *forever. Eternally.*

Part of me wants to block all this from integrating. It is fighting very, very hard against integration. I feel slow and sleepy, thick.

Libby Maxey

If I were a Pentecostal I would say it is a demon, *but in truth it is race consciousness thoughts.* Loving God, I give these thoughts that would prevent my evolution to You. Remove them from my consciousness, and transmute them in the Light You are. Get thee behind me, Satan! (Just to cover all the bases, God) Thank You, Beloved Abba. And so it is. Amen.

Now the birthing vision, child of Light. What, no rest? *There is work to be done, a harvest to be gathered.* Yes. I can feel that time is of the essence now. *The quickening is upon you, and the whole of the lovely Terra.* I accept my place in Your Mighty Plan. *Ahh. Music to my ears. In you I Am well pleased, beloved Liberty.*

Onward. I could bask in that feeling forever, but I get the idea that will come, too. The birth vision, now. This vision involved me on many levels. Me as parent, me as my own child, *and me reborn as Christ* (again with the italics!) I was also the dreamer, the participant in the dream, and the *idea behind the dream* God, could I do this? I really think I get it! *Remember throughout: Ye are Gods.* Okay. I do get it, because my next thought was that I was Creator, creating newness through my beloved Creation to bless all of Eternity. *Yes, indeed, you understand. Now for the integration of that knowing.* Well, that is the tough part.

The symbol of the trees, the many and varied trees. They were so beautiful, so full and lush and alive with Life, sparkling. The harvest time symbol seems quite appropriate. The harvest of Spirit, the evolution that is upon us now is the reward we have sought since the beginning of time here. The symbol of the many windows confirms my opened vision and the reward to me of witnessing the Great Harvest. The symbol of giving birth, of course, the birth of Christ in me and in all. But I am also midwife to the birth of the Christ in all those I touch, in my life and through these words. The jewel shaped room; I get the feeling You will have more to say about that to me in another experience. *So lovely to be known again; you melt My heart, beloved.* And You have reduced me to a puddle, too! The "eternal treasure of the superconscious" is God mind – that's what the room means to me. Color symbols now- the prana colored gown Laura wore mean the restoration of wholeness, the total rejuvenation our harvest holds for us and for the Earth. White, our own pure Spirit fire; cleansed.

136

The symbolic kiss of the Christ child's forehead: that gives me chills just typing the words. What a magnificent experience. I felt, in that moment, as if I were truly One with God, blessing my own child-self as I sent this Perfect One into the world of experience. "An anointing blessing bringing peace" is very appropriate. And to kiss the third eye; I felt as though I was Divine Wisdom bestowing Divine Wisdom, while in that same moment receiving Divine Wisdom. And that, too, is a trinity of experience. The sky blueness opening up in consciousness, too, as my consciousness, Laura's consciousness, the child's absolutely pure consciousness, God consciousness, Christ consciousness, Holy Spirit consciousness - there were no divisions, no separations, no edges...but no blurring, either. All was as crystal, pure, clear. And I know that I know that I know - I am a trinity of beingness, a wholeness created to accomplish God's work of manifesting Liberty for the sake of the world. I surrender all. I surrender all...

The Jewel of Christ

Earlier in this writing, in the chapter titled "Meditation", I describe a being entirely composed of eyes. I experienced this being, which I knew in that instant to be my God-self, in 1994. Boy, did I resist that image, calling it something a great prophet or apostle from the Bible would see, but not something for me to see or understand. But now I see and understand that the image is Truth, and it must be seen as Truth for Jesus' great prayer that we be one with the Father as he is one with the Father to become our reality.

This eye-being meditation experience occurred prior to the great explosion of metaphysical education in my life. It was, therefore, a pure experience, similar to the Melchizedek experience when I knew almost nothing about Melchizedek or what the Order of Melchizedek might be. At the time, I wrote about the experience in my journal and then simply filed the experience away under "unbelievable" in my ego mind.

The roses, the spiraling dance of fire and water and the birth vision have awakened the eye-being image in a new way for me. The eye-being is not only I, but also the entire body of Christ, fully awakened. So it is I, but it is also you. And everyone else, too. We **are** one. And we are one with all things. And God has made this invisible Truth visible to me. Here we go.

~~~

Image-in that you are a small child and you have a magnificent, sparkling diamond in your chubby hand. This diamond is large, round, with what seem like thousands of tiny facets, all reflecting light in a way that mesmerizes you with their beauty. It is fiery, too, lighted from within, it seems. To protect the diamond, you place it on a shelf and because you are a child, you forget about it. It becomes dusty and grimy over time, mixed there on the shelf with the collection of stuff you have found. One day Mom says, "Clean up your room!" and you put the diamond, now covered in grime, in a box, which goes under the bed. In a later clean up, the entire box is thrown out with the garbage. Neighborhood dogs tear up the garbage bag and the diamond falls to the ground, rolls down a small hill into a muddy ditch.

Years pass. You are now an adult, making a sad final visit with your dying father at your childhood home. You wander down to the ditch and notice a faint sparkling something there in the dried mud. You dig around it with a stick and lean over to pick it up, realizing it is the diamond of your childhood. It seems much smaller, is encrusted with dirt and God-knows-what, but you put it in the pocket of your jeans anyway. It stays in the jeans through the wash cycle, but you hear something banging away in the dryer and go to find out what it is. It is the diamond, sparkling like a smile of recognition. But you don't look at it. You put it away in a drawer, hiding it once again.

This jewel is the Christ self. We each hold that sparkling Truth in our childhood innocence, and then let it become dulled and grimy, often throwing it away as easily as garbage. The Christ self re-emerges in troubled times, but again we often look away.

On a cosmic scale, the jewel of Christ comprises all humanity, all Christ potential. Each one of us is a facet, looking out on our world from an individual and unique perspective. As little children we dance with joy at our uniqueness, but know we are safe and protected, part of a larger whole made up of parents and siblings, other family members and friends. Over the course of our lives we allow our viewpoint to become narrow, shallow, clouded, and darkened by negative thoughts and attitudes. We continually look out, not realizing that we are part of one whole jewel, but thinking we are a tiny and separated facet, small and helpless and worthless. Until the day comes when helplessness becomes so deep, we cry out for belonging to something bigger than our small selves. Then perhaps, just perhaps, we will turn our viewpoint and look within. There, though our facet of perception is dark and clouded, we see the fiery dance of Spirit. But perhaps it is shadowy, and in fear we look away again. But maybe, just maybe, we will look, and look again, and keep looking until we see with our own eyes what we knew was true in our innocence - we are part of the whole, and the whole is the Christ. Then our facet becomes clear, and the dance of Spirit shines through it instead of being blocked by it.

Libby Maxey

Then maybe, just maybe, the facet next door sees the shining of Spirit through you, and asks how you became so clear and pure. And the next, and the next, and the next; and in a Mighty rush of hope the remaining facets cry themselves clean and behold! The Christ is reborn, whole. We are one being, with multitudes of eyes. Our vision, Christ vision, will re-connect us.

This deep knowing of our oneness will allow an impassioned compassion so profound we will gladly and miraculously drop our perception of separate selves. From within the jewel of Christ-heart and Christ-mind, each individual and unique viewpoint is but another magnificent outlook on the Creation, a new and different set of eyes with which to see and experience the Universe. Each facet, perfected, equally important to the whole jewel, singularly clear and brilliant, out-picturing Spirit from within.

The View from the Center

From the center of Christ mind, all facets are of equal size, shape and importance. From the center of Christ mind, in fact, all facets merge together like the pixels of a computer screen to form a whole, holy and seamless vision of what is real and true. Seen from within the consciousness of the living Christ, the world is a miracle of Light and Sound, a manifestation of Ideas magnificent and profound, continually outpicturing.

While driving to church on Sunday, I was listening to a favorite CD, Avalon's "A Maze of Grace". The last song on the CD is "Dreams I Dream for You" in which God talks about His Vision for our lives, in contrast to our own puny ideas. In listening, I realized with shock and amazement that I was listening from the perspective of GOD, not Libby, dreaming and visioning dreams for people I saw out the window, family members, people who crossed my mind, people at church, the body of people who make up our church. I was listening from the I AM presence. **I realized with shock and amazement that I am who I am, present moment**. Further, I realized that I am answering Jesus' great prayer, that we be one with the Father as he is one with the Father with my own life. Gratitude washed over me in great waves, and continued. I felt elevated to a new level of awareness, fully awake.

Vibrating madly but with physical control I walked through the door of Unity Church and saw the faces, seeing with fresh eyes the reality, the isness, of each person. I was seeing each person as God sees that person - sometimes just in a flash of presence, but there just the same. I could not look deeply enough! I could not see enough people! It was like drinking cool water from a well, so satisfying was the experience. I was filled with inexpressible Joy just being in the presence of these people, knowing who they truly are, and truly, deeply **knowing**. *And here, beloved Mine, is the fulfillment. Here is the At-One-Ment. You are fulfilled in Me, and I Am fulfilled in you. My Gratitude flows to you for believing Me!* Yes, that's how it felt. So fulfilled, so satisfied. Such joy underlying all thoughts, as if negativity could not touch me. *So it is with Me.* It is such a profound relief, this Oneness thing. *It has been a long time, beloved Liberty.* And You, God, with that amused manner You have...*it is Joy, purely Joy, in observing your reactions and your wonder - I Am your Abba, you* *know.* I know. It's a parent thing, isn't it? *In you I Am well pleased, little oneness.*

What was most revealing was the absolute naturalness of being in that space, of observing from Your Perspective. It isn't the <u>entirety</u> of Your Perspective, of course, but it is perfect for the circumstance. And as I draw closer and closer to the center point of Christ within, the perspective will widen and deepen, will it not? *It seems only natural.* There You go with the God-chuckle! I love that! *It's the language. You have inherited My sense of humor in this regard. I love that!*

The shift in consciousness I have experienced can be very subtle but is also very significant. It brings up a whole new set of dissatisfactions, too. For example, one of the songs in church, written from the separated self, had no meaning from the state of At-One-Ment. This is hard to explain. *The Course in Miracles could be of assistance here.* Yeah, the end of duality stuff. Give me a page number, God-self - how about it? *You think I'm going to make it that easy? What do you think chapter headings are all about?* Kidding! *Knowing!* Banter with God...what a concept! *This is My concept of Self-talk.* Yeah! Self-talk with the I AM! Talking to my Self takes on a whole new meaning. Still, I'd better not do it out loud....

Stepping Stones

Beloved, it is time. It is time to step with courage and faith all the way through the valley of the shadow of death, through the open door, into My house of many mansions. Up until this now moment, you have been stepping on stones following the leader, the way shower I have given you. You have followed a narrow and steep path, but one that is well worn by Lovers of God throughout the ages. Now is the time to take that leap, stepping out in complete commitment to that which you most desire. This step is into the vastness, the totality, the entirety, the wholeness of the I Am you most truly are. You have fears, child. Walk through them. They are but shadows hiding My Glory from you. Do you not desire to look upon My Glory? Glorify thou me, Beloved Father! I believe You, I desire You - *I will help your unbelief, I will shine away the refusal that remains in your being...*before I have asked, Glorious One, thank You.

I come to you too, Beloved Child of our Holy God. Lord Michael, thank you. I have felt your wonderful, protective presence with me. *It is my function, one who is named Liberty, to protect you in your transformation, to balance the above and the below, to restore the Christ Light. I attend you now.*

I am here too, my own Liberty. I attend you as well in this time beyond time. I bow to you, Lord Melchizedek. I breathe in your mighty presence. *We honor you, Liberty, word of God; together as the Ascendant we will re-program the consciousness in order to re-establish harmonious communion with God and thus open heaven's gates to all who will come.*

The Manifest Presence of God is preparing to burst forth within and around the world, beloved Liberty. Together with you as Ascendant will the Presence be dramatically manifested: as above, so below. Only this time will the energy fields above and below merge and blend. At-one-ment is in full swing, beloved Liberty, thanks be to God for you and all the other devoted beings expanding to Christhood.

Glory be to God in the highest. You are the Glory of God, Liberty. But I note that you are not in full awareness of the meaning of the word "glory". No, now that You mention it, for some reason that is not a word I have examined. Would You care to suggest a good place to look this up? *Use Fillmore's "The Revealing Word"* Okay. Here, "Glory: Realization of Divine Unity; the blending and merging of man's mind with God-mind." Then, "Glorify: To magnify with praise; to enhance with spiritual splendor; to adorn. Glorification is the highest spiritual state of consciousness attainable by man." *Ahh.* Oh, Geez. Oh, my God. Why is it that even though I have worked and strived and sought for this that I cannot believe You are actually meaning me here? *It is perplexing. Close your eyes, beloved one. Put on the Alleluia CD and the angels will sing to you. I will show you something you have not remembered.* Okay. I need to breathe anyway. My heart is pounding.

Thank You for inspiring Robert Gass to record all these wonderful chants. This one, "Alleluia", is so very conducive to breathing deeply and rhythmically. *Just breathe. Resist not.*

~~~

And something happened in me, in my emotional body. He said, "resist not" and fear rolled over me like a dark cloud.

Resist not? Are You kidding?

For two months all I can seem to do is resist! The resistance has even taken up physical residence in my left neck and shoulder. I have resisted God at every turn. I have resisted others. I have resisted my self. I have resisted even re-reading these writings (since I know that I know they are truth!) I have resisted meditation, prayer, and quiet, blaming the busy-ness and noise of summer. I have been resistance, even in sleep...angry dreams, nervous negative whisperings in my head. The one outcome I have desired more than any is within my sight and all I can do is fear! What is this about? This is most definitely a valley of shadows. But I am ready for the resistance to end; for a new and radical acceptance of what is the truth of my being. Living in resistance is living in lack, not the abundance of God. I don't want any lack of any kind. I want the fullness of All That Is. I want to be of use in God's plan. And I know that my truest nature beckons, calling me into the complete Christ I am. At the same time I feel drawn to awaken and enliven God's children, for I have found You. I no longer seek You. I have found You.

That is beautiful music to Me, beloved. Now I can no longer be lost to you. I want the fullness of Liberty. I choose you, beloved, to heal my beloveds. I beckon you, calling you into the fullness I Am. I Am found.

I feel as if I'm on the edge, on the verge: no, it's more than that. I feel as though the **collective human consciousness** is on the edge, on the verge of Greatness; our collected resistance about to collapse and the infilling, the great outpouring of God's Self, Divine Unity, to fill us up. And I feel the Presence of God so strongly, so often, so unexpectedly, that something new **absolutely must** be coming. More and more people, astonishing numbers of Your people, are claiming healings and seeking prayer and simply stating their willingness to "see" what You're about. It fills my heart to overflowing, seeing Your wonderful people opening and awakening. Like last night, when all those people showed up for the Jesus class at Unity Center! Jesus, your presence was so awesome.

Rev. Patricia gave us a scripture to meditate on, and to change and re-arrange to suit our individual desires. The scripture, from John 12:32 "...and I, if I be lifted up, will draw all men unto me."

Libby Maxey

This has been a cornerstone scripture for me for a long while. But You, God, have that wonderful way of breathing new meaning into even the most studied phrases. From the Jesus perspective, I see that this statement reveals Jesus' choice to be lifted up and yet he is completely surrendered to the will of the Father, knowing that the current plan is that he will be lifted up, but the plan is subject to change according to the highest and best good for the All. By making this choice, Jesus points us to the choice we all must make to be (or not to be) lifted up in Christ consciousness as well. From our perspective today, the choice Jesus made was also completed. Now we are assured that all souls will be drawn unto him, or into the Christ consciousness. In this way, Jesus has truly redeemed us, because he has made of himself a bridge from separated to unified consciousness.

And for me, Jesus, it is such a marvelous relief to submit to my desire to be with you. For a time I seem to have been away from you in my day-to-day life and also in my quiet time. I have been concentrating my efforts on being equal to you, as a sister is an equal to a brother. But I see with such gratitude that it's okay to sit at your feet in adoration, to look to you and to look up at you in surrender to your experience as Christ, to allow you and to trust your assurance to draw me to you. Realization has dawned that I can turn to you in any circumstance; that you are not too busy for me; that you are indeed omniscient and omnipresent, available not just to those who have great needs, but also those who are simply after a smile and a hug. I was limiting you to think otherwise. I surrender to you, beloved brother. Draw me to you. Draw me through the valley of the shadow of death, Yeshua, to everlasting life in the resurrection and ascension, to being a flame of the Holy Spirit. So I believe I will change this scripture to suit myself: Lift me up! Draw me unto you.

Ever curious for more meaning, I stood before my shelves filled with sacred books. Immediately I pulled out "The Complete Gospels" translation, compiled by the Fellows of the Jesus Seminar and edited by Robert J. Miller. These are direct translations of the scrolls from the Dead Sea discoveries. The wordings can be frank and startling. I read that Jesus made this decision or statement on the evening of the day he arrived in Jerusalem, that day when he was greeted by the throngs in the streets of Jerusalem as the

146

Messiah. The day was a day of victory, even though Jesus knew the plan that was in motion. He must have been feeling a tremendous responsibility and certainly some apprehension. He was in the epicenter of a mighty spiritual wind and he had to know it. He knew the end of his physical life was nearing when he said the following beginning at John 12:27...

> "Now my life is in turmoil, but should I say, Father, rescue me from this moment? No, it was to face this moment that I came. Father, glorify your name!" Then a voice spoke out of the sky: "I have glorified it and will glorify it further." The crowd there heard this, and some people remarked that it had thundered, others that an angel had spoken to him. "That voice did not come for me but for you," Jesus rejoined. "Now sentence is passed on this world; now the ruler of this world will be expelled. **And if I'm elevated from the earth, I'll take everyone with me.**"

Elevated! That's interesting. That word adds more twists and turns to the statement, because "elevated" has more meanings than "lifted". Elevated can mean magnified, glorified (that's the word I'm looking for!), raised (another biggie) levitated and exalted (!) So still, in this translation, Jesus makes his decision even while leaving the decision in God's will, and provides the assurance of his promise. Christ is the open door. Jesus is the shortcut. Oh my God. All we really **do** need to do is call on his name!

So, Beloved Jesus, lift me up! Draw me to you.

Build My Kingdom

Unity Church for Positive Living voted unanimously two weeks ago to sell the church and purchase 8.5 acres of lovely, level property to build our new spiritual center. It was an awesome unification of minds. There was almost no discussion (everyone had the facts prior to the meeting) and absolutely no dissension. All was joy. God is so awesome - it is so obvious that we, as a spiritual family, are building the Kingdom of God on earth, right in Nashville. What a tremendous privilege. There is a wonderful sense of excitement, anticipation, and expectation.

Just last August, just one year prior to this momentous vote of agreement, there was lots of talk - about buying land and building and oh no! We can't leave this church! And oh my God! This is going to be too expensive! Mixed thoughts, lots of lack thinking and a good bit of attachment. To be in a group, discussing the idea of a new, expanded church would give me a headache. I expressed my thoughts to Jesus in the manner that follows:

Me: Just why am I so dissatisfied, so discontented with the churches' building dilemma and the way we are dealing with it?

Jesus: You are discontented, Beloved, because you are not, as a group consciousness, asking the question central to the process of building your "church".

So what is the question?

Asking the question requires some new definitions. First of all, it would be most helpful to the group consciousness if your quest were not for a church at all, but rather for a true spiritual home for everyone. This is more in accord with my idea of "church" as a concept. It is broad; it is open. Also, this question presumes that all are willing to be aware that the Kingdom of God truly is at hand.

Are we, as a group consciousness, ready for that leap?

I would not tell you if it were not so. But I need human help to build the Kingdom. You need to believe me like never before, to focus on the Kingdom like never before. Remember like never before.

I've been feeling that need to stay very focused.... Oh! Why did that flash in my mind? Sunday night Patricia came to me in the dream state and she smiled her beautiful smile, saying "I love Him as you do, you know" and I was so filled with delight. We had a wonderful holy instant.

Patricia came to your dreams at my bidding. She is also feeling the need for a new question. Are you ready for the question? Actually, I may get carried away and give you several questions....

Go. I'm ready.

Ask your holy selves this: If the Kingdom of God were at hand, right here in Nashville, right now, what would my true spiritual home look like? If money were no object, what wonderful features would my true spiritual home have? If all the knowledge in the universe were available, what would my true spiritual home teach? Ye have not because ye ask not! Oh yes, many of you have prayed, and your love is most beautiful and sincere. That is the reason for giving you these new questions, these new opportunities. Will you, as a group consciousness, believe me? Or will you shrink away from my plan for you? I am giving you the recipe for manifesting heaven on earth. And I give it to your Unity Church.

I feel like I'm choking. Like this is where I've choked you off before. Why did I type *that?*

You have reached this phase in your growth before. But before, it was not the fullness of time. Now is the fullness of time.

He came on a cloud of light!

The Sunday following the vote, a whole new experience of Jesus happened in the sanctuary. I began to feel a mighty and powerful presence soon after the service started, and it grew and expanded through the meditation. When Rev. Patricia began to speak, there was an atmosphere; I felt a new vibration; a pure crystalline energy filled the room. I rubbed my eyes when I "saw" what can only be described as a cloud of energy, resting at about the heart-level of all those seated in the sanctuary. It was a cloud of Light, pristine, pure - finer and more alive that what now appeared to be the "ordinary" daylight in the room. The natural and the electric light seemed dull and drab in comparison, and even the sunlit sky in the window above the altar looked dark and veiled.

I was suddenly aware that the Light "came in" from the back of the room, and I knew that I knew who was back there. I was so certain of Jesus' presence that I expected to see him fully manifested when I turned my head to look. I did see his spirit-form, standing beneath the stained glass window, and he was also as a "face" filling the back wall and entire room. I turned back and met Patricia's eyes, and she said, "He's here" and somehow maintained her composure. It just so happened that the architect for the new church building project was in attendance, wanting to get the "feel" of our congregation! Such times we are living in. Thank You, God, and oh Jesus, I love you so.

I must see what the symbols of this appearance mean. I feel like I'm being dense about what this manifestation might signify, like I can't think about that yet. So I will analyze. Still so very human of me. Go along with me here. Symbols.... nothing in "Watch Your Dreams" resonates, I'll get the Keys of Enoch. Okay, the Bible too. That's the one I'm resisting. Okay, the Bible. And it opens to...Matthew 24. Okay. I'm going to breathe here; something is coming. Oh, God, there it is, at Matthew 24:30

I read the scripture and dropped the Bible on my bed. I couldn't read any more just then. The computer was on so I decided to check my e-mail. I wrote a message to Rev. Patricia, congratulating her on being able to function so beautifully in such a magnificent presence, and then described my experience. This was her response to me:

What a day it was!! I really did have a challenging time because I was feeling such intense energy, and I was being physically touched by him on the stage. I was listening to HIM, feeling HIM, and trying to keep talking!! Several people asked me after the first service if something was wrong with me...ha. In the second service he was standing on my right - several people saw the aura and one person came up and had it drawn out on their bulletin. Amazing.

Hang on...here we go.

Blessings, Patricia

A little later, Patricia forwarded an e-mail that came to her from another visionary congregant, Sunny. This is Sunny's e-mail to Patricia:

Patricia,

I still am in awe of the image I saw in church yesterday. I can't get it out of my head...When I first noticed it; I assumed it was simply a part of your aura. But when you stepped aside and it remained where you had been, there was no question in my mind. There was a bright white form standing within a few feet of you, head turned as if watching you, with an arm outstretched as if protecting you... I knew in an instant that the spirit of God was with you; with all of us...it took my breath away.

I fought the tears only briefly, then allowed a few to slip past. But, not wanting anyone to think I was sad, I tried to contain them. On the contrary, I was exhilarated! I was witness to something that others can only imagine. I saw, with human eyes, what so many search for. I felt what I have felt countless times at Unity [Unity Center] - the absolute pure love of God.

You are indeed blessed, Patricia. And I am blessed to know you. Thank you for letting your light shine on all of us...

Love,

Sunny

Reading Sunny's description left me stunned with joy for a little while. When I regained some composure, I e-mailed Patricia my thanks.

Patricia - Wow. Thanks. Did Jesus let you know when you got this calling it was going to be so outrageously astounding? Me either! I tried for two hours today to study my revelation, but over and over found nothing that resonated, until I finally picked up the one study guide I was resisting. And opening to the very page, there it was - Matthew 24:30. That resonated. Read it and weep.

Love ya! Lib

And Patricia responded with this:

No, I didn't know it would be like this...it is better than I could ever have known to be doing this work and feeling his presence. Did you read Mt. 24:31-33, especially 33.... know that it is near, even at the doors.

Several others felt the energy rush through the doors and up the aisle so for once, we were not the only two having the experience - it was so powerful that most everyone felt something.

Love you,

P

Through chapters 24 and 25 of the Gospel of Matthew, Jesus is answering the question of the disciples: "Tell us, when will this be, and what will be the sign of your coming and the close of the age?" Jesus' answer is prophecy at its' purest. Here is Matthew 24:30-33 from the Revised Standard Version: ·

"...Then will appear the sign of the son of man in heaven, and then all the tribes of the earth will mourn, and they will see the son of man coming on the clouds of heaven with power and great glory; and he will send out his angels with a loud trumpet call, and they will gather his elect from the four winds, from one end of heaven to the other.

From the fig tree learn its lesson: as soon as its branch becomes tender and puts forth leaves, you know that summer is near. So also, when you see all these things, you know that he is near, at the very gates. "

Okay. Okay. Still breathing. The next step, then, since we have seen the son of man come in on a cloud of heaven would be to listen for the trumpet call and keep a sharp lookout for the gathering angels! Better open the gates, too...because he is indeed near. He is indeed here.

Flying Lessons

It's been three days since He came in the cloud. Earlier today I was in the shower, and I realized that I had not taken a deep, cleansing breath since the occurrences of Sunday! I had been so immersed in the exhilaration of the experience, breathing excitedly, shallowly. So I took some deep breaths, and my mind wandered to Sunday school and how to really interest the children in deep breathing. Then it occurred to me that if they had wings, their shoulder blades would rise and fall, similar to the rise and fall of deeply breathing. In that moment I could see all the smiles on their faces as they flapped their "wings" with each deep breath. Yes, I'll teach this, I thought, and then I fell into my own deep breathing, peaceful and joy-filled.

I was curiously inside and outside my body simultaneously, and the me that was outside observed my own shoulder blades. *There, in the center, beloved, that's where the wing attaches. See? The plates, the shoulder blades are bases for the wing sockets. See how the wings swivel there? They have marvelous flexibility. Their greatest flexibility is that they are completely composed of thought.* I am getting wings? *They are a conveyance and an appearance. They are fun. They give you a certain look. It can be very impressive; thus useful. And yes.* In this moment I was not in my body at all, though showering continued. Autopilot. My consciousness was in space, in the sparkling deep. I observed my spirit-self, wings in place, flapping and lifting off, clumsily flying about. In the same moment, I was also within my body of light, feeling the sensations of flapping my wings and lifting off, flying about crazily. I felt that I would bump into something and *you can't bump anything. It's all thought. But still it's a good idea to practice. You want to look good!* He said this so like a brother, teasing, cajoling, eyes twinkling. *You like it when I draw you to me this way.* Oh yes. I love it. *Follow me and I'll give you some more flying lessons. You will be Grace.* Help me! I'm melting!

Tonight I attended the next-to-last Christ Jesus class. Patricia, also very much filled with the ascending Christ energy, gave us a particularly powerful assignment. We were to stand, face a beloved, clasp hands, lock eyes and speak "I behold the Christ in you" three times, then "The Christ I am sees the Christ you are" three times. I partnered with Denise. We moved closer and closer toward each other, until we were forehead to forehead, speaking as one person with one voice. Our hearts beat in the same rhythm. In the same blinding flash, we were one soul - I saw myself in her face, in her eyes. We were one: one body, one mind, and one spirit. Denise had the exact same experience, simultaneously. We felt an incredible vibrating Grace in that intense, remarkable moment. Next we changed partners, and I hopped up to the stage to face Patricia. We both shared a delicious laugh, feeling almost drunk with love for God. She mentioned that she needed to keep her feet firmly planted, and she wasn't ready to leave the body just yet! Like I have control over that! We gazed into each other's eyes, and completely forgot what we were supposed to say! What joy to be united in spirit!

The same week, Friday, was the second holotropic breathwork session. I had gratefully agreed to be a "sitter" after the last session so that someone else could have this healing experience as a "breather". On the way to the session, I briefly gave voice to the hope that there would be too many sitters and not enough breathers, and I would get to have the experience again. Just a simple hope. And guess what? There were too many sitters and not enough breathers and I got to have the experience again!

Breathwork II

For the two weeks preceding this second breathwork session in late August, the "Mighty I Am Presence" had been constantly "with" me; that is, I have been consistently in Christ awareness. A new level of awakening, a speechless awestruck place where my consciousness will only occasionally "fall" into my ordinary human awareness (even though Spirit reminds me that all consciousness is of the same importance) rather than momentary flashes of God-mind sprinkled in ordinary awareness! It's no doubt a good thing I had little time to think about what might happen if I were to breathe in this way in such a presence. For a moment I considered reading again about my previous breathwork experience, but God quickly put that out of my mind. I had no expectations, so in calmly excited innocence, I put away my ego and breathed.

It seemed to take a long while to enter the silence, but in a wild rush of electricity like molten lava roaring throughout my body, Lord Christ made his Presence known. He stood before me and within me. I observed my kneeling body, trembling hands uplifted, vibrating, and chest heaving with powerful jolts of the cleansing, healing Presence. Then a soft comforting indigo darkness came over me, and I remember nothing but this womb-like void of no-thing, rocking gently in a sea of utter tranquility.

My consciousness awakened to gentle Jesus' beatific smile as he leaned over me, and my body sat up to a cross-legged position, comfortably limp and relaxed. Jesus, brother Jesus, began instructing me again in the art of flying with my wings. Many, many other wing-ed beings gathered 'round to watch us, their sparkling eyes mirth-filled and tender. In this lesson, my consciousness was entirely within the marvelous body of light I am, and I knew what it is to "mount up with wings like eagles". Our wings, the wings of our light bodies, lift us quickly high, and then effortlessly, we soar. It is pure wonder.

The flying lesson receded and I resumed the deep rapid breathing. Again the soft indigo no-thing enveloped me in pristine sanctuary. It seemed a long while and no time at all when Jesus abruptly entered the stillness and demanded of me *and when will you heal the sick, raise the dead, cleanse the lepers and cast out the demons*

156

which torment my beloved children? Yet even in his demanding, he was sweetly compassionate. He said it with an I-know-it-is-scary, hold-my-hand tone in the thought-picture that he wove in my mind, as beloved souls stricken with illness of body and mind appeared on the screen of my consciousness. Some beseeched me, eyes calling me to speak the one word that would break the chains. I was broken, sobbing, quivering...wondering how I would ever **do** that...and he lifted my chin, and looking deeply into my eyes, forehead to forehead, breathing together...we were one being. *Surrender knowing what happens next, beloved. It is beyond your imagining.*

Again the velvety indigo space. All things of the world disappeared. Then a light appeared, a bubble of light, and Yogananda's splendid image, his living face, was before me. He smiled his charming smile of fulfillment. Then my own Dad's face, warm and tender, eyes soft with love. Then Mother Theresa, saint of the poor, her face fresh and radiant; glowing with Truth. Then Lady Diana, Princess of Wales, stunning in her power. Then my beloved Granny, grinning with excitement. Each being took a place in a choir arranged in a circle that went all the way around me and continued up and up, level after level above me and over me. It was something like being inside a gigantic round flower bud just before it bursts into blossom. Again Jesus, commanding: *Resurrect the dead.* What? *Resurrect the dead. Now is the time.* Me? *Me in you. You in me. You are in me and I am in you.* Kneeling, I raised my arms and fell forward on my face, **completely** surrendered. Of resurrecting the dead I know nothing. Yet my mouth moved in prayers, words of origins unknown to my human mind came forth. Yielded, unguarded, all ideas of separation from I AM who I AM gone, together as one being, Jesus and I raised the dead. The mighty song of praise from the great group of souls surrounding me grew and grew, the light expanded and expanded, and in a blinding flash of Divine Light the flower opened; the lotus blossomed. The souls flew forth like wisps of dandelion fluff, lifting beyond their earthly constraints, into the Golden Light of ascension.

With a snap I realized my body again. Thirst! *Where you are headed, beloved, you will neither hunger nor thirst.* I tried really hard to ignore that as I gulped. Body satisfied, I lay back and closed my eyes, breathing deeply and rapidly. Peace drifted over me like a security blanket. I curled up, deeply and profoundly relaxed, like an infant child in utter safety, softness and warmth.

I was in a dry place, an arid place with outcroppings of rock. Rolling hills and small mountains...oh, I know – this is the Holy Land. Simultaneously this place was also the soft indigo nothing...and lifting my eyes, there was Jesus, hands softly folded, leaning gently forward on a large granite boulder. His eyes beckoned me toward him, and I joined him there. He clasped my hands in his and I saw tears in his tranquil eyes. *Agree with me now, Liberty. Pray with me and join my prayer; that you would be one with the Father as I am one with the Father.* When he said "you" I felt something open in my head and images, hundreds of thousands of images of people all over the world cascaded in a rushing wave through my mind, until the images trickled away, and I looked fully into his wonderful face. I agree with you, beloved brother. So be it. And somehow, somehow, the trickle returned, but the faces were changed; opened, lighted, delighted; and then the rushing wave of happy, blissful images melted and merged into the One blazing jewel; the diamond of Christ made whole and complete.

I gasped in utter astonishment, amazement and awe. The breathwork session was over.

So near to me

Of course I began to wonder just when I *would* begin to heal the sick. I feel all the gifts of the Holy Spirit right here, within the grasp of understanding; yet I am inexperienced in the how's and when's. Further, I have been holding myself back, waiting for God to tell me when it was my time. It's now. I know it is now. And so I'm just willing.

Friday while cleaning the church, as is my usual practice, the phone rang and a beloved member, Rebecca, was on the line. Rebecca has numerous health challenges and even more emotional challenges. And Jesus demanded: *Heal this beloved, Rebecca. Heal my beloved!* I spoke to Rebecca for a while and told her a little about what had transpired between Jesus and me. She wept, dumbfounded. We arranged that I would come to visit her early in the morning the following Tuesday. We agreed to tell no one.

Hanging up the phone, I continued cleaning the church. In Patricia's office, I noticed an intoxicating aroma. A small measure of frankincense oil remained in a glass dish. I touched my finger to the warm liquid and transferred the scent to my hands and wrists, temples and throat. I felt a tingling sensation wherever the oil touched, and the scent transported my consciousness immediately to the very presence of Jesus. I shook my head and returned to my daily consciousness - there was work to do!

That glass dish of frankincense oil beckoned me again and again. I wanted to be surrounded by that marvelous fragrance. It was a strange sort of hunger, this frankincense desire. I felt as though the fragrance itself had substance, a presence. It satisfied something very deep in me. But I had work to do.

At our communal lunch that day we were discussing the Jesus class and my sweet friend Ruth asked me what was different now about my relationship with Jesus. I mentioned that he was now, truly an ever-present help, constantly available to my consciousness; and it occurred to me that our relationship was something like the newlywed relationship - constantly together, of one mind, intertwined, blissful. *So this is our honeymoon, beloved; and I am so close to you, sweet Liberty, that you smell my fragrance. You desire*

159

Libby Maxey

my presence above any other. Oh! Your fragrance - the frankincense!
And so I seek your presence, even in the natural world. *Because
there I am, as well.* Yes. Oh yes. Even to the end of time. *Which comes
soon, soon. Watch. Listen!*

Of calendars and prophecy

At this time in the cosmic cycle things are jumping. It will soon be September 17, 2001, a big day according to varying prophecies; a day heralding a season of initiation and evolution. Energies are building, time is undulating, minds and hearts expanding, vision opening to truth. It is a time of naked trusting. Prophecy has one use, and that use is to call forth decision. If the prophecy is of a negative nature like Armageddon, then decide this is not the desired outcome. With prayer, image-in the desired outcome, and call that forth. In the case of positive prophecy, call it forth! This or something better, God!

Barbara Marx Hubbard and her co-author the son of man himself, in the book "Revelation: Our Crisis is a Birth" illustrate this essential idea on prophecy in a brilliant way. In this marvelous work, Jesus presents what he has imaged-in as a positive alternative to the Armageddon of John's Revelation - a peaceful, aware birth into universal humanity. He draws us to this New Jerusalem, a place in consciousness so beautiful I weep to contemplate it. By our conscious, intended listening to his voice, the One Voice, the voice of the Holy Spirit - we are guided, unmistakably, perfectly, into the vortex of our own evolution, through atonement, to ascended Christ beingness.

September 17, 2001...I wonder what we will be saying after that day occurs. Right now the calendar says September 10. I can certainly feel the energies escalating. September 17, 2001 marks the "ending" of the calendar stone inside the pyramid of Giza. This calendar stone has marked all previous dates of world significance - birth of Jesus, world wars; like that. Does this mean, then, that measurable "time" is coming to an end? September 17 is a big day in Mayan prophecy, as well, not to mention the new moon and the one of the highest of the Jewish High Holy Days, Rosh Hashanah (new year) that day. Rosh Hashanah begins a ten-day period called the "Days of Awe" culminating with Yom Kippur (Day of Atonement) on September 27. So is that to be the day of at-one-ment?

~~~

161

Libby Maxey

Today is September 12, and unbelievably, the title of this chapter has itself become prophetic. For just yesterday, shortly after dropping little Isaac off at kindergarten, I walked into the living room and said "What's in the news today?" to my husband Gil. Then I looked at him and followed his stunned gaze to the television. There, before our eyes, the second jet slashed into the World Trade Center. Ashen, he looked at me and said in a whisper "Oh my God, these must be suicide bombers" and we watched, horrified, stricken with pain, as the remaining events unfolded in their relentlessness. It was if all the doomsday movies, all that we had collectively imaged-in with our hatreds and unconscious beliefs had suddenly been created in reality. And that's exactly what it was. *So do I have your attention? You have mine. What I am really after is your un-divided attention. I want your attention, united. I want your eyes single to the One Truth. God is. I AM. And ye are Gods, whether you believe it or not. Do you see the power of god-lessness? Perhaps you will now choose to wield the true power of God-fullness.*

I closed my tear-puffy eyes and surrendered. Father, forgive them, for they know not what they do. Thy will be done. Over and over, breathing in and out until I escaped into an uneasy peace. I saw the earth and the energies surrounding the planet, and saw the immense hole in the ethers created by the collapse of thoughts in race consciousness. Thoughts of safety, stability, sanctuary, freedom - countless thoughts held in world consciousness, now collapsed, shattered and destroyed. The hole was like a vortex, massive and dark, drawing energies downward into the spinning center. I looked to the center of the vortex, and realized that the center was much lighter and clearer than the edges, as a hurricane often shows a patch of blue sky in the eye. Then I saw the energy above the vortex - another vortex, but this one made entirely of Divine Light! As the above-vortex joined the below-vortex, an explosion of light and sound; in the same instant, radiant, radiating, radioactive Light burst out in all directions, sending a shock-wave of realization throughout the world consciousness while the magnificently blended sounds of crashing water, blazing fire and a angelic voices joined together to soothe, cleanse and illuminate all beings in this mighty rush of Love energy. Then all was soundless, and in the stillness, I saw again the twin towers of the World Trade Center falling, falling, silent witnesses to the end of duality and the beginning of Unity.

162

Heaped up, pressed down, shaken together and running over

This is what is happening to energies all around me and in me as well. Emotions are shaking us together; old, negative imprinting long pressed down in everyone is running over, and in the midst of all that God's grace is heaped up everywhere we turn. There is not only a vortex of negativity and fear in New York City being cleansed, but also a vortex in every soul, and the Light of God is exploding in us individually and collectively. Our evolution is at hand; that is very clear.

This has become crystal clear in my vortex of a human life. My nearly 25-year marriage may be ending as of last Friday. The very same day I sent this manuscript, called "Imaging God" to the first three publishers, I asked Gil why he was acting so coldly toward me. There it was, a volcano of his hurt and anger toward me going back to the very beginning of our relationship! I was struck dumb. The old, dead Libby would have agreed with the saying "no good deed goes unpunished", but Liberty, the real me, expects reward beyond my imagining for gracefully accepting what is. Suffice it to say that we have come to an impasse that appears impassible. He believes in the past, in his humanness. I believe in now, in my (and his) divinity. It feels like an ending. So again I am trusting. It does hurt; we do have three children and money stuff. The money stuff is another so-human difficulty. He sees us as lacking while I feel blessed by the abundance in our lives.

In church this morning we were treated to a wonderfully wise skit that made the analogy that God (good) is a river flowing through us. Obstacles and challenges in our lives were described as boulders in the river. One of the actors noted that the river flows faster and with greater power around the boulders; and faster still when many boulders group together. So that's what I'm expecting, God, that You are flowing faster, with greater Power than ever before around this challenge that is before my family and me. This challenge, this obstacle is my stepping-stone to next level, I know it.

This is my prayer, Wonderful Alaha. Heal Gilbert at depth; reveal his divinity to him. I bless him and release him to Your care.

Libby Maxey

Guide us both in our actions and reactions. Your will for this book, Father, is to awaken and empower those ready to take the next step in Your plan. I acknowledge and accept my role in that plan. Bless me greatly, Father, pour down Your abundant Grace. Manifest Your plan through me. So it is.

~~~

A week hasn't changed much of anything in the physical realm; divorce looms as a potent possible, I will have to update my resume and look for a job. My great desire and fervent hope is that God comes through (and what do You say about coming through before the last minute?) and the right and perfect publisher calls me, delighted and excited about this work. In my spirit, I know that all is in Divine Order. Much of that doesn't transfer into my moment-to-moment thought-realm right now, but I do thank God for knowing. In some moments I feel a tremendous freedom, and it's not freedom from Gil or from marriage, it's a freedom to really be. The floodgates of good are open; the vortex of my being is spinning out all that is not God. It's happening not just in me but also in Gil and in everyone.

Getting ready to go to the doctor this morning, in a moment of anger I stripped off my wedding ring and flung it into a drawer of my jewelry chest. I fished around in another drawer and found my amethyst ring – a small, rectangular violet stone. In Unity, violet represents power. In symbology, violet represents power as well; power as transmutation. I slid the ring onto my ring finger, muttering "I guess now I'll be the bride of Christ by default". And then it occurred to me that nothing at all has changed. I have always been the bride of Christ by default, and that is the one, perfect fallback position, every time. In a rush of energy, I realized the amazing, blazing Truth of the core concept behind "A Course in Miracles", which is "Nothing real can be threatened. Nothing unreal exists. Herein lies the Peace of God." The reality of Love cannot be threatened, ever. All that exists is Love, even if it looks like a distortion of Love. The distortion is the unreality. Herein indeed lies the Peace of God. On this core belief I will stand, vortex whirling around me. Therein stands the Peace of God.

164

At my physical exam, my doctor noticed what she thought might be fibroid tumors in my uterus. I was totally unconcerned by that statement, and then she said I would need an ultrasound exam. I had no fear of any kind. When I got home, I looked up the condition in Louise Hay's "Heal Your Body" and amazingly, the probable cause is this: "Nursing a hurt from a partner. A blow to the feminine ego." After a hearty, astounded laugh, I firmly decided not to be hurt. A hurt is a perception of body consciousness, and nursing a hurt would be unforgiveness. I forgive him completely, Father, help Thou my unforgiveness.

~~~

In general when my Unity Church holds healing services, I am one of the givers of healing. For obvious reasons, this night I asked to receive healing. During a healing meditation, we were asked to find the right and perfect affirmation to release, heal or cleanse our individual blockages. "I release all attachment to my human life" came as a direct "command" from the Voice. Mindfully, determinedly, on each out breath I released all attachment to my human life, and observed numerous little clouds and tiny dark swirlings leaving my being. Later in the meditation I found myself encased and surrounded by gigantic gem of a transparent, gel-like light; something like a force-field yet also intelligent, protective. *More like a Source-shield, beloved one.* Yes, absolutely.

After the meditation, my dear friend and wonderful chaplain Eileen balanced my chakras with a healing touch technique while I rested on her table. At one point she removed her hand from my solar plexus chakra, and Jesus immediately placed his hand there, whispering with sweet gentleness "I will protect your joy, beloved." He kept his hand there like a promise, and I was filled and surrounded by profound Grace. Thank God.

He knew how much I would need that Grace. The next morning, Gilbert actually asked for a divorce.

I'll die to all of it, God

Tuesday, October 9. We talked about money today. It was a tearful meeting. He is a truly good man. I feel such sorrow that he doesn't want to be a partner in this journey any longer. But in terms of our spiritual journey, he hasn't wanted to be a partner for some time, and I have really known that. God has given me plenty of signs. I hope we can be better friends than we are partners.

After some talk, I walked outside into the bright and beautiful October day. I noticed a purple flower in the grass, and thinking it might be a violet (yes, even in October – I expect miracles!) I bent down to look. It wasn't a violet. I walked further, into the patchy grass under some trees. This was an area of the yard where I thought violets might grow when I walked there in the spring, but no violets grew there. But then I looked again. Patches of violet leaves! And then there it was, in October – a lone violet. Just for me. This is a symbol that I know and love: the violet is symbolic of spiritual healing. God is so very good to us to give us what we need when we need it. Oh, if everyone would just look…

~~~

November 15, 2001. I haven't been able to see Goodness very well for a while. So much pressure to get a job in the world and I have real difficulty seeing myself out there, doing some office job. Yet until I have an income, Gil cannot leave the house and get his own place. We both want him to have his own place. He has his own reasons; my main reason is to be free of his continual rejection. To be "reviled and persecuted" in my own home is very tough. My truest vision of income for me is to have a publisher excitedly pick up this writing; to open up God's incredible blessings to the evolution of humanity contained in these pages. I want my abundance to come through the vehicle of these words. I want this abundant prosperity to bless me, my children, and my church family; to touch the world. I want to remodel my kitchen! I want to install new windows! I want to know financial peace. Since time does not exist in ultimate reality, dear reader, agree with me in the consciousness of the Living Christ that the desires of my heart are fulfilled! Even so, Wonderful God, thy will be done. It is finished. Amen.

The outer experiences of uncertainty have recently been overwhelming – September 11, the grief of my own situation, the ups and downs in the sale of our beloved church and moving to a new space, the income challenges, war and rumors of war, plane crashes, anthrax and every other ugliness, all the uncertainties everyone around me is facing – this list could go on and on... The tightrope walk of staying balanced is extremely challenging. And yet, balance is the perfect lesson for maintaining unified consciousness. So in uncertainty, seek Divine Certainty. The times of late when I have, finally, exhaustedly, just given it all up to fall into His Peace the Grace has been astounding. And if shedding tears is truly an act of cleansing, I am cleansed! My feeling is that we need to embrace and trust the Certainty of our oneness with God. So doing, we have the strength and humor to see the uncertainty as temporary and temporal. Certainty is real. "What is real cannot be threatened. What is unreal (temporary) does not exist. Therein lies the Peace of God." God knows we certainly need the Peace She has planned for us!

He moved out and we bought a Christmas tree anyway

Yep, he did it. He didn't wait until I have a job. How does that work? He rented an apartment and moved out last Tuesday. He didn't take much stuff, but we didn't have much "extra" anyway. We live lightly, with as few possessions as necessary. The kids have decorated a little Christmas tree for him as a gift, and we bought a lovely fir tree from North Carolina for home. It's been over a week now. Today is December 6. The first couple of days were strange and hollow and dark. I didn't like that place at all. It is a place of grief and mourning for what has been and what will not be. But it is a place of illusion, because now comprises neither what has been nor what will be. In this now moment, I declare that the ending of this relationship has no power over me. And that will be true until it is not, eh God?

You know waves of mourning will come, little one. There are still triggers in your consciousness; most connected to our children. But know this, beloved Liberty, that your desires are so close to fulfillment, you are so near to Perpetual Consciousness...oh, my darling child, if you could but see all that I know for you.

It's hard right now to believe anything great and wonderful is coming, You know? *Yes, that sums up My difficulty quite well.* And yet, I do know it. You know, God, that You leave few signposts letting us know where we're going in Spirit *entertain the thought that perhaps you don't see all the signs* well, okay. No argument. You know how much I desire that the perfect publisher pick up this manuscript submission and know that she knows this is You. Waiting sucks, and I'm tired of it. That's the plain truth. *Continue on, beloved of Mine, for instantaneous manifestation comes* and there You go again, interrupting with a great and wonderful stuff that I KNOW is on the tip of my experience, like a word on the tip of my tongue.

This experience of my marriage relationship breaking: this is the harbinger of the greatness and wonder of Christ manifesting fully in me, through me, as me. I have to KNOW You are my Source, my Abundance, my everything **in my experience**. I still had some dependence on marriage, on sameness, on physical security. These are illusions to be shattered, so You did. Thanks a lot. But really, thank You. This is liberation. I'm for that. I am that. *You said it. The word was made flesh and dwelt among us. Within us. As us.* My love for You knows no limit. It grows as I lift it to You, praising You, loving You, faithfully waiting on You. *That was a "One Voice" revelation, lovely one.* Oh! Oh! Thank You! I feel warmth, a liquid vibration flowing over me, the tone it makes lifting me in His Love.

I'm supposed to go and sign the divorce documents tomorrow. If I did not know in my heart that what is happening is good, if I did not know what God is up to in all of this, my heart would be breaking. And it is, in a way, but what is real cannot be threatened. Why is it I feel so threatened?

Knowing that my Source is You, Wonderful God, I ask for Your abundance to rain down on me and my family. It is clear that our marriage is over, God. Please bless Gilbert beyond what he can ask, think or imagine. My family requires income from a new and wonderful Source. You have given me a dream, a desire deep in my heart, to publish the words You have given to me in our book. I ask that our book be published, and that this be the avenue for Your abundant blessings to flow to and through me. The right and perfect publisher is right now calling me (or e-mailing me or sending me a contract and a check special delivery). Confirm Your plan for me by making this so. The abundance that flows through the publishing and distribution of our book will enable me to bless my children, my mother, and my beloved church. The greatness of Your plan for humanity will flow through our book, awakening and enlightening hundreds, thousands, millions of Your beloveds worldwide, bringing them to their own evolution in Spirit.

Father Mother, I want my children to attend the learning institutions of their choice, based on their desires. I want the financial Peace to know this will happen. Mother God, I want to remodel my kitchen. I want to install new windows and landscape the lawn of my home. I want to re-decorate my home to reflect who I am in You. I want the financial Peace to know my mother will be comfortable, all the days of her life. I want to be able to give freely from my abundance. I know that You desire for me more than I could ask, think or imagine, so having placed my desires before You. I surrender to Your Will. I desire above all else to know You, to see You, to be one with You. Thy will be done. In the precious name and one with the wonderful consciousness of Christ Jesus, my sweet Yeshua, I ask and know. This or something better, Lord I Am. And it is so. Amen

And then there is the Gene situation. My sweet friend Gene Elizabeth Ross, wife of Roy; now dying, quite clearly, from cancer. In March she told us about the recurrence of cancer; this time it was a lesion on her liver. We sat, holding each other's hands, in the violet light cast by the stained glass window at our Unity Church. We prayed, and I told her what I was seeing. I saw a youth-filled, vigorous Gene, fiery, passionate; with an honesty, a devastating sweet honesty about her - I saw the image and likeness of God, manifest as Gene! And I knew that this beingness was coming to her.

I went to see her at the hospice yesterday. I walked in, and noticing that she was asleep, took off my jacket and pulled a chair near her bedside. I closed my eyes to pray, but quickly opened them as I heard, then saw her sit forward, expectantly. Her eyes, though closed, danced…she smiled a blissful smile, filled with wonder, and nodded three times. I knew, I just knew – in that moment, she answered to Jesus. And her answer: yes, yes, yes. Suddenly she roused, looking me full in the face. She said " No, it wasn't you!" and returned, eyes closing, to her blissful place.

When she later awoke I asked her if she would counsel all of her Unity family, if she would coach us and guide us from beyond the open door. She said "Oh, yes!" with pleasure and finality. I knew that she was very near the open door. I knew the veil was very thin. She walked easily now between worlds.

Today she walked on through the open door. She is guiding us already.

Life is so very strange. In such a short time the world and my life have changed so dramatically. And I feel dramatic, darting from darkness to light in consciousness, from death to life. And then I see that death is the same as life, as with the appearance of trees in winter, and then so joy is the same as sorrow, and love the same as fear – all appearances. Finding balance is a constant need. *Balance can be found in breathing, you know. You treat breathing as a luxury.* God? *You have treated breathing as if it is something you cannot afford. It's been tough getting through, my beloved one, very difficult.* I have been in the soup. But I want You so much *then take the time to seek Me!* But God, I already found You *I will let you know when you have reached permanency of Christ consciousness. Still you retreat, eh, beloved?* Yes, I do. I know it. In the current time of my life, I find it difficult to trust experience. Since You are the provider of all experience, I am a little gun-shy. *I understand. Truly.*

God, tell me more about image and likeness. I saw Gene's image and likeness; the perfect "Gene-ness" You envisioned and created her to be. I know that she has returned to that state of perfection. I have glimpsed, once or twice, my own image and likeness. I want to so purify my being that all of my "Libby-ness" *Ahem, your "Liberty", you mean* okay. Correction. Purify me, sanctify me; reveal through my being the word Liberty made flesh, fully manifest, fully awake full time, to do Your Work. *That is a prayer. That prayer calls for agreement. That prayer calls for declaration.*

God, I am so scared. I am just petrified with fear. I feel like a traitor to You. I want to trust You completely, to just fall into that wonderful childlike trusting. I feel like a rat in a brand-new maze, except now it's dark, and someone keeps opening trap doors in the floor. The floor keeps falling out from under me. And I know all this stuff is just stuff, just appearances. I know You have a marvelous plan for me, waiting just over there, just beyond my visioning. It's more than just a little difficult to trust experience. How can I trust? And yet what else is there? Because if I do not trust You, then I block understanding. Trust brings understanding. I need understanding.

I know your need. I love you tenderly, devotedly. Close your eyes, darling child, and come to Me. I long for your closeness. You long for me? *Oh yes…it's a parent thing, you know? I crave your touch, your fragrance, your holy desire for Me.* God? This is where I'm most afraid. I know You are calling me to completion, and I am praying myself to completion…it's like jumping consciously into a black hole, and I'm the only one nuts enough to jump. Am I nuts? I feel so crazy, sometimes, believing I am ascending in consciousness, becoming Christ right here and right now in my silly little life. All I have is You. You are entirely everything. And You are not visible, yet appear everywhere. God, I want to be conscious of You, conscious in You, conscious as You. *So the rant is over, and we again have agreement. I want you and you want Me. This is where I get to take the final step.* Do You mean the "final step"? The "A Course in Miracles" final step? *That's the final step to which I refer, yes.* Oh, God. Oh, my God. My heart is pounding. I want You to be close like this and I'm terrified at the same time. Oh my God – I'm afraid of You! Oh God, Oh, I don't want to fear You! I want only to love You!

Then be who you are! That is how you love Me, that is how you do My will, that is how you become the fullness of Christ Liberty, the word made flesh. You have been sent as a messenger of written and spoken word: the word liberty! You are a writer – write! Display your frail humanity, accepting your feeling nature in full view of the beloveds who will read these words. Your humanity is important. Remember Jesus? You love his human-ness. Take on that which you are. My beloved and wonderful one, know that I have people lined up to give you My Abundance. Trust in the truth you KNOW and I will eliminate all fear from you. I want you only to love Me, holy Liberty, with more intense desire than your energy fields can possibly contain. This fear will leave you. That is My promise.

Use what you know

The life of my physical and emotional natures has been completely re-ordered. As of today I have no job and no income save what is deposited to my account by Tennessee divorce law. God has even called me to give up the small income I have received by cleaning the church on Fridays, my "celebration of service" day. Every Friday has been a celebration, too, because everyone at the church on Fridays is serving in some way, and we celebrate with a communal lunch and lots of laughs! The income I can be "certain" of will in no way cover the expenses of maintaining this wonderful brick home nor the feeding habits of my wonderful three offspring. My three offspring are facing angers and resentments and uncertainties, each of their own. This is heartbreaking, too. When little Isaac prays for his daddy to come home, I cry, devastated for him. Please, God, please, don't let him think for an instant that You will abandon him. My elder son Aaron is chasing strong angers, avoiding them, looking away. He has learned to "suck it up" all too well. Loving Father God, teach him to face his feelings, to allow his emotions, to express his pain in the highest and best way for him. Laura seems fine, for now. She has learned many tools to express and allow her emotions. Mother God, hold her lovingly, gently. Keep her heart and mind open to You in her life. Let no-thing block Your Presence from her.

And me. It seems I haven't had time to pee alone since well before Christmas. I doubt seriously that I have processed even half the emotions surrounding September 11 and those outcomes. I know I have processed little of the emotion surrounding September 28, my own personal day of destruction, and that batch of outcomes. I feel very much like You have let me down, like You have just dropped me because I didn't do something right, some unspoken something that I should have known better…I want to trust You. I guess I'm just transferring all the feelings I have toward Gil to You. *Very human of you, beloved. And it's okay. I can take it.* That's good, because Gil can't (or won't) take it. Even honest expression of feeling he will not accept. *I know his struggle too.* Forgive me if I don't give a shit. *Forgiven. Again, it's a human thing.*

And this is driving me nuts, too. God, why would You want me out there working at an ordinary job when You have given me this tremendous gift of words and humor to share with the world? Why would you want me hanging out with the unawakened when I could be helping You bring initiates closer to You? *Why would you think one group has value over the other?* Oh. Oh. Oh my God. I have been arrogant…oh, God, please forgive me. I only want to serve You in the best way possible *and you are not in the position to see the best way possible.* NO SHIT!!! I CAN'T SEE ANYTHING! I CAN'T SEE THE PURPOSE YOU HAVE FOR ME!

Well! Now we're getting somewhere! And where is that, exactly? *We're getting closer to unity than ever before in time. You are closer to Reality than you can imagine right now, but that veil needs to stay in place until My Divine Timing. You can feel the veil, can you not?* Are You referring to this "pressed to the wall" feeling? *Describe that.* It's like I'm pushed face-first into some kind of membrane, very thin, almost transparent, but extremely tough. I'm pushing, pushing, squirming in the tightness. There are others, many others, pushing up behind me. It reminds me of the star gate in the movie of the same name. When the scientists figured out the codes and activated the structure, a gel-like watery substance formed in the center of the gate. The innocently curious scientist that cracked the code walked up to the gate and touched the gel, and there was a stretchy surface tension that held him back from pushing through, even though he wanted to push through. *And how did he finally push through to his new experience?* I'm not sure he pushed through at all. What happened was that he returned to the group, they thought and prepared, and after a while, he and some others just walked right through. *Ahh. He returned to the world, gathered others, and walked through the gate.*

So I am returning to the world, gathering others, and walking through the gate? *So it would appear. That would be an excellent purpose.* But God, what about the purpose of this book? What about that? So far those answers have all been rejections, too. Am I to abandon this writing and the good that You have shown me that will come from sharing it? And what about all the abundance issues? Right now I have to decide whether to pay the electric bill or the car payment! How can that kind of angst serve this purpose?

You have to use what you know. Right now, you know you have to provide income. Use that knowing to serve the purpose of providing income, while using what you know. That's some conundrum. *It is what you have right now. Use what I give to you. You have received more knowledge from Me than most, yet you do not use what you know. You say that you do, and sometimes you actually do, but not really, and lately not so much at all!* It is very difficult to maintain spiritual sanity in the midst of such madness. It is very difficult to desire to eat properly, sleep properly, meditate, read, pray, or even be nice to my kids! *My beloved daughter, I am so very aware of all this. Why do you think I have lavished you with such Presence?* I did wonder about that. Even though my entire life is wobbling crazily, every Sunday You have filled me with such Presence, such assurance...Oh! I just had a vision! *Yes?* (He said with a wonderful God chuckle) I saw a line of people, hundreds maybe, some holding small baskets, some holding paper in their hands, all lined up on a grassy ridge overlooking a beautiful meadow. They were all coming up to me, one by one, giving me money from their hands or from their baskets. Some cried as they gave me their tithe (tithe? me?) Others gave to me laughing, turning to run or skip away, totally joyful. Wow! So when does this lovely parade begin, God? *Look again, wonderful child. It has neither beginning nor ending. My abundance has neither beginning nor ending. It is most helpful to notice, Liberty. All that you need is provided.* Yes, that is so. Now to unload all the doubting.

Crucifixion, 2002

By mid January 2002, having had no luck responding to advertised jobs nor with internet job searching, I decided to direct market. I found 23 area lawyers specializing in areas of the law in which I had some paralegal experience, and I sent all of them letters and resumes. In the first week I had one interview and found out what the pay really is in this area, and it ain't what's reported by the information-gathering websites! But I realized that I can do job this thing. I realized that it's a temporary measure; that nothing between God and me has changed. The Plan is still rolling, *even if it doesn't seem so, sweet Liberty*. How do you like that, interrupted by God again. Right after the interview, which was kind of rushed and weird, I made a wild decision to cut my hair. All of it. Short. So I did.

Anyone who knows me and my spiritual story would say that I flipped out in the moment I decided to cut my hair. I have had my hair shoulder-length for several years, ever since the night Jesus "superimposed" his body of light over my own physical body. I felt his hair touching my shoulders, gently curling in the hollows created by my collarbone. It was an exquisite moment, and from that moment I wanted my own physical hair to touch me there, just to keep me in remembrance. But cutting my hair, shaking my short hair, running my fingers through this new look was freeing somehow, and I couldn't understand that.

The last day of my church cleaning service I arranged to see Rev. Patricia for a short visit. I mostly whined about not understanding my purpose anymore, about lack issues, about avoiding my human feelings. At the end of our talk, all cried out (at least for the moment) she commented again on how she liked my haircut. I asked her if she knew my story about Jesus' hair (she didn't) so I related it to her. She apparently understood how wonderful his lightbody feels, because she gasped with delight when I described how it was for me...then she blurted "You cut your hair because you don't need him to be superimposed over you any more. You have the strength to stand as Christ on your own!" And we both burst into tears and laughter...and I realized: It's true.

A couple weeks passed and I sent out a new batch of letters, this time to insurance agents and insurance claims offices, then to lawyers further away from my home. But the first batch of letters came through again, and I got a call from a lawyer's office in the town I had really decided would be the best for me. The interview went great, almost two hours, ending in being introduced to the whole staff. I felt this was it! I like these people, they like me; the boss seems to be a great guy with a terrific sense of humor. I can do this and be okay with it. I can do this and Gilbert has no power over me. The only problem was the contract with the temporary agency that had been providing temporary and potential employees. I would have to work as a temporary until the contract was up, then I could be hired outright. The boss said he felt very good about the whole arrangement; the rest of the staff was relieved. I agreed, and we set a date for me to start, 10 days later on the first Monday in February.

There was a lot to do in a short time. Isaac's after school arrangements had been set in motion earlier, but now I had to get everything done. I wrote a note to his teacher, telling her my new daytime phone number and what our plans were for bus riding and after school care. For a minute I wondered if I was jinxing everything by putting all these plans in writing, but I felt satisfied about the job and the people, so I laughed at myself. Besides, I knew that when I started working, any doubt they might have about my abilities would quickly vanish.

All in place, the last Friday before I was to start my job I planned on a day of meditation and peace, work on my book, and going to lunch at the church with my dear friends the last Friday for some time to come, I was sure. At 11:00 the phone rang. It was my new office-to-be. The boss had one of his paralegals call me. She told me that a woman they had offered the job (my job!) to in December had called to accept, and she had been hired! However, they still needed me to work the two weeks as a temporary.

I was destroyed. I managed to choke out that I would still take the job as a temporary, because I needed the money. Somewhere deep there was a shred of hope in me that during the two weeks something would change; that something somehow would work out...I didn't know how, and I didn't care. But I was destroyed. I was betrayed again. I could not believe what was happening.

This could <u>not</u> be God. I wanted my hair back. I wanted my life back. All I could do was cry. I dragged myself into my bedroom and collapsed on the bed, chest heaving, uncontrollably sobbing. I couldn't even move.

Gil came that night to pick up the kids for his visitation. For the first time in a long while, I felt that he cared about me, which was a little better and a little worse at the same time. Aaron and Laura were very concerned about me, having never seen me so upset. I had never seen myself so upset. The emotional pain was excruciating; I was humiliated and dejected, betrayed and rejected. I knew that I knew I was crucified, as surely as if the nails pierced my skin and I was hanging on a cross, misunderstood to death by the people around me. Then everyone left and I was alone, crucified on a Friday night. There was nothing good about this Friday.

And the beat goes on

Yeah, the beat goes on. The heartbeat, that is. Fragile, puffy-eyed, I went to church on Sunday morning. Hope was beginning to re-build in me; I know what comes after crucifixion. I was accepting, accepting; that's all I could manage. The first dear friend who spoke to me hugged me close to her and whispered in my ear "You know, Libby, you can allow your crucifixion to happen with me. I will support you through it." Taken aback that she would know my thoughts, astounded and relieved, I did…I allowed all of it to wash over me, the entirety of the meaning of crucifixion. I breathed deeply, abandoned-ly, allowing the process of dying to happen, knowing the process was not as it appeared to the human mind. I felt the life of Libby slipping from my consciousness as my physical body slumped in Suzanne's arms. *Father, forgive them, for they know not what they do* and I saw my life, my children, my friends and my family members; authority figures, all the faces of judgment in my lifetime, and then Gilbert and the recent events and players. Father, forgive them, for they know not what they do, I whispered, then breathed out - a long, lingering expiration. Suzanne held on. I truly "gave up the ghost", totally surrendered to the death of limitation. Libby is dead. Long live Liberty.

I don't know how long Suzanne held me up there against the purple wall at Unity Church. I just know that when I came around, I was changed. I was light, I was free. I began to feel the resurrection. God was gentle with me, coming over me in the service with a merciful, comforting Presence, speaking of renewal and rebirth. He held me in softness the rest of the day. He knew I would need to remember that softness the next day, because the next day I would be going to work. Temporarily.

5:30 Monday. Time to get up and get Isaac out of bed. The morning bus comes between 6:15 and 6:25, the bus company said. Thank God they will stop for him at the end of our driveway. It is still dark when we take our walk up the driveway, out in the cold morning air. Isaac holds me tight, apprehensive about his day. I reassure him, feeling tightly wound and apprehensive myself. He bravely boards the bus, smiling broadly when he realizes that his favorite Miss Darlene is the morning bus driver. So far so good.

My new hair won't cooperate and my eyes are still puffy, but this is what they're getting. Discomfort and anxiety accompany me as I make the drive to the office, even as I listen to God music all the way. I have no idea what I will say. I decide to say as little as possible, but to just listen and be open. I decide to forgive them, because I know not one of them would have purposefully hurt me as they did. In a kind of fog of forgiveness, I learned what was taught that day and performed well, beyond their expectations and my own, for that matter. The day passed. I picked up Isaac at his after school program, and it was already dark. He cried about losing his days. He cried, asking me how he could get his life back. I explained acceptance of what is happening now, but still we both cried all the way home.

Things continued. Isaac was sad. One night after reading his nighttime story, I asked him "What do you want to pray for, sweetie?" Isaac gave me a long look. "I want to pray to God for my life back. I want to pray for us to have money to get me a fort and swings for the back yard and I want to pray for you to get a new kitchen, Mom, and how will this happen?" He looked straight into my eyes. "How?" I told him that God had another purpose for me, and it was time to pray that purpose into reality. I told him that our abundance could come through this writing; that the right and perfect publisher would hear God and decide any day to pick this up. He smiled, satisfied. "That's it! Let's pray for your book to be our money!" A sweet rush of Love came over us, and we hugged and prayed. Surely God will answer the prayer of a child, I thought. I hoped. I prayed. It had to be true, or why would He show me all that He has shown me? It must be true. It must be Truth.

I convinced my boss to take my resume with him to the local bar association lunch on the Wednesday before the end of my time as his temporary employee. He came back, looking a little worried, and said to me "You know, there aren't any jobs available right now. I asked everyone. It seems they are all just sitting tight right now, waiting for the fallout from September 11." I looked at him, and could see the concern in his eyes. Feeling strangely okay, even blissful, I reassured him that I would find something.

The next day there was a quiet flurry of activity and an impromptu meeting of the permanent staff. The boss came to me just before lunchtime and said that he was amazed to find himself in the position to offer me the job! It seems the person that he had hired decided to stay put and now it was truly mine if I still wanted it, although he would quite understand if I didn't want to stay. But you know, by now I had begun to love him and everyone there. So I stayed. I was glad, rejoicing, because I had known, deep in my heart, that forgiveness would save me in this situation. I had not notified Isaac's teacher that we would be changing back to our former schedule, but waited instead. Now I could relax. The pain of humiliation was gone, lifted entirely. Thank God.

On the way to pick up Isaac that evening, the Presence of God flooded over me as I drove. I had to pull over, the vibration was so strong. I was grateful and thankful, praising God for all the relief I was feeling in my human walk, and God spoke, clearly: *You were given that job in that way to teach you about the immediacy of forgiveness. As much as the early circumstances were hurtful, you forgave and forgave completely. And you forgave for your own sake, so that you would no longer be wounded by your own thoughts. You decided to extend grace, even when you were feeling humiliated. And immediately, the entire picture was transformed in Goodness, everyone was given their highest and best outcome.* Ineffectively, I sobbed Thank You, God, as I trembled in the powerful, the wonderful Presence. He went on. *I have my reasons for keeping you busy, you know.* Huh? *I have kept you preoccupied with all that is going on in your life is to keep you in MIND. For if right now you were in your heart and soul, which is where I know you want to be, you would be far too overwhelmed with the enormity of your growth to function in the human realm. I am not quite ready for you to be solely in Me. But just know, my beloved child: This is your time.*

Part Three – Truth

The Ease of Forgiveness

So now I'm in the working world. To the extent they will allow themselves to be known, my coworkers are beginning to come to me and talk about their lives. I see the sweet compassion they have for the people who come in; the retarded man who cannot read brings a ticket in, thinking he is in big trouble. One of the lawyers sits down with him and calmly explains the process, walking him to the door to point out to the courthouse where he needs to go to pay the fine, helping him count out the right amount of cash. It is awesomely sweet. Then the boss hires a homeless guy to wash all the windows of the building, gives him $100 cash and drives him to a restaurant to get him a good meal. These lawyers represent clients in criminal cases, but their representation comes from a knowing that all these "criminals" have done is made a mistake, sometimes for the umpteenth time, but still it is a mistake. I cannot find contempt for the clients even in the way they speak after the clients leave. I find myself praying that all lawyers come to represent clients from this state of mind.

Still, for all the business of working in the law office, it is only my mind that is engaged, and not so much of that. I find that very little of the wholeness of who I am is required to be present at the job, and still I am extremely effective and efficient. This makes me wonder about Gilbert again, how he can be so consumed by his job that it has become who he is, by his own admission. It makes me wonder about people in general, about how people get so trapped in thought patterns that limit their very beingness, and how our world supports that entrapment. We are told to go to school, go to college, get a job, start a career, get more education, advance our careers. People who work long hours are "dedicated" and "loyal". We give these people raises and bonuses. We continually reward them until they collapse and burn out. In our society, we use people up and then discard them when they no longer perform.

Most fortunately (well, it is Your Plan, after all) my new boss allowed me to take two days off to attend the annual chaplains' retreat in mid-March. I didn't really need to take extra time off since the retreat was Friday night, Saturday and half the day Sunday, but I knew that I would need both time to prepare and time to "recover". Boy, was that the right thing to do.

This year our Unity chaplain team has 17 members! The gathering on Friday night was wonderful and tough. We all shared, deeply, what we were feeling and going through. Everyone had been experiencing wildly shifting emotions, volatility in relationships, just plain craziness. Thank You, God, that we have a safe place to empty ourselves of our selves, and open to the One Self that is You. We all brought sacred objects again this year, and Lee Ann brought a wonderful print of Jesus' smiling image. I sat gazing on that wonderful face. I brought this book, my offering to God, for the first time all 170 pages or so printed book-style on both sides of the paper, in a notebook. After the sharing time, I led a chakra opening and balancing meditation. The Presence of God came in, and all was Peace.

The next day was cold and stormy. I realized I forgot my jacket, so I wore two shirts and a sweater. It was still cold; raw wind knifing around corners. But even nasty weather cannot dampen the Spirit, so very present in even the stones of the Gothic buildings on this beautiful campus. So very many Spirit-led gatherings and retreats and classes and meditations have been held here; there is a unity of consciousness in the atmosphere. The sleeping rooms are adequate but very small. The dining hall is magnificent, with wonderful dark woodwork, arched Gothic windows and doors, beautiful heavy tables and chairs, marble floors.

Our morning was spent in laughter and tears. We discussed grief and change, and we all were dealing with plenty of both. Our congregation had been through a large number of deaths and divorces and break ups and lost jobs and of course, September 11. So we laughed and cried, hugged and prayed. After lunch I went to my room for a short private time with God. I knew that I knew something was coming to me, some new revelation, a great burden lifted. In a word, forgiveness.

In the afternoon Rev. Patricia decided to follow God instead of the schedule, so she led us in a forgiveness meditation. The synchronicity of the plan and the speed at which the plan is manifesting leaves me breathless, even as I type about this past event. Before we closed our eyes, we had to choose the person we desired most to be able to forgive, and answer three questions. Gilbert came to my mind immediately, of course. The first question was "when you first were with this person, how was it?" Images and memories flooded over me, snapshots of life. It was hot when we first got together; also opening, magical, sweet, mysterious, synchronistic. There was awe at the instant bigness of our relationship, the instantaneous knowings that occur when those who have traveled many lifetimes together reconnect. He was honest, accepting – he allowed me to be what was then all of me. It was wonderful to feel all that again.

The next thing we were to do was to list disappointments, disenchantments and difficulties in the relationship. The vibration in the room shifted. The earlier expansive love gave way to anguish and guilt. The great disappointment for me was that he did not support me in my growth, my purpose or this writing, the opening that I was choosing for myself. The disenchantment came out as his promise early on never to hold a grudge against me, but he revealed massive grudges going back to the beginning of our relationship anyway. The difficulty in our relationship was his way of shutting down emotionally, how he could turn cold. I felt cold myself. Chilled to the bone.

Patricia then asked us to describe how we felt about the loss of the relationship. I wrote, stream-of-consciousness style: saddened, relieved, sometimes gleeful, angry over "injustices", resentful, pissed off that I have to have this experience, grandly pissed that the kids have to experience divorce, grief over "what could have been", even though I haven't been able to see that for some time, and anger over Gilbert's insensitivity to even his own pain. Whew. She ain't so saint like, this Liberty, is she now?

Then my true self spoke, like a mantra: Father, I forgive Gil, teach me to forgive. Mother, I forgive Gil, teach me to forgive. Jesus, I forgive Gil, beloved Yeshua, teach me to forgive. The prayer spiraled around me, reverberating, rising like smoke to God. In the smoke, revelation came. He came. *My beloved child, see this one, this Gilbert my son, as a person unknown to you, standing up to introduce himself at Unity Church one Sunday morning. Do you see? Can you forgive him his story, my Liberty?* And Oh God, in my vision I turned and saw him with new eyes, standing there a little nervous but cocky, giving his name and the reason he came to our Unity Church, just like all the new people. The ease of forgiveness came over me with profound simplicity. Choose once again. See afresh. Father, I forgive this one. It is simple, effortless, childlike. And You have said it over and over in A Course in Miracles that forgiveness redeems everything, now. It redeems the moment, so that there is no past and no future, only now. That's how You do it. That's the immediacy of forgiveness. It corrects the past – oh my God I see it now! That's how children behave, until they forget...*Beloved, when you see anew in each moment, this is truly forgiveness. See all as sinless and you behold your own sinlessness. When you see only innocence, you clearly see the face of Christ.*

I was already overwhelmed with the wonder of this revelation, but there was far more coming. Patricia was just beginning to calm our breathing, preparing us for meditation. Bathing now in His wonderful Presence, I breathed deeply, expectantly.

Patricia asked us to visualize the person we desired to forgive. We were to pick up, hold and carry our person in our arms. When I picked Gil up, his body had the feeling of Isaac's little body, still heavy, but not a serious burden. The idea of potentiality in Isaac that also once existed in Gil came in. I felt sadness that he was choosing not to be his potential. We were to face a flight of seven steps and carry our person, one step at a time, to the top to release the person to God. At each step Patricia said something awesome, unloading all the baggage of the relationship, lightening the load at each step. At the sixth step, I think, Patricia said to look in our person's eyes. I looked down at Gilbert's face, into his eyes, and we became a melded being, one life in that moment. I felt cleansed, clear, purified. Then on the seventh step, we were to release our person to God. I did so, knowing that my God is his God, and God loves Gil. I love Gil. I turned, breathed deeply, and flew away on white wings!

I was not the only person in the room who had a powerful, life changing experience – everyone did. Patricia, knowing full well by our sobs that we were all having tremendous experiences, was still overwhelmed by the enormity of the breakthroughs.

That night, alone in my room after the evening meeting and meditation, snuggled under the covers and finally warm, I opened the one book God guided me to bring. It's always this book She suggests when something big is coming. For some people, it's the Bible, and sometimes that's true for me, too. But most often it's "A Course in Miracles", my worn old friend. All bookmarks and papers removed, I opened it. To my everlasting amazement, this book that is not a book opened to a place way in the back, in the section "Manual for Teachers". The subject at the top of the page? Why "What is the Resurrection?" of course. As soon as I read the word, I knew. It is really happening. I am truly resurrecting, even as Jesus did. And more, because through his example, my resurrection does not even need to follow actual bodily death. I am resurrecting, alive! From glory to glory, he promised. And it is so. As the enormity of Jesus' meaning swept over me and the Mighty Presence filled me, I read on, drinking deeply. I know I have read this before, but never with this understanding. Oh my God. Each sentence is an eloquent description of resurrection, each phrase a poem, then midway through the first page I read "It [resurrection] is the invitation to God to take His final step." Oh God, my God. The final step.

Tears streaming, filled with His Power and Glory; in that moment I feel certain visible light is streaming through every cell of my body. The aroma of frankincense drew my attention, and our wonderful Savior leaned over my right shoulder and draped his arms around me from behind me. His face close to mine, we read on with one mind, one heartbeat. With each phrase, each meaning deepening my understanding, we are nodding in Divine Agreement, up to the last paragraph. There I felt Jesus' consciousness "draw back", leaving me reading alone, still in Christ mind. The last paragraph begins "These things [all of what the resurrection means] await us all, but we are not prepared as yet to welcome them with joy." My thought, immediately, was "Oh yes, I am. I welcome resurrection with joy!" A crashing wave of intense fiery Divinity came over me. I remember nothing else until I awoke to a thunderstorm Sunday morning.

The Light of God

The wind was howling, thunder booming, rain pounding the slate roof of the dormitory building. I looked out the window. The grass was brilliantly green and alive; I noticed that the buds on the tree outside the window had swelled and several had burst wide, revealing bright pink blossoms. I pondered on the idea of resurrection. Could it be as simple for me as it is for that tree? The tree simply drinks in the spring rain, and following a pattern of renewal and rebirth, puts forth blossoms and leaves, forever lifting itself up in praise to God. The tree is. The tree simply is. It has no past or future, only now, perfectly accepting of how things are for the tree in every moment. *You have described the state of sinlessness, my child. You have described also following the Will of God.* Oh! It is such utter simplicity! I suppose now all I have to do is click my heels together three times and say, "I want to go Home, I want to go Home, I want to go Home." *That or something better, yes, it is a matter of intent.* I was kidding! Just being a smart ass to break the profundity of the moment! *Truth wears many faces, tells many stories. Likes a good joke. You know Me!* Yes, I think I am truly beginning to know You. I Am is my dearest friend. *I Am my dearest friend. Look in the mirror, child. Look upon your sinlessness.*

Breathing deeply and rapidly, beginning to feel the overwhelming vibrational Presence once again, I climbed down from the window ledge and sat in the chair, facing the mirror. Then I looked.

With astounding tenderness, I saw my own face as if for the very first time. I loved that face with the same love I felt for the beautiful image of Jesus from last evening's sacred gathering. I saw in my own face all the changing images from early childhood to teenager to young adult to now. There was nothing in that image, that wonderful image that God's Love has made, that could be blamed or judged or attacked in any way. I saw my own self, perfect, pure, sinless, innocent. I beheld the face of Christ. My own face is the face of Christ! Weeping soundlessly, lifted above all things human for the moment, I basked in the Glory I Am. I am Liberty, the Christ. I Am Christ Liberty. I Am the resurrection and the life. I Am the Will of God. Manifest Your Will through me, Oh God. Collapsed once again in sobs of Joy, I lay my head down on the desk, caressing my own cheek with a Love I had never before given to me. From down the hall, I heard voices, doors opening and closing. It must be time to go to breakfast. I roused my human flesh and dashed for the shower, thinking for just a second that I'd better not click my heels in the shower unless I want to present myself to heaven naked.

I couldn't eat much at breakfast. I barely dared speak to anyone, much less look at their wonderful faces. I knew I would burst into tears if I looked anyone fully in the face. I was teary, overwhelmed with the innocence of even sidelong glances my way! Thank You, God, that all these people accept me as I am. Actually I think they enjoy the show. I know it is obvious to most of them that something profound is going on with me. I walked out of the dining hall alone, and went back to my room for another moment with God before we began our chaplain day with a short church service. The experienced chaplains had alerted the new chaplains that it was their duty, as newbies, to put on the church service for the rest of us. What a blessing that the newbies were all from the choir! Down the hall from my room, I heard someone singing, and I thought, "Oh, they are practicing for our church service" and my face grew hot when I listened again. The song, accapella, was "Over the Rainbow". Once again a mighty wave of that glorious energy washed over me, and I felt entirely, completely Loved. Such wonderful gifts God gives to me. God must love me, to do all this just for me.

This year the chaplain retreat was really open to Spirit. Not following the schedule at all, we were treated to an opening exercise, before we began our little church service; a relaxation/ opening/therapeutic technique called "scuddering". Betty, our very own Healing Touch practitioner, led the group. One person was the receiver, the other the giver. The technique is all about energy and balance. I was receiver first, and my sweet dear friend Carolyn the giver. She is very open, especially with me, and curious. I was on fire with Spirit before we even began, and Carolyn was definitely in the Flow. She increased the energy in my fields at least a hundredfold, opening me wider than I have ever been before. I could feel the energy pouring from her hands, crackling as she nearly touched me, and coursing from her when she actually touched my body. Part of the procedure is to massage the hands, then the feet while kneeling in service. We were both weeping with the intense Joy that flowed as she served me. Then it was my turn to serve her. I really wanted to do it, but I was not so sure I could even stand up. Betty looked at me, knowing yet concerned. She did not want me to fall, I knew. But I looked deeply in her eyes, and nodded that yes, I could do this. Yes, it is my desire to serve Carolyn.

I was absolutely on fire. I could feel and "see" Divine energy flowing through my crown chakra, a blue-white electricity like a river of liquid lightning. It smelled like lightning, too, like the way the air smells immediately after a thunderstorm; clean, clarified, rarified. The energy enveloped Carolyn and me, kind of encapsulating us, yet it also filled the room. I could see similar energy envelopes around the other chaplain pairs. I followed Betty's instructions, and the energy zoomed from my fingers. My fingers and palms so tingled that it was almost like itching, hot and intense. I felt that nothing outside God's Will could possibly stay in this energy, and directed all that was outside God's Will for Carolyn to leave her. At that moment, she sighed deeply and smiled a blissful, contented smile. Thank You, God. Massaging her hands and feet, I was overcome by my desire to serve God's wonderful people, to awaken all people to the Truth, to the Light. To remembering. To our evolution. To the resurrection.

Scuddering over, we circled our chairs for our impromptu church service. Wonderful Beth, one of our new chaplains, opened the service singing "Over the Rainbow", according to Plan. Thy Will be done. Our Will be done. So is it click three times or knock three times or what? I do want to be Home. And it must be that simple, because our Home is Christ mind. That is heaven in our world. That is how the above becomes the below, and it is one thought away. I Am one with God. I Am one with God. I Am God. God is I Am. Completely relaxed, Oneness came.

As I write this nearly a month later, I am still just beginning to remember the Light, so completely engrossing, such a totality of experience. At its' most transfixing, the Light was an intensity of violet, a shimmering fire that burned all around and through me, yet it was just before me, about a foot from my third eye chakra, where it burned most brilliantly. The Light was also like a diamond, a jewel of transparency and translucency at the same time, but without edges of any kind. I could feel the energy vibrating everything in me and all around me; the Light had depth and breadth and vibration and sensation and sound, voices and laughter and song, the perfection of harmony. The Light had fragrance, like wondrous newness, reborn continually; like flowers and sunshine, like frankincense, like Him. The Light is indeed all in All. The Light of God stayed and stayed, wave after wave of bliss crashing over me. My eyes were open wide throughout the entire experience – every organ of sensation in my body supercharged with Presence, with Power, with Glory. I could see, hear, feel, smell, taste and KNOW that God IS. I saw the Light of my own resurrection. I stood and declared: I AM the Resurrection and the Light.

The Light slowly withdrew. I wept, brokenly, grieving already, pained by apparent separation beyond my wildest imaginings. The Light is everything to me. I had no idea.

Chain of Remembrance

From very early on in my spiritual quest for full remembrance I've had momentary flashes and some longer experiences in a place that I now know to be somewhere in Tibet. When I was young woman, early in my marriage to Gilbert, we went to Chicago for the weekend. During a drive around town, we wound up at the B'hai Temple in Willmette. In my memory it is an unusual and marvelous white marble structure, intricately carved, and I remember being captivated by the beauty and peace of the building and the grounds. I have never forgotten the strange feeling of familiarity that came over me while I was there.

Later, when I began attending Ernestine's meditation classes, once in a while Ernestine would play certain music that was extremely evocative for me. I asked her about this strange and powerful music, and she told me that the music was an ancient Sanskrit chant. That meant little to me then. But she played it that evening for us, and I had a vivid, moving meditation. In my vision I stood apart from a rather large gathering, listening to the chant being sung by a blissful group of souls while I remained in silence. The imagery of the meditation was strikingly beautiful: wonderful mountain scenery, lush green valleys, piercing blue sky, fresh and fragrant air. This was one of the first meditation experiences that involved all my senses. It was truly me, though not Libby, in the place where I stood, leaning back against a carved white marble wall, feeling the coolness of the marble; viewing the scene, hearing the chanting and the sounds of the musicians, breathing the invigorating freshness of the pure mountain air, feeling the bliss and peace of God there. For some reason I was impressed that I stood there apart, separate from the group and silent, but I didn't know why.

Perhaps a year or so went by. One night at her meditation class Ernestine was in a playful mood, and decided we would do a past life "experiment" she herself had been given in a meditation. She turned off all the lights. We prayed for guidance and protection, did some deep breathing and became still. Ernestine lit a taper candle, giving it to the person at her left to be held with the flame just below chin level, to light just the face of the holder. All in attendance were instructed to speak out any impressions that came. We were all

193

simply amazed at the abundance of impressions that did come! My girlfriend Elizabeth found out about a lifetime she and I had spent together as Mayans, in which she had been a male and I had been his wife! What was so striking about that revelation was the truth of it, the knowing. When it was my turn, Ernestine began to speak in a voice not her own, low and raspy. She told me about three lifetimes I spent in silence, one as a nun in England in the 1600's, once as a Franciscan monk, and once, many lifetimes ago, she said, in an ancient sacred place, high in the Himalayas.

At some point I purchased a CD with that same Sanskrit chant, "Om Namaha Shivaya." The other chant on the CD, however, was "mine". As soon as I heard the first chorus, "hara hara guru deva, parabrahma parameshvara" (I purify myself and discover the Oneness that is everything), I knew this had been my favorite chant in that enchanted place of my meditation. I hummed along until I caught the melody, then sang along with the chant – and burst into tears! Knowing there was something to learn, I re-started the selection and sat down to meditate. Immediately I was there again, and again I watched and listened in silence. More details of the calm, peace-filled place came this time. I saw how the marble structures were constructed, marvelously, into and on the side of a mountain, overlooking an enormous, breathtaking valley. It looked like paradise; like some fabulous heavenly place in a movie. The air was pristine pure. There were bells and the sounds of stringed instruments, voices and birdsong, the tinkling sound of falling water along with the rushing sound of rapid mountain river. I found myself again standing apart, listening to the chanted words. In "my" consciousness, the words were huge, expanded thoughts that radiated Love from the group of chanters (and me) from this mountainous place into the entire world consciousness.

In the same time period, I attended a t'ai chi class. I found t'ai chi wonderfully relaxing, refreshing, dynamic; and there was a familiarity about it that I couldn't quite figure out. It came quite naturally to me, more like remembering than learning. In one session, our group was practicing the long form, and for quite some time the silence was broken only by the sound of our tandem breathing and movements. We were one being, moving together. My eyes were closed, concentrating. In my mind's eye I saw our group, moving together, except we practiced in that same peaceful place, in a large, open grassy space just below the marble structure where the chanting took place! This remembering was so vivid, so true that I gasped in astonishment and broke the concentration of the long form. The intensity of emotion that washed over me overwhelmed me then and I broke into tears. I got some pretty strange looks that day.

Then I "found" a book, "I, the Christ" by Dolores Pevehouse. Highly recommended, but not for those tied to the religious and/or purely biblical image of Jesus. This book is written from the first person. It is astounding, breathtaking and entirely wonderful. How it is possible to love this one, this Yeshua more and more every minute, I don't know. But in this book he is so human and so Divine and so <u>real</u>. The book is his autobiography, from age 12 to age 30. The "lost" years, though it's a hoot to think anything about him as being "lost". Through the instrument of Dolores Pevehouse, he tells his story in a remarkable, intimate and provocative way: his adventures, his thoughts, his impressions, his childlike wonder, his relationships, his massive faith, his doubts, his fears, his worries, his joys, his errors, the ways of loving, listening and learning from everything and everyone around him. I was captivated by Yeshua before, but now I'm totally in love with him, as a human person and as the Christ he is, too.

In the book, at about age 19 or so he goes to the Himalayas and stays with some lamas for a time, learning their ways, adding to his wisdom and openness. In his marvelous descriptions of the mystery and wild beauty of the place, he described "my" valley and "my" white marble structures there. Totally taken aback, overwhelmed by God one more time, I dropped the book and cried out Oh, my God, what could this mean? And do I dare ask?

~~~

I dared ask, though, in the company of my dear Unity friends, that the sadness and all that I have held back during my times and lifetimes of silence and keeping my mouth shut, forever be healed. I dared ask that the one thought that keeps me silent even today be lifted from my mind. I dared ask that God heal my mind of the idea that His Word is not mine to speak. I dared ask God to speak

Libby Maxey

His Word, directly, through me, as me. And all those who heard me speak these words agreed in prayer with me. It is, therefore, so.

Shortly after the asking, we closed our eyes and opened our hearts in meditation. Immediately I am transported to the wondrous mountain valley. I am seated, myself but not this self (the self in the Himalayas is male), on a white marble bench. In my meditation I am meditating, aware of all the beauty surrounding me, feeling the strength and warmth of the sun-baked marble, bare feet touched and tickled by the tiny flowers and grasses, the cool refreshing air sighing with pleasure as the breezes lift my robe. A presence approaches the bench; I cannot decide if it is an angelic presence, if it is in a body or not, but in my indecision, the presence sits quietly beside me and touches my right hand. Electricity leaps from the presence; my eyes fly open. It is a young man, not much more than a boy, really. I don't recognize him. He is beautiful. He draws me into his eyes; I feel myself falling into him, into this consciousness he is projecting and holding around us. Somehow I know that something is eternally sealed there in that timeless moment; a deal is struck, a covenant is made. We stand; bow in service to God, and part.

Realization bowled me over; waves of his marvelous presence enfolding me as I sat, both in my present body and in the other body-self, feeling both lifetimes becoming one life. I felt that I would pass out with the enormity of this knowing. Oh, my God. I met Yeshua; I really met the man-boy Yeshua! He sealed in me the covenant to become who I am right now. I am the at-one-ment with him. I am one of the 144,000. I will not fail in my purpose, because it is his, also.

The Sacred Heart

He only gave me a couple weeks to ponder on the Light experience before I had another. This one was so beyond my ability to fathom I blew it off, calling it "unbelievable" and made every attempt to block it from consciousness. But this God of ours, well, He just doesn't give up.

The second Light experience was triggered by something Patricia said on a Sunday morning two weeks after the chaplain retreat. Patricia was Catholic as a child and young woman, so occasionally referenced "Catholic" thoughts. This time she mentioned something about the "sacred heart" of Jesus. But I was in dire need of some human love, I thought, not some far away cosmic love that cannot hug me. I observed a loving couple in our congregation, and wondered, directing my thoughts to Jesus, who will love me? I drifted away from that thought when Patricia began the Sunday meditation. I was in a place of hope, though feeling momentary despair. Patricia guided our breathing, so together we breathed in the Presence of God and breathed out the heart of Christ to the world. That felt so wonderful, so true. My heartbeat pounded in my chest; somehow I knew that as those gathered breathed together, our hearts were beating as one. Relaxing, softening into His comforting Presence, I felt a warm tingling inside and on my chest. My eyes flew open – I know that vibration! I glanced down, almost fearful of what I might see, and as I did see, my fear vanished. The Light, the beautiful Light of God was pouring from my own heart.

I will love you. I will hold you. Will you be my bride, beloved Liberty? I **could** feel my Yeshua holding me. His arms surrounded me from behind in an embrace of softness and comfort, while at the same time he knelt in front of me with a penetrating look of pleading hopefulness. *You will be my bride, and I will be your bridegroom.* Wanting more than anything to shout Yes! Yes! A thousand times, Yes! Instead my fears came up again, and I asked, tentative, tears flowing "but what does it mean to be your bride?" With what seemed like relief, he chuckled, then threw back his head and laughed! I swear he seemed throughout this experience to actually **not know how I was going to answer his question!** I knew that

197

he truly would be broken hearted if my answer was "no" (like that would happen).

Oh, my beloved, when you are my bride, I am your constant companion. You will never again perceive my "leaving" your presence. You will go where I go. I will take you to my Father's house, beloved Liberty. Remember I have told you "in my Father's house there are many mansions" and it is so. You will share in my abundance. I will be your shield and protector. I will be your confidante, and you will be mine. We will play and laugh together. We will be in Joy together, my wonderful bride.

As he spoke in my heart, already filled with Light, the Light expanded to enfold me entirely. I felt sure it must be visible to everyone in the congregation. With every heartbeat the Light grew, and throbbed out from my heart center in larger and larger waves. I felt so In Love, so Beloved. I am the Love of God in manifestation. The Truth of that statement was entirely obvious. He was already taking me on the journey with him to the Father's house, and one of the mansions is my very own heart! Yet, as he spoke his wonderful words of love, I was also with him, seeing in Spirit the "places" he spoke of, the abundance he knows. I did not want to leave, and I did not want to leave him. Like a bride, constantly wanting the companionship of her Beloved, I never wanted to leave his side. He still knelt before me, immense pools of Love in eyes. I leaned over to whisper in his ear "yes, yes, yes and amen!" His eyes filled with tears!

He knelt there, holding me with his eyes. It seemed like forever was contained in his unwavering gaze. *You will live with me in timelessness. Duality will be ended for you, for you will live eternally in Christ mind with me. You will see, holy one, that all your momentary visions and revelations are Truth. All you have dared to dream with me, my wonderful Liberty, will be manifest for you, and more. All He has is ours. All of the All is ours. Here is the decision you must make, and it is the key to becoming "adorned like a bride for her bridegroom". Will you make this decision?* I am not turning back. I cannot turn away from you now, so yes, whatever it is, yes. He leaned toward me, as if to tell me a secret: *Simply, my child, it is this: Let nothing come between us.*

The words had that melded feeling, like the totality of a huge cosmic thought contained in five English words: Let nothing come between us. Let no-thing come between us. Not a thought, not an attitude, not a moment, not a breath, not a heartbeat. I felt his own promise in the words, and I knew that for over two thousand years and even before he became the man Yeshua, he had let nothing come between us. In truth, there is no "between" except what we create with our "sin", or error thoughts. This is awesome in its' simplicity. *My hallmark.* Yeah. I decide to let nothing come between us. I am sure I will need your assistance. Help thou my indecisiveness.

I will do more than help thine indecisiveness; beloved; as One we will heal indecisiveness! There is only one decision. It is timing, you see, that makes all the difference. Share in my sacred heart, Liberty mine. Today is your own heart alive with the sacred Light-fire. You have opened yourself to readiness. Today is born in you the same heart that dwells in Christ Jesus. Behold Christ Liberty, my beloved bride.

Imaging Jesus

The Mighty Voice I love suggested that I next write down everything I know about Jesus. He indicated that by doing so, I will have a much better idea of how to draw that reality into my being. I will have a much better image to image-in. I know a good deal about Jesus – where to begin? *How about at his beginning?* I guess You want me to start writing this now *someone, somewhere has said, "there's no time like the present"* Oh! I just had a wonderful image of Mary holding the baby boy, holding him close and whispering "Yeshi, Yeshi" as she kissed his tiny neck. Okay, so first is his nickname – Mary called him "Yeshi". Wonderfully sweet.

He's a beautiful baby. I'm sure it was very hard for Mary to take her eyes off him. He is the sort of child you could watch for hours, so peaceful and restful it is to be in his presence, even as a tiny child. I imagine her looking into his eyes, knowing who he has come to be and how he fulfills prophesy. She must have wondered how his life would be, wondered if he would play like other children; no doubt she was filled with wonderings along with her wonder.

If he's anything like all the other little boys I have known, and we know he was a human boy, I know he loved the outdoors. He was able to see and feel the underlying Unity in all things from birth, so he certainly appreciated nature in a way the other boys could not. He also appreciated other children, their essential beauty, in ways unfathomable to the other children. He probably seemed quiet and observant, maybe aloof – but alone, running freely in a meadow or under the stars, his exuberant dance with the Creator clearly evident.

There are some stories about him as a child in the Infancy Gospel of Thomas, from "The Complete Gospels". He was breaking Sabbath rules even as a five-year-old! He and other boys were playing with clay and water on the bank of a stream. He was forming sparrows with the mud. Someone tattled on the boys, particularly Jesus, for playing in this way on the Sabbath. As the "adults" came to chastise the children for their wrongdoing, Jesus commanded that the clay birds take flight, and they did! Another time he was helping Joseph in the family's carpentry business, and a beam was cut too short for its intended purpose. Joseph was distressed about it, but Jesus

200

merely lined it up with the beam it was supposed to match and stretched the beam to the perfect length. As his parents, Mary and Joseph must have been continually astonished by him, frequently perplexed by him, often frustrated with him and entirely in love with him.

His education was for him not so much about learning facts, since he already knew Truth. I think what he sought to learn were ways of expressing and of manifesting Truth that would make Sacred Unity and enlightenment simple and joyful for everyone. Jesus, as the first fruit of the Spirit (what I think "only begotten son" really means) was born without the cellular baggage most of us carry, imprinted by beliefs over numerous lifetimes. He was profoundly connected to God ("crowned with many crowns") even as his body grew in Mary's womb, and his physical birth did not diminish that connection, but strengthened it. It never occurred to him that he was separate from God, from love, from the natural world, from other persons. He saw with inclusive vision, knowing that everything he saw, heard, smelled, touched or felt, was part of the All. And he was one with the All.

His Hebrew name was Yeshua. Yeshua ben Yusef. Yeshi, sweet Yeshi. He is Jesus to us now, son of man. Son of God.

I don't think he knew his mission all along. I think his mission, the totality of his mission, was revealed to him incrementally, according to his ability to acknowledge and accept each new level of meaning. This is how God reveals His purpose in every person. In me he does it one sacred word at a time, interesting me in, for instance, ascension. Liberty. Glory. Fire. Light. Praise God, He never stops drawing me forward.

For a long period I relied upon "The Aquarian Gospel of Jesus the Christ" by Levi when I wanted to know more about Yeshua as a youth and young man. Although filled with information and beauty, this book did not, for me, reveal the personality of the man Yeshua. Then I found "I, the Christ" by Dolores Pevehouse and I discovered the beautiful story of his youth. This "novel" feels like his marvelous Truth, for it reveals who he is and was and forever will be, ever expanding. Who he is in this novel also revealed me, for I am as he was and I am as he is. I asked the same questions, I wondered the same things; we have learned the same lessons. Oh, my spiritual progression is not nearly so dramatically linear as his, but accepting his experience as my own lifts me to him. I would have been so drawn to him, had I known him while he lived in a body; I would have loved him so completely.

Who he is today is a wonder and a puzzlement; too big a thought to fit in my mind. He is still the personality of Jesus, our wayshower. He comes to me as Jesus in gentleness, in sweetness and comfort. He is truly the Comforter. The wonderful, forgiving elder brother, ever watchful over us, his little sisters and brothers. He comes to me as Yeshua to court my soul, to win my heart for the Kingdom. Yeshua is to me the personal personality of the bridegroom; this beautiful complete man, wholly integrating all aspects of human experience in the very Love he is. Yeshua brings freedom, today. Yeshua is the one who attained Christing. Yeshua is the one I follow.

He has attained to omnipresence. He is the same for you in your individual need as he is for me in my individual need. He plays no favorites except that each child is his favorite. He cares not what name you call him by. He cares that you call.

His home is everywhere, in everyone. He is a universal being. He is Light. He is Love. He commands our universe, our solar system, our sun, our moon, and our earth. He beats your heart; he breathes your breath. He is the breath. He commands the grass to grow, the rain to fall. He created you and holds you in his Love. He is not whole without any one of us. He is one with the Father/Mother. He has attained to the Christ; the Universal Christ.

The bridegroom is the entirety of the Christ being, the personal personality of Jesus/Yeshua and the Universality, the impersonal wholeness of the Christ, the Love Child of God the Father/Mother. Wonderful, powerful Creator, make me worthy of this honor, to be the bride of Christ, to take on his name and his power. This is your area, God, I am trusting. Amen.

Betrothed

For a couple of weeks I thought the whole "bride of Christ" thing was completely sweet. I thought about it a lot, but kind of giddily, not really with any depth or attempt at understanding. Christ Jesus, my Yeshi, seemed more present, more attentive; expectant, somehow. Over and over I played a love song to Jesus, on the Phillips, Craig & Dean CD "Let My Words Be Few"…the words to my beloved Savior so beautiful: "I don't know how to say exactly how I feel / And I can't begin to tell you what your love has meant / I'm lost for words / Is there a way to show the passion in my heart? / Can I express how truly great I think you are? / My dearest friend / Lord, this is my desire / to pour my love on you". The chorus: "Like oil upon your feet / like wine for you to drink / like water from my heart / I pour my love on you / If praise is like perfume / I lavish mine on you / Till every drop is gone / I pour my love on you".

One Tuesday morning after taking Isaac to Grandma's house for the day, I was on my way to work, admiring God's glory manifesting as the beautiful Tennessee countryside. This song began. My personal, sweet love for Yeshua, my beloved grew deep and strong in me, sweeping through my body in a rush of joy – I pulled over and stopped the car. Closing my eyes, breathing deeply, he opened scene after scene of my life on the screen of my memory, showing me his presence with me every day. In a wave of remembrance, all those times I have known of his presence tumbled through my mind/heart. Then all the times I have asked for his presence out of need came. These remembrances were more powerful, more purposeful. Then the more recent times, when I have asked for his presence, humble, desiring only his presence. These remembrances came on a wave of inexpressible tenderness. I wept at the beauty. I spoke aloud "Oh Jesus, I so desire to see you as you are. It is not enough knowing you are there, it is not enough knowing you will answer my needs – I want to know you as you are."

The song was over. Silence filled the car. In the space between songs, he revealed himself in a new way. Images of what is coming in my life filled my mind, and he is there, beside me as always, but I KNOW THAT I KNOW I can truly see him, manifested, beside

Libby Maxey

me. We share secret smiles and knowing glances, minds and hearts linked by light. I see myself, Jesus at my right, on a large stage, speaking to an audience; then speaking in another place, touching people, hugging people, laughing. He is there, beside me, sharing every moment. I realize that others around me see him as an aura near me, many feel his presence, some do not yet know he is there. The scene shifts, and I kneel at his feet. It feels like the end of one of our speaking engagement days. I rub and caress his feet. I know that his feet do not ache from standing because he is still vibrantly full of energy, and so am I. I want to serve him, to touch him, to join with him in a tender, loving moment. *When you are my bride, you will see me as I truly am.* I have never known such depth to love until I fell in love with you, Yeshi. *When you are my bride, you will see me as I truly am.*

Another scene sweeps into my mind, filling me full. I see myself facing him, vowing forever to love him, letting nothing come between us. *Arrange a ceremony, my love. I will be there. You know I honor commitment, Liberty.* Instantly I know what he wants me to do: ask Patricia to invent a sacred ceremony for my mystical marriage with Jesus, the personality, and Christ, the I Am of my own heart. My only thought, reverberating with every heartbeat, is yes, yes, yes...

~~~

This whole bride of Christ thing - I always thought it was just a symbol of union with the Divine, not something of this world. *Liberty, as a bridge of consciousness between the human and the Divine, do you not see my purpose? As above, so below, lovely one.* So my decision, as spirit, is made manifest, in the physical. *Ah. You do see. I will deepen and expand those thoughts, beloved.* Yeah, I was afraid of that. Just kidding (he smiled broadly at that) *Yes. But I know you better. You are a student of God's word, and you will look for understanding.*

204

Humdrum Conundrum

There is a wonderful thought offered by one of Yeshua's many teachers in "I, the Christ", and it is "Do you think the Divine All put this wonderful idea into your head only to make it impossible to follow through? Is our God so impotent?" I truly appreciate this thought, but putting it into practice in my life seems, well, impossible. At least now. God has given me this awesome idea; I have followed through. I cannot make anything happen; that is God's territory and God's timing. In the meantime, I remain deep in the trenches filled with human mess, feeling like my feet are stuck in muck. You have told me You're keeping me busy doing this stressful, sometimes awful law office work. I love the people I work with, I see the Christ in them and sometimes, to my amazement, in even the criminal clients who make the same mistakes again and again! But this is kindergarten! It seems I'm just babysitting Your spiritual babies when I could be of far greater use to those who actually **want** to wake up. Also, there is the matter of me. I deeply need the fellowship of like minds. I long to be with people like me, to converse with, to meditate with, to breathe with, to have sex with *Did you think I wasn't listening?* Well, that's fellowship, isn't it? *Indeed!*

Plus to find all the time to do this writing, God, is extremely challenging. The single Mom day is overly long and crammed to the gills, every day of the week. No Sabbath for single Moms. *My darling child, I have told you that you do not require sleep.* God, that just seems like bullshit. Can I say that to You, God, that what You've just said to me is bullshit? *Apparently so* (He chuckled) *since you have done it, Liberty. Still I will tell you again – it is your perception of a need that keeps you in need. The same is true with food.* Why is it, then, that I am so tired? *Perhaps if you will look at exactly what you said, child. The "I am" part, in particular.* Oh, geez, how could I be so ignorant? *Not to worry, beloved. Change your mind.* Still, God, I don't want to experiment with not sleeping and not eating, not while there is so much to do in my human experience. If I still perceived a need for food, even deep in the unknown recesses of my being, I could still get the screaming hunger headache and stomach cramps. *That is not My request, beloved. This is a process. I agree in your current circumstances even Yeshua would find such an experiment difficult.*

Really? *Really. You do, after all, still live in the world, in your body. The circumstances will change, though; you know this. When you are more in Me, with your focus each day on Me and My purpose for you; that will be the time. You will know. Soon.*

These "soon" promises really bite. *I feel that with you, child. I know your needs, each and every one. I love your consuming desire for Me. I placed it in you, Liberty; this fiery desire for Me is My own desire for you. I am using everything about your current circumstance, Liberty; the overwork, the stress, the lack of benefits on your job, the divorce worries, the responsibilities, the money troubles, the appearances of lack. I am using all your challenges for the highest and best good I can imagine. You must appear extremely real and ordinary to the beloveds who will read this work and pretend their own ascension **because** you are as real and ordinary as they. Look with me, child, at the beloveds who will mirror you, following you as you follow Yeshua through the valley, through the open door. All my prodigals, running into My arms; that is My plan, beloved one. Your task is Holy. Soon.* And here the God of the Universe broke into a hearty laugh.

~~~

In the midst of all the daily life goings-on, I'm dealing with the most major spiritual stuff anyone; **anyone** has ever dealt with, knowing it is my choice to do so. You must be helping me mightily, God, otherwise, how could it even be possible? I could not even conceive of arranging my "marriage with the Lamb" unless my mind was one with You; isn't that true? *Yes, my beloved child. You still allow the anti-Christ thoughts to come in to your mind from time to time, but that is the challenge: to know unity even while seeing separation. I feel your resistance. Is it My reference to anti-Christ?* You know it is, and I do want to have this conversation with You, God, but could we focus on the marriage thing right now? *Certainly!*

In July I met with Patricia about the ceremony. She didn't know the reason for our meeting beforehand; she probably thought I had some problem I wanted to discuss until she saw my excitement and exhilaration. She was delightfully receptive to the idea; somewhat stunned, I think, but very willing. We talked about the "hows" of such a ceremony, agreeing that Andrew Harvey had written some definitive work on the subject, agreeing to do some internet searches using various Bible translations. Then in one serendipitous moment we both said "Barbara Marx Hubbard" at the same time! Patricia remarked that she didn't know I was a Barbara Marx Hubbard fan. I reached in my bag and retrieved my copy of "Revelation – Our Crisis is a Birth" lovingly worn, full of papers and bookmarks, all the pages with references to the marriage marked with yellow post-its. We shared a laugh together, rich with meaning. We continued our conversation but could not decide on the "when" of the ceremony. I was looking to September; she had commitments. September 28, in particular, would have been my choice, to turn that otherwise ugly anniversary of Gilbert's rejection into the ultimate positive. But we parted, not having set a date. As I stood to leave, Patricia came forward and we embraced, both of us weeping softly in the Joy that surrounded and enfolded us there. I whispered to her, not knowing why "I apologize, Patricia, for being such a challenge to you." She drew back, seeming a little surprised, and answered with great seriousness "It's okay, Libby, you stretch me and make me grow."

That was the final time I spoke with Patricia. Soon thereafter she became quite ill and left the area to rest and heal. She will not come back. Due to the incredible stress of being a minister in these days and times, the church construction and expansion and all of her own personal stuff, she knew she would not heal if she returned. I couldn't help but think the spiritual challenge I placed before her was a pretty large contributor to the stress. I love her and I will miss her fellowhip. I pray her wholeness. And once again, God: now what?

~~~

Of course You know about all the psychic children information, the "Thomas Messages" coming to and through James Twyman, God; that seems of importance to my purpose also, I just don't know how. In one of the early messages Thomas commented with such wonderful Truth on the concept of "pretending what is true", and quite naturally realized that is what I've been up to for so long, with my life and with this work. <u>I know that I am a messenger of this great, liberating Truth</u>. Later in the messages Thomas revealed (as if it were hidden!) the cyclic nature of our existence in this dimension in a wonderful, simple way: we **descend** (into matter), we **pretend** (what is true), we **ascend** (into that Truth). Neale Donald Walsch got into the Twyman/Thomas act around the time of the descend, pretend, ascend revelation, and an e-mail of his commentary made it's way into my mailbox.

Descend, pretend, ascend. That's it! Calling this book "Imaging God" is still the pretend phase! That's descriptive of the process, and the title should reflect the outcome, the Truth I am pretending. No doubt this also explains my vague dissatisfaction with the title "Imaging God." What shall I call it, God? *How about naming the book based on the outcome of your desire, beloved?* The outcome I desire is the allness of my ascension. *If now you are imaging-in what you are doing, the result will be a fullness of being. Who are you planning on being when the pretending comes to fruition?* I will be complete. I will be Liberty, manifested. "I Am Liberty!" That's it! Oh, oh God....thank You. Oh, this feels wonderful, this wave of Truth that is flowing. You are so awesome. I love You with all my heart, with all my mind, with all my soul. I love this title. *I just knew you would, beloved Liberty, sweet child of the evolution.* God, are you choked up? *Think you that I do not live for these EUREKA! moments, my darling? Each moment is a homecoming, a movement my own child makes toward Me.* It's a parent thing. *Yes.*

September 28, 2002

This is the anniversary of my personal "date of destruction." I was hoping it would be fantastically wonderful, but it was a pretty ordinary Saturday in my household.

At one point in the day, I took a cup of coffee outside and sat on my front steps in the warm sun, admiring the beautiful clarity of blue the sky was presenting. My neighbor approached his driveway. He and his wife, both at about the same ages as Gil and me, are now having marital difficulties. He is behaving in much the same way as Gil; sullen, withdrawn, snarling; gone "to work" much too much. I realized with a start: I am glad and thankful Gilbert no longer drives into my driveway. For the first time, with truth and conviction, Thank You, God, that Gilbert is gone! Thank You, God that this relationship is over! Thank You, God, that I AM free!

For the first time in a long, long time, I slept soundly. I dreamt sweet dreams, heard the "tape" of God music that lives in my mind. But in the early morning hours, I had another dream that was neither short nor sweet. Or maybe it was forever and the ultimate sweetness. It was vivid; it was real. This dreamed evoked intense fear for me, but I am in awe of it as well.

My family was gathered at a vacation place. We were attending some sort of a reunion being held at a beautiful outdoor park. Isaac excitedly grabbed my hand, pulling me, wanting me to come down to the water with him. We ran together to a rocky area, to a large irregular pool of sparkling clear water. It seemed to be a spring-fed pond, the clarity of the water indicating constant movement. The water was surrounded by rock walls of layered stone. One of the rock walls formed a shaded cave-like area in the water; Isaac was particularly attracted to that spot. I watched from above as he descended some old man-made concrete steps into the water. He splashed and played in the cool water, then asked if he could climb the rocks. Knowing the futility of telling a young boy no, I said yes, but only there (pointing) where I can see you. The place I pointed out looked safe, like stair steps. Isaac climbed nimbly up, and down, back and forth.

He came to where I sat, asking me to come down in the water and watch him climb another wall, a more jagged looking part, more steep. I went with him, laughing at his exuberance. The spot was next to the concrete steps, at the top perhaps twelve feet above the shallow water. Isaac, scampering about as boys do, took one step too far and down, down he fell, slow motion, down into the shallow clear water, down between the concrete steps and the rock wall, down in the water shaded by both. I could not see him in the shaded darkness, but only heard his earlier laughter as it echoed off the rocks. I raced down the stairs, feeling nothing beneath my feet, glancing over to where I thought he landed, finally catching a glimpse of his blond hair. Without thought I was there, reaching into the water and gathering up the body of my lifeless boy, cradling his smashed and bleeding head there in the shallow rocky place.

I knew he was leaving. With the last life left in his little body, he looked at me and smiled, green eyes shining, face glowing. His beautiful little boy smile, filled with infinite gratitude and eternal love, filled with His Peace. We closed our eyes together, Isaac and I, and I watched as his spirit-form scampered up the rocky wall, up and up, to the top where we could both plainly see the Light of God. At the top was a grassy, flower-strewn plateau, and a form, a beautiful, familiar being appeared, standing with his back to us, about ten feet away.

He turned, Isaac shouted "Jesus!" and flinging a last adoring, excited smile over his shoulder at me, ran flying to Jesus, who knelt to catch him in his waiting arms. Jesus looked up at me, smiling that same smile filled with All of everything, and they merged as one being. The dream ended.

When I awoke suddenly from this dream, I felt different. I felt adrift, as if cut loose from everyone and everything. It was a good feeling, mostly, very liberating, even joyful. Apparently I am even giving up my mommy's attachment to her baby boy. I cherish him, but he is forever God's child. I relinquish all control of everything. I never had any, anyway. I guess this is the part where I "loose all the chains that bind me" that I may be lifted up.

I walked around in a daze that day and the next, the dream images haunting every thought. On the third day, Isaac was particularly quiet on the ride home from after school care. We had traveled perhaps a mile when he spoke, finally, with a gravity in his voice I had never heard. "Mom, I need to tell you something", he said. I waited, expectant, glancing in the rearview mirror at his little face, so serious. "Okay, sweetie, I'm listening" I said.

"Next time I go to heaven, I'm not coming back." He spoke with confidence, with an air of decided finality totally unlike a six-year-old. I nearly wrecked the car, the entire dream flooding back into my mind. I knew, I knew absolutely, that Isaac and I had participated in a real event, a shared experience only God could provide. "So what made you come back, anyway?" I asked, my voice shaking, hoping he couldn't hear my emotion. "It was you, Mom, I love you and I am here for you. I came back to you. You called to me. But I wanted to stay with Jesus, Mom, 'cause he's so beautiful and nice. Everything was so beautiful and nice. Nobody needed anything, everybody was happy all the time. The flowers even smiled there, Mom. I love it there, Mom, and next time I'm not coming back. Okay?" Tears streamed down his little face. "Okay, Isaac, next time you stay with Jesus. Can I come, too?" "Oh yes, Mommy, please come with me too. That would be perfect." He sighed with great relief, a burden too big for his six-year-old consciousness lifted.

He sat there in silence, eyes glowing with remembrance. I regained a small amount of composure, glad that I had the distraction of driving the car, happy there was no traffic. "Tell me about heaven, Isaac" I offered. Eager, he sat forward. "Oh, Mom, it's just like I remember. The light feels so good all over. Nobody thinks about what they want or need, everybody has everything all the time. The flowers and trees are alive, Mom, it's like they're little people. They look at you and follow you around there. It's weird, but I like it. There are people and angels everywhere, all around. It's all like, soft, or something. I want to stay there, Mom."

Ahhh, me too. The whole world wants to stay there.

As you can well imagine, for the next couple of weeks my emotions bounced wildly from elation to despair. I wondered what exactly God wanted me to surrender now. I seemed to revisit every thought about life and death I had ever contemplated. But mostly, I was just pissed off.

So, what do you want from me, God? Am I to be willing to give up even my sweet little boy? You said in "A Course in Miracles": *You give up nothing to receive everything.* It is very difficult to see Isaac as nothing, even though I know his body is not him. I realize, too, that human life is a reflection, an out-picturing, of spiritual life. I realize that my human life is a perception and not the whole. So are You meaning I am to be willing to give up my own life? You know that I am willing to leave this body. And truly, God, if I cannot fulfill my purpose, and soon, I am willing to give up my human life, and even want to do so. *I want you to give up your ideas surrounding your purpose, beloved Liberty. These ideas need to be relinquished to make way for expansion.* God, don't You think I could get some relief here? You want me to take on even more?

You give up nothing to receive everything. Think again of A Course in Miracles. Do you remember also, beloved child, the meaning of what is real? As in "What is real cannot be threatened, what is unreal does not exist"? Yes. What is real is eternal and cannot die. What is real is Life itself. You surrender attachment to all that is not eternal, such as a body, such as a limited idea. You surrender all attachment to all things. You give up no-thing, do you see? Just all attachment, which is simply perception!

You give up knowing the ending. Do you think you can hold in your finite mind My Idea of how this evolution will work out? Do you think you can really envision the totality of My Plan for your life? Do you imagine for just one moment that you can see My Purpose for your Unity Church family? Be willing in each moment to give up your idea for My Idea. You must empty your mind of limited ideas, not matter how expanded the idea has seemed. Even those ideas are not big enough for now.

*You have entered God territory. As humanity, your birthing is imminent; even now the Christ child that you are is crowning. All of humankind is today in a tight place, feeling wedged in all around, feeling as if darkness is closing in, fearing the worst. Oh, my precious beloved child, Rejoice! This is your birth! Crowning begins the final phase of birth, beloved. The next phase is beyond your comprehension, beloved, for when you push free of your confinement, free of human limitations, you will see! You and all my beloveds with eyes to see and ears to hear will see Truly, and hear Absolutely. And I **shall** wipe away all of the tears. Rejoice! Tell everyone to rejoice! Now is the time of your birth!*

Where are You, God?

It is dark here, very dark and confusing, God. Where are You? Why have You forsaken me, Your beloved? I do the God-stuff. Why is my life so hard? Why aren't You blessing me? I can't give any more! My son Aaron has now been without a job for six months straight. I have been paying his car payment and insurance, and my savings is going, going…it's jeopardizing my tentative hold on any financial stability, even though what I had was not adequate today…not with three people depending on me. And Gil just blows off the idea that his son might need his financial help. Aaron needs a job, God, and You know it. I know he is depressed and feels like he can't do anything right, has lost his hold on what manhood means; has lost his dad and his best friend. God, he is deserving, too. He is goodness. Please help him Father, You're his True Father. This one little step, Father, to boost his self-esteem, and then he will be able to look forward, toward his true purpose. I know that's what You want, too! It must be Your Will that Aaron move toward his purpose!

And why, in the midst of darkness, do You catapult me into an experience of Light so precious, so wonderful; God, the spiritual mood-swings are mind-bending! In prayer at church this morning I rehashed and released all of the Aaron stuff to God, praying manifest abundance for my family. I want so deeply to move into my good. I long for my good, for my God, with all my being. Every cell longs for the experience, the presence of the Living God I am, all the time. In worship, my conscious experience of loving God with all my heart, all my mind, and all my soul, I opened my eyes to behold beloved Jesus step out of the print of his beautiful form that hangs above the altar. His right hand upraised, he leaned out toward me and stretched out his hand to me, sending me the thought "Will you come?" I was paralyzed, awestruck, **unbelieving**! Can you stand it? Unbelieving!

I can see the parallel, too; Jesus holding out everything to me, saying, "Will you come?" and life is doing the same with Aaron. He is unbelieving, too. *Just who does he not believe in, my beloved one?"* Why himself, of course, he also does not trust. *Will you look at this parallel as well, child of light?* Oh God! I am not believing in myself? Yes, that's true. I am relying too much on Libby, and not on

213

Liberty, my true Self. And I have been distrustful, too. Waiting for the other shoe to drop. *Feeling squeezed on all sides, pressured beyond any pressure you have ever felt before, knowing that something is coming, but that something is as fearful as it is potentially joyful.* Yes! *Sounds like birth to me.* God, I get that the Isaac dream is about birth. That's what I kept coming back to in my own mind, that this "death" that Isaac played out was no less than rebirth to true consciousness. God, I have a longing for this rebirth that is so deep, it's like a well within me, so very deep, so very empty. Fill me, Father, fill me.

The Gift of Revelation

I gave myself a gift for my birthday (well, **somebody** needs to love me!) and it's the best gift ever. It's a gift that will keep on giving into eternity. In December I received a mysterious e-mail from someone with the screen name "mallell". This was intriguing in itself, kind of superman-esque. As it happens, this "mallell" is a genius of a person who seems to have met the same quirky spirit guides I've met and she's offering a class called "Christ Consciousness". Turns out that my sweet friends Jamie and Denise are taking the class, too. It starts on my birthday, fortuitously, and THANK YOU, GOD ALMIGHTY, that I now have a new guide and helper in human form! I think that Dr. Louise Mallory-Elliott is as intrigued with me as I am with her. But I feel and I know that she will be my guide and companion on this final step.

Dr. Louise's classes were part instruction, part meditation. From the time in Fort Myers until Dr. Louise's classes, I had been primarily meditating alone, so the group meditations were a great treat for me. Immediately I began to have overwhelming meditation experiences, revelatory, prophetic, the whole nine yards. I had two outstanding interrelated experiences in February 2003.

Revelation, February 3, 2003

Yeshua, appearing manly, muscular and robust, purposefully strode toward me. As he approached he raised his right hand, coming right into my space. In his hand was an object, a clear crystal about eight inches long, which he proceeded to push into and through my third eye! I felt and saw the entry of this shimmering clear, pulsating crystal, which I now knew to be an obelisk. I felt little but surprise as he lovingly looked into my eyes, humor sparkling from his wonderful face. He sent me the thought "That takes care of you; others need me now." I felt his focus turn from me and his presence divide as he went to every other person in the room, simultaneously.

Returning my own focus to the energetic obelisk in my head, I noticed a deepening, widening, opening sensation, as if truly my physical skull had been opened. I could feel the air breathing in and out of the "hole" made by the obelisk. I knew that a powerful

215

new level of awareness was downloading into my being; it was filling every cell of my physical body with vibrating Light. I wept with the staggering enormity of what was being revealed, although realization has not yet filtered through my ordinary awareness. As this process continued, I observed myself spontaneously rocking, breathing deeply and rapidly, and shouting to the Universe in a whisper "I accept all that I am I accept all that I am" over and over. I observed that Louise' helper, Carol was touching my forehead at that point. I felt her desire to keep me grounded, and I wanted to say "don't try to keep me here" but attempting to speak anything but what the Holy Spirit was putting in my mouth was futile, so "I accept all that I am" kept coming out.

There was a soft blackness, a resting that occurred then, followed by a rush of presence. Lord Christ Sananda filled my awareness. Overwhelmed and overtaken with the majesty of this presence, I spontaneously obeyed the desire to be on my knees. I knew a revelation was coming that would knock me out of the chair anyway.

He opened the space now created in my third eye. The earth appeared there before me, about the size of a basketball as compared to the size of my consciousness-body. He was beside, within and all around me. He showed me the love humanity has received and created, surrounding the earth like a pink gelatinous mass. *Notice that the love does not flow, beloved. Notice that although humanity receives constantly, it has not yet learned to give. That creates the stickiness. Look now.* I watched. I noticed that there are numerous sparkling vortices in the pinkness. I noticed that I have created one of the vortices! Fascinated, I observed the vortex that I am. It is deep, going straight and true into the very center of our wonderful earth, like a well created by my very desire for God. I have been building this well with each lifetime on earth. I realized that my love for God nourishes our wonderful Terra, as does the love of every other co-creator. With this realization my vortex blazed with Light, from above to below. I heard someone cry out in the room, and turning toward the sound with my consciousness, the blazing Light jumped from my vortex, connecting with his, which connected with another's, and another and another and another, blazing Divine Fire over all the earth, Lighting every heart IN THE TWINKLING OF AN EYE.

The Love that surrounds the Terra began to flow, iridescent, building, growing; and a song of Joy exploded from every living being. "I am the vine, ye are the branches" took on a whole new meaning as Christ Love branched out to heal everyone and everything, all at once.

Revelation, February 10, 2003

I had barely enough time to remember the first vision when the second phase opened to me. This time, without the discernable presence of the Master (or any masters, for that matter) I stood alone, massive beside the basketball-sized earth. I saw her tremble; I heard her cries; I felt the immediacy of her need. There were dark patches in the gooey pink light surrounding her. I felt a compelling, intense love for the earth mother and great thankfulness for her patience with us. The light brightened, but quickly faded. I knew it was up to me to heal her. Inexplicably, the enormity of the job didn't even occur to me until now! I stretched out my hands, prayer after prayer for healing and wholeness, for resurrection, for peace, for God's will to be done spilling from my consciousness, flowing through my hands. Then it was as if I could see all the faces of all the people on the earth, like a tapestry composed of faces. Each face a beloved child of God, and intensely, completely, in a rush of extreme joy, I loved every single face. I longed with all my heart to see every face alight with bliss. I longed with everything in me to see all these faces explode in that song of Joy.

In the most heartfelt, complete act of my lifetimes, I asked God, knowing with absolute certainty that God's will is that all His children know Joy, that the Joy-song begin on earth NOW, as above, so below. Divine Light-fire flamed from my hands, from my heart, and in an exquisite slow-motion vision all the faces lighted, starting in each forehead and spreading into a smile, glancing around shyly and then, enthused, beginning to laugh! The Light spread again as before, slower this time so that I could notice the sweet faces, all around the earth, connecting everyone, re-membering and re-creating. I could hear the wonder and excitement in the crackling electrical energy. This whole experience was the definition of fun.

It was then I realized Yeshua was at my right, with masters and angels surrounding the earth, standing there with me where they had been all along. Simultaneously the song of Joy from all the

217

smiling, laughing Christ-faces burst forth. I knew the song! It is a brand-new release on the Christian radio stations. I had only heard it four or five times before, but I loved it, and each time I heard the chorus, I knew it was directly Inspired, so filled with Holy Spirit energy it is. *All God's children singing Glory, Glory! Hallelujah! He reigns! He reigns!* Simultaneously to hearing these English words, I could feel and know the melded meanings of all the words, mixed with the same ideas in Sanskrit and Hebrew words, and the same meanings in angelic languages; all mixed and the same and entirely understandable, all at once. All beings, all together, one mind, one heart, we sang it over and over, building and building, wave after wave of bliss crashing over me. Oh my God. Oh, my wonderful, personal Jehovah I Am.

The Egyptian Initiation

Ahh, another Monday, another Christ Consciousness class! My meditation began on the way over – while driving, I was holding the truth that all the drivers were truly their Christ selves, right now, driving and practicing forgiveness and compassion. This thought was making me feel really good; tingly and delicious. There was a song playing on the CD I had chosen and the lyric, sung to Jesus, was "you are good, you are good, and your love endures today" except the Master himself put his wonderful twist on the words and sang them back, now connecting the lyric thought with my Christ drivers thought, and I had a vision. I saw every driver, smiling, enjoying, **singing the lyric thought**, and simultaneously I saw each Christ self, angelic, high "above" each vehicle, index finger gently guiding the vehicle as if playing cars like Isaac does! I have never felt so safe driving my car, I must say, vision and tingling and all.

Louise had a wonderful surprise for our now "Intermediate Christ Consciousness" class – the marvelous privilege of leading us through the sarcophagus initiation in the Great Pyramid. Our class of perhaps 15 willing souls lay prone, open, trusting. The trust and willingness were palpable energies. Louise was in rare form, a powerful goddess herself. Our group gathered, standing in the dusky light on the day-warmed sand before the Sphinx, who is to me the manifestation in stone of the lion lying down with the lamb. That was strange. I referred to the Sphinx as "who". We are all robed in white, ready to be presented to the Hierophant for the ceremony (and actuality) of living death. But first, breathing deeply of the last outdoor air we would breathe for some time, our group stands together in a circle, creating the peaceful hearts required for entry into the Hall of Records beneath the great paw of the Sphinx. I am rapt, exhilarated.

Louise asked us to visualize the symbol necessary for our personal entry into the spiritualized energetic structures so identified with Egypt. I could not think of a symbol. A symbol would not come to me. I heard a rushing sound, a familiar sound almost like a word…it is a word! Ehyeh..I Am. Hebrew for I Am. Then the fire letters appear, golden, shining: Ehyeh Asher Ehyeh, I Am that I Am. More than symbols, these "words" shimmer and dance with Life, right before or between my eyes; I can't tell. Now

219

I am chanting, over and over, Ehyeh Asher Ehyeh Asher Ehyeh Asher Ehyeh, vibrating every cell of my body; the sand beneath my feet feels like liquid, and I am propelled inside the paw of the Sphinx with my own breath and God's own breath; there is no distinction.

We travel downward, into darkness. There are swirling energies all around, darting between us, coming right into my space. I feel inspected, sniffed out; and I know these are watcher energies. Their sole job is to protect that which our group seeks, so they are not letting just anyone by. They test our every intention. We are grudgingly allowed to pass. It seems we have walked downward in the suffocating energy for a long time, sometimes down stone steps, sometimes down a gradual slope, but finally we arrive at another massive stone doorway, which Louise pushes open with one finger. It is a vast room and I am amazed to be familiar with it, having been here before. The room is light and bright, cleaner than clean. There are scrolls and books and instruments and art, exquisite sculptures and a perfect replica of our solar system. I am reminded of a clock, and immediately know that the replica is exactly that: a timepiece. I also realize that its usefulness is nearly over. We don't stay in this room but pass beyond to a place with what appears to be a mirrored floor. Louise says something about looking deeply into the self; looking into the mirror of consciousness we have created. I keep looking, but see nothing but clarity. For some reason I almost hope to see something, a ripple, some roughness; something there to mar the perfection, but there isn't anything. I wonder if this is my mirror. Louise says something about cleansing the mirror with fire, and giggling, I lift my hands and command Fire! Blazing violet fire roars to life, flowing from my hands and coming up from the mirror and I am surrounded with flames, tickling my flesh. I feel exhilarated, purified, rarified. I am ready for everything. I realize that I am still chanting Eyher Asher Eyher Asher Eyher and I still see the fire letters, but they dance around me, living fire. I am one with the Word of God.

Apparently we are now ready for the Hierophant, so we start on our upward climb toward the Great Pyramid. I realize we are walking the same pathway Yeshua walked for his sarcophagus initiation. I feel free; I feel like shouting to him Yes! It's my turn now! I will do it too! I feel his promise never to leave my side, and

I am calm, unafraid. The most predominant feeling is curiosity, followed closely by a wild, almost primal excitement. I feel very childlike, totally open, untamed. All strictly human thought is gone, forgotten, unnecessary, ridiculous. All is blackness. I am aware of other bodies, but we are truly one mind, now focusing on our purpose: initiation from death to Life.

The last part of the journey is difficult and narrow, up the ladder into the King's Chamber. All is blackness and stone and stone and blackness. I find myself shivering; quivering. Perhaps it is cold in here, but it seems a complete waste of thought to try and see if I'm shivering from cold or quivering from excitement. I really don't care. Suddenly the Hierophant appears before me; I think for a second he has appeared there by the power of thought because I'm ready to meet him. I feel/see his nod of assent. He holds out a golden ankh on a staff; I am absolutely mesmerized by the fabulous, huge lapis lazuli stone centered in the cross of the ankh. The golden veins in the stone are pulsing with life. He touches my throat with the ankh, and a warm liquid fireball bursts open in my throat chakra. I feel the lapis lazuli stone-energy, warm and pulsating, vibrating there at my throat chakra. I hear the stone singing; or is it me? I am singing praise without making a sound, and in the silence all I can hear is joyful praise all around me, lifting me, echoing and vibrating the stones of the pyramid. He glances toward the sarcophagus, and I nimbly climb in and lie down. There is a marking in the stone beneath me; I feel/see a caduceus engraved in the stone. I have the idea that the stone encases the caduceus of light. I have the idea that my body encases the Caduceus of Light. I feel the Hierophant's nod of assent again. The black granite lid comes down over me. I am complete trust.

I feel my muscles tightening, tendons becoming shorter. I feel rigidity coming into my body. I feel the cotton wrappings, especially on my hands and feet. I wonder when it was that I was wrapped; I don't remember that at all. My breathing is very, very shallow. Then I realize that there is no more oxygen in the sarcophagus. I am completely unafraid. I wonder why people worry about being dead. I have never felt more alive, my consciousness more aware, even though all there is to be aware of is blackness. Here I am, crucified, dead and buried, and I don't care in the least! Three days here; that's what I need, Yeshua; then I'll be rested! It's like a silly joke, my human life, a crazy wild game. I like the sarcophagus. I feel the Light of the caduceus blending with my body now, my lifeless form. I watch it happen, my awareness one eye looking at me, observing what I will do or think next. I feel an undulating movement travel through my body; snakelike my body writhes up and down in a wave, again and again. It feels good, primal, natural, necessary.

I begin to wonder if I my body is truly dead. I wonder if I remember how to resurrect my body, and I think then well, if I don't remember, I'll just call on Yeshua. The writhing stops and my body is totally at rest; even the tightening has relaxed. I feel a soft touch on the right side of my neck, like someone is nuzzling close, then I feel his body, full length next to mine. Yeshua is in the sarcophagus with me! He is so delightful, so playful. He pulls at the silver cord attached to my navel chakra, and says "Come on! We've done this before; let's get out of here and go heal the sick and resurrect the dead! Come on!" and he pulls me right out of my still body, right through the granite lid, right up through the capstone of the Pyramid into the indigo star-filled sky. Some of my consciousness has stayed behind with my body; I still have that awareness, but off we go! We travel out, pulling hundreds, thousands of souls right out of their still bodies. Adon Mashich Cumi, Lord, Christ, Arise, Adon Mashich Cumi, again and again. Sometimes we pull them out to heal the body, and then send them back, other times they decide to leave the body behind. It is joyful, beautiful service. I am quite familiar with this practice, I am puzzled to realize, like it's something I do with him all the time. We travel around Egypt, and I realize I am seeing sights from ancient days and present time, condensed into one seamless reality called now. All of time has collapsed into now, and I realize it is one story, told from every vantage point and from every timeline: the story of Creation, of God breathing. Expanding, contracting, but ever God, breathing.

Once again I am solely aware of my body. It is very, very cold, as cold as the stone that surrounds and encases it. I am not bothered. I look upon it from above the granite lid. I can see through the granite lid, and the moment I notice this capability, I also see the carving on the lid. Again, it appears that the carving of light was there, and the granite is there to protect the carving. It looks like someone carved these words, these fire letters Eyher Asher Eyher, into the molten stone with an index finger, smoothly tracing the words, then pouring liquefied gold-Light into the groove, filling each letter to perfect smoothness with the stone. The words float just above my heart as I lie there, content to be dead, more alive in death than ever in life. I see the caduceus, also golden light. I see the sarcophagus, and through the sarcophagus, my body, and through my body, the entire pyramid, and through it also. There is truly only God: I see the visible Light in every particle, everything, even the dust sparkling in the moonlight streaming through the crystal capstone. I see through that, too, through to the constellation Orion, mirrored on the Giza plateau. Orion beckons to me, actually appearing to crook a finger toward me! Orion thunders Adon Mashich Cumi and I feel my consciousness hurtling to him. I enter his spirit, and feel the star-form enfold my form in a galactic embrace, enmeshed, home. I feel at home with a constellation! The tiny idiocy of my little life convulses us with laughter. It seems so utterly ridiculous to have even learned to worry!

My consciousness contracts, spiraling toward my body-mind. Louise has just mentioned resurrection, feeling the cells fill with the energy of the resurrection. I remember how much I love these body rushes, like it's an old memory from somewhere else. Strange. It occurs to me that one reason I have returned to the body again and again is because I love the manifestation of feeling in the human body. I'm like a spirit junkie for a body rush. Funny. When I'm in a body I want only God. When I'm in spirit with God I want a body to feel God with. Breathing in and breathing out, there it is again.

The resurrection energy is rising in every body around me. I feel myself to be lying dead in the sarcophagus, with Yeshua wandering the Earth, resurrecting the dead, standing silent with Orion, watching, watching, and also in the room in Nashville, feeling the resurrection energy in the here and now. Divine energy is vibrating me in the here and now. Waves of bliss crash like feathers over me, over everyone in the room. I see the sparkling God-Light in everything, everywhere. I don't know if my eyes are open or closed. It doesn't seem to matter. Feeling this is all that matters. I allow myself to feel every cell, to see my body filling, filling with this marvelous Light, this Fiery Divine Light. This is what I'm after, Yeshua, this is what I love so much; Oh Yeshua, I want to be as you are. Yeshua, you. Yeshua, yes, you. Yeshua. Yes,

Libby Maxey

you are. Yeshua. Yes, you are. I am completely Christ, as you are. Yes, you are. I cannot tell if I am speaking to him or if he is speaking to me; we speak as one voice, mirroring this Love; oh, Yeshua. I love you so. I feel our energy, combined, spiraling upward, lifting, rising, as naturally, as spontaneously as breathing. Oh, I need do nothing. I need only be willing. I am willing. I am willing. Ehyer Asher Ehyer; I am all that is. Oh Yeshua, it is so simple. God is breathing in. There is no resistance in me. Adon Mashich Cumi, Abba, I come.

Holy Week

We're quickly cruising into Easter '03. It's Good Friday right now. Ooh, the resurrection energy...it is rising! And that is a major understatement. At night I have been consumed with praise. I have not been able to shut it down; one thought or phrase or mantra of praise after another is the Heart behind every other thought, even in sleep. I fall asleep in constant praise, and wake up the same. It's different than the continuous recording of God music; somehow, because it is completely me. Praise without ceasing. There is music mixed in there, but all the praise comes from, through, as me. This year, again, the Christian Holy Week is perfectly combined with the ancient Hebrew celebration of Passover, and we also have the full moon on Passover. Passover began on Thursday night at sundown, at the exact time when Yeshua's lifeless body was taken down, lovingly cleansed, wrapped, entombed: the stage set for his resurrection.

Earlier this week at his bedtime I read Isaac, now six, a sweet rendition of the Easter story; sweet because the story began "The disciples were very sad because their beloved Jesus had died" so the cross scenario was already over. Thus far in his life Isaac's ideas of Easter revolved around candy and bunnies and such. But since the divorce, he had become very aware of Jesus and his constant presence, asking more questions, lapsing into thought about him more frequently. Tonight Isaac listened intently, very interested in the angels, enthralled with the idea of resurrection and how that works. I explained that Jesus knew that death had no power over him and how his death and resurrection proved it; how anyone who is close to God can do this. Isaac looked directly in my eyes and said, "I'm close to God." We went on reading.

We got to the part where Thomas touched the wounds and believed, but that's not what got Isaac's attention – what made Isaac sit straight up was how Jesus suddenly appeared and disappeared. His eyes glittered with tears and he got a funny look on his face, like realization dawning. Isaac said in a breathless whisper "Oh, Mom, that's what I've been praying for, in my heart, when I say, "teach me, God" over and over". I stared at him, realizing that he was praising constantly, too. He pointed at the book and we read on. The next page was Jesus' ascension. When Isaac heard that word, he fairly shouted, "that's it! That's what I want!" and he excitedly explained what he knows about ascension, about shape shifting, about materializing and dematerializing, being able to go and do and be anything he thought about. And a little child shall surely lead us. With knowing like this, with little children praying for their ascension without even knowing the word, our evolution to ascension must certainly be at hand.

Things move quickly in our world these days. Louise now teaches her classes at my Unity Church as well as maintaining her other classes; in fact, her biggest class by far is at our church. I was glad to be able to join with my own "cloud of witnesses" and bring the levels of spirit up with our bunch, and oh my, have the levels climbed! My first meditation with this wonderful group mind happened yesterday, on Passover. On the drive over, the Christ energy was already overtaking my consciousness, my body quivering with anticipation. The energy was high in the group, a fever pitch of excitement underlying the laughing conversations and following us into the meditation. The resurrection. That was our excitement.

James Twyman is today offering himself as Jesus/Jeshua/ Yeshua's medium of expression in a series of e-mail lessons titled "The Art of Spiritual Peacemaking". In these lessons he is (to me) expressing the same perfect voice he expressed through "A Course in Miracles", very direct, completely trusting our ability to understand him, now. And I do, generally, to my great delight. But, there is one thought that I had not gotten my mind around. He said in one lesson that we are to expel the idea of "you" since there is only one: one mind, one heart, one Spirit. It is difficult, though, to think thoughts without the concept of "you". It makes everything entirely personal. I guess you can see I was having trouble comprehending.

Meditation time began. I sat on the stage, the raised platform that also served as the altar. Immediately as I closed my eyes I could see the violet fire leaping up all around me. I remembered that I wanted to tell Louise, in answer to her question of a week ago, that I no longer left my body when I meditated; that it was more like the whole universe came into my awareness now; as if my willingness now allowed all of everything into "my" mind. Just then a rush of energy whooshed into my crown chakra, and instantaneously Louise spoke the words "breathe the white Light of the Living Christ into your crown chakra".

I was deeply immersed in sound and vibration; hearing the meditative tones in the music Louise had chosen for the evening, the ongoing praise in my mind/heart stream, the common breathing of everyone in the room, Louise's bewitching voice. It was all one sound, perfectly blended, totally harmonious. The sound of peace, intended. My body felt weightless, as if suspended. I heard Louise mention "the perfection of balance" and that's where I was, except Balance and Perfection were beings, individual and yet in every particle of everything. I felt the particles consume my body, or enhance it, or something; it is not describable. My body felt as a fetus, still my body, but as if suspended in a fluid place of complete, perfect peace. While within this place, I was also able to observe this perfected self, as yet unborn in totality. I am within a seed; it feels as if I am suspended in a sweetness not unlike golden honey, a gel-like Light that is the definition of comfort and wholeness. There is absolutely nothing to do. I am pure being. From observer mode, watching, the perfected one opened her eyes, pulling me into the Balance and Perfection I am, suspended in now and no-where, yet everything, balanced in no-thing.

Again hearing my thoughts, from somewhere beyond this awesome timeless suspension, Louise mentioned the particles of creation, creating, and us, co-creating. I remembered from the Kryon teachings that particles of creation are at our beck and call, creating our desires as we speak with pure intent; how there are zillions of particles imprinted with my name! The particles of Balance and Perfection seemed to bow to me, if that can be imagined, and in so doing, they became Liberty! From deep within me and seeming to bounce and echo from the particles of Liberty, like a booming drumbeat the mantra ADON MASCHICH CUMI (Lord Christ, arise) vibrated. ADON MASCHICH CUMI, **ADON MASCHICH CUMI** *ADON MASCHICH CUMI!* He is calling me. I know he is calling me! Adon Maschich Cumi; it is he, Christ Sananda, calling to me. I am the Lord, the I am, he is calling to arise. *Liberty, arise, Liberty, I am.* The vibration is so strong, I am on fire; I cannot fail him. My shoulders feel a shuddering pain; my legs feel weak and wobbly though I sit on my meditation pillow. The honey from the balanced place flows down my forehead, dripping onto the ground below. I am still suspended, but this is not the place of balance, though it is symbolic of balance. I hang with him, within him, on the cross. Yet in him, breathing there, knowing fully the outcome, the balance remains, untouched. He is perfection. He is balance. Even in this, he is. And I am, too, because he is the way. Deeply within his eyes, I lend him my strength. From this time, I send Christ Light to that time. We will heal this, too, Yeshua. He nods and expires, relieved.

I could not consciously tear myself away from him, so God must have shifted things in me; a wave of intense gratitude came over me, as if God were praising ME instead of the other way 'round. I had the intention to thank God for creating in me the desire to follow Yeshua all the way through the ascension, but before I could form the word "Thank" in my mind (actually, I didn't get beyond tha.., and not even that far) God was already blessing me for being willing to follow Yeshua all the way through the ascension, covering me with waves of bliss, cradling me in feathery softness, pleasure explosions in every cell. I tried again. I had the intention to thank God for the unfoldment of His Presence in my experience, and again, before the "tha.." the mighty waves of bliss, His gratitude to me feeling like great tears of Universal Joy that I would have the guts to be willing to accept such an unfolding… I realized something. Giving and receiving **are** the same activity. Perhaps what I can give to God is really something God wants. *My child, my desire is so intense, so one-pointed.* My God, my desire is so intense, so One-pointed. That was when realization came. I and the Father are One. It is True in my experience. There is no "you"! There is only I AM.

I heard Louise's voice again, this time calling the angels and archangels, announcing the nurturing presence of Mother Mary. Christ Sananda was already present for everyone in the room, and had been so from the beginning. The energy of the resurrection was palpable, creating a rising heat and almost a hissing tone as negativity burned away in this mighty energy. The drumbeat sound of Adon Maschich Cumi reverberated around me; this time all were included. My eyes were wide open. Everything looked as normal to my physical eyes, if a bunch of middle-aged seekers meditating can look normal. Yeshua, Lord Christ Sananda; the fullness of his being, stood to my right, and from there and beyond and within me as well, he spoke.

Behold, he said. Behold! He said. Behold what? I wondered... Commanding now, *Behold! Behold the New Jerusalem!* Absolutely transfixed, eyes open, I beheld. The room, our makeshift sanctuary in a dilapidated storefront building appeared suddenly to be filled, filled beyond capacity, with living people and living beings, beings in spirit and in bodies, angels, archangels, all interposed and intermingled in various dimensions, but all facing toward the stage, expectant, waiting. *Behold the New Jerusalem!* He commanded again, this time breathing out the command, his breath a purposeful wind. The faces, the gorgeous faces of my beloved spirit-family, exposed by the breeze of his out-breath, looked up, and above each and every head, the white Light of the Christ exploded into a flaming crown. Astounded, speechless, I beheld the New Jerusalem. *The pentecostal flame, the Light of Christ, is open to you now. You are the bridge, the liberator. But do you see, my beloved Liberty, that your work is already complete? The imprinting of this moment will bring it to experience. Are you yet willing, beloved?*

I am. I am willing. I AM!

The Perfect Word

Being a closet Pentecostal Christian has its' effects. For example, it has made me want my own "scripture to stand on", you know, that perfect Word from the Bible, just for me, pointed out by Himself just in the nick of time. That's what I thought I wanted. I thought, several times, surely God would give me my scripture NOW: oh, God, don't you know this is the worst moment in my life? I would whine.

Then on August 16, 2002, I got my scripture. There isn't even a story around it. I heard the evangelist Benny Hinn read it and I knew that I knew. No revelation, no fanfare, no trauma, no nothing: just words that sear my soul. This scripture is so big, so incredibly huge, that here in late April 2003 I still cannot deal fully with it nor understand in my experience why this one would be mine. It is Isaiah chapter 60, verses 1-3 (NRSV)

> "Arise, shine; for your light has come, and the glory of the Lord has risen upon you. For behold, darkness shall cover the earth, and thick darkness the peoples; but the Lord will arise upon you, and his glory will be seen upon you. And nations will come to your light, and kings to the brightness of your rising."

I'm beginning to understand now. Trust becomes a greater and greater factor, every day: as I see more of His Plan unfolding, I realize more that I am nothing at all without God, and pray more and more that others realize their own frailty and utter dependence on our Creator. This scripture is not about me at all, though it is certainly about I Am. The glory of the Lord (I Am) rising upon me refers to the visible Light becoming apparent, even to those who see only with the physical eyes. The Light could not become apparent (come upon me) unless I first was filled with the Light. The inner becomes the outer, in other words: this time, visibly. The nations and the kings? Is this symbolic or literal? That part of the plan is not so clear, and I'll most definitely have to Trust if it is literal! But really, I don't care either way. I'm just a junkie for the Light.

May I interject? Certainly, italics master. *I would like to give a personalized translation of this scripture for you.* Okay, breathing deeply, go ahead, I think…

Adon Maschich Cumi, beloved, shine thy Light! Thee are the vessel, and thy cup runneth over. Thou art the glory, risen with me, in me, as me, thou beloved child. Thee have seen the darkness and know it is not real. The Light is Real, and expels the darkness. All will turn toward this glory: nations and kings will cry out in praise and thanksgiving when they, too, behold the brightness of the New Jerusalem. Thou art that.

Wow. Beautiful. I hope it doesn't take me eight months to come to grips with this translation. Why are you using thee and thou? Does that have something to do with eradicating the concept of "you" from my consciousness? *Yes! Excellent!* I guess I have fewer perceptions, fewer mind-connections, with thee and thou *and the connections you have thee and thou are very sweet, positive* connections Hey! Quit reading my mind! *Not likely, sister, thee have let me in, and I'm staying.* Okay. Thee can stay. Why don't thee remember Thursday's meditation for me, while thou are digging around in my mind?

That's funny. No answer; no witty retort. No matter, He will help anyway. He was there, directing.

Louise seemed to mold the meditation, every spoken word, to me. I'm certain everyone else felt that way, too, but I know that she was using the evening to create and build the ascension energy directly for me (and for her!). She was conscious of this, while at the same time, allowing Christ Sananda to speak through her directly into my experience. I'm also certain every other meditator felt the same way, on some level. Awesome. Intensely personal yet universally impersonal at the same time. It was the final evening of the Christ Consciousness class at Unity Church, and she was going to make it special. Pure intention such as that creates pure power.

I was very excited, very in my flesh, when the meditation began. God was pulling out all the stops, sweetly drawing me to Him, coordinating the tones of the music, the rhythm of the room sounds, Louise's voice, my breath, weaving the experience, calling me to fall into Him. *Come with me into Creation, beloved one. Follow me into the vast no-thing. Breathe out thy desires, Child of God, and create.*

"Create in me a clean heart, oh God" Louise and I intoned these words simultaneously, just then. I was absolutely electrified by the power. *I Am that*. Yes. *Yes*. Yeshua. *I Am that*. Yes! In that moment I knew beyond any doubt that my heart was cleansed and purified; made new, both the heart of my spirit and my physical heart. The power, the life coursing through me was astounding, breathtaking. Louise was talking about resurrection and ascension; about rejuvenation and healing and wholeness happening for all willing beings. Louise talked about the sacred heart of Jesus being born in each of us, now, and asked us to envision the newborn baby, the Christ child, at heart level. I love this image anyway, and while gazing with love at the tiny child, the beautiful I am of balanced perfection from last week's meditation looked back at me.

I Am that. Breathing deeply, profoundly aware of the very life of God, the particles of God, creating, flowing, saturating me in every breath, every pulsation, every energy movement of every kind within my body, inside my mind, surrounding me, everywhere present. Profoundly aware that to every thought of every kind of every being God says *I Am that* because that is what Yes means to God. God fulfills every thought by manifesting God self, God particles, as that thought. I was in a vast place, totally aware of the minute, utterly simple and immeasurably complex process of creation. It can be summed up as *I Am that*. I feel a deep sorrow, a great sadness that we give God such lousy thoughts to become, followed by an intense desire and passion to think God-thoughts that create delight in God when He declares *I Am that*!

This huge knowing about creation, about co-creation, took hold of my mind and my body in a new way. I felt the immense power of this knowing deeply in the core of my being, like a secret key opening me, filling my entire body with this electrical energy, alighting every cell with *I Am that*, really knowing that this, this entire body/mind/spirit I know as Libby and God calls Liberty is GOD'S OWN THOUGHT, and **I Am that.**

Feeling perfectly balanced, breathing God, I relaxed into a new awareness, a different softness. It felt like a returning, though there was no movement of any kind. Totally in and aware of my body, yet not attached to the idea of being a body at all, I welcomed the entirety of all that I am in my awareness. It was as if the entire universe filled my senses, and my senses extended to the "edges" of the universal knowledge. I felt filled, energized, whole, Real. The story of the Velveteen Rabbit hopped across the vast movie screen of my expanded vision, all in one thought. Just like the stuffed rabbit, once fully aware of the love of his beloved owner, became a real rabbit; now I, fully aware of the Love of my Creator, am Real. "What is Real cannot be threatened. What is unreal does not exist." (from A Course in Miracles). I Am Real. *Ahh, Beloved Child of my Heart, I AM THAT!*

Weeping softly, vibrating, rocking, *I AM that* echoing in every cell, my heart-voice began calling out those thoughts I desire to manifest. Breathing out, intending with all my little might, I declared to the vast audience of Spirit "I am purified" and simultaneously returned *I Am that*. "I am Thy beloved child" mirrored back on an intense wave of Love energy *I AM THAT*, with a chuckle. "My heart is clean and new; innocent as the child Yeshua", his infant self held to my heart, and I could feel God's Joy washing over me, the velvety softness of the Mother God embracing me, whispering *I Am that, my beloved child.* An intense swirling energy awakened in my solar plexus. *Thee are opened to fullness of Joy, child of God.*

The power, the energy swirled around me, and I was part of it. Somehow I had sprawled flat on the floor, vaguely aware that my hands were making spirals, acting as birds again, acting on a will that creates energetic forms for manifestation. Breathing, drawing upon the breath of God breathing me, I declared "I am Divine Courage" but I didn't really feel so courageous. *I Am that*, He thundered, low and powerful, sending me His En-courage-ment, filling me with the knowing that God is the source of all courage, Divine and otherwise! I became extraordinarily aware that I, my personal being, had totally stepped aside, and was observing. My entire focus was on God, like one eye. *Thine eye is single, beloved child.* Yes. Yes.

"I am the resurrection and the life." *I Am that. I AM THAT.* My consciousness was so completely magnetized by the vastness of the Presence I AM THAT. There were no edges of any kind; I don't think it would be possible to conceive of edges in this Oneness. "I am the ascension in the Light." It was the barest whisper in the indigo no-thing of Creation. My hands were still making spirals and clouds and in my awareness, they burst into Light forms! My vision filled with my own form, my ascended form, the new and improved, wondrously beautiful Self I am, clothed in a garment of Light, a lovely violet and gold mantle draped over me, both garments flowing Light, shaped by Love energy flows. I stood in a doorway of emerald and gold-veined marble stone, rough-cut yet smoothed by eons of loving touch. I had seen this doorway before. That time, there was a golden sign hung on the top-most stone that said "Christos Victorios" on the doorway. But this time, no sign, and I knew it is because now I know this is Truth, and need no outward signs. *I Am that.* I knew God was including the whole thought, the whole image, all that I can see and all God can imagine, in this *I Am that.* There was a tenderness that felt like tearful gratitude that came in a soft wave then. My consciousness was, truly, exalted.

"I am the purifying fire." That statement was pure Holy Spirit. Fire leapt up all around me, I breathed in fiery elemental Light that energized every cell with tiny blue-white flames, crackling. God breathed *I Am that.* Oh my God, I have never felt like this in my body, God; even my body feels expanded, like You are surrounding each cell, immersing every particle in Love-Light, with Intelligence. I am being lifted up; there can be no mistaking this feeling. *Ahh, my Liberty, I AM THAT.*

So completely enfolded in Divine Love, I whispered to God, my mother-father, my beloved "I accept all that I am. I accept all-ness for everyone. I am Liberty, God, I will be Liberty for You." Tears flowed from my eyes, my purest intention pouring from my heart. A fiery white-Light wave of Divine Love crashed over me, lifting me into Awe. The vision of my ascended Self, my Completion, stood huge before me, filling the screen of my vision, while simultaneously filling my being through my toes, energetically bonding with the Earth through my feet. I felt intensely connected with everything, everywhere. *I Am That, Liberty Mine. Thou art that. The crucifixion is forever over, holy one. You have defeated death, my beloved child Liberty.* My body was rushing all over, Omnipresence all the way to the bone! Wholly God, wholly my Self, I knew: death is not real, therefore it does not exist. Life is Real. God is Real. I Am Real. *And oh, I Am so That. You cannot know in your present experience how great is my Love for thee, for you know, little one, when one of My children gets it there is a quantum leap in the Universe.* So I get it? *You got it back in 2001, actually, but you can just now realize that you get it.*

Oh, my God. I'm not so sure I want to ask anything just now.

I was coming back to the room, becoming aware of what is apparent while maintaining what is Real. There is such power in that. I want to hold it, always. I knew, I know that my body and my mind and my heart and my spirit were woven together and simultaneously unbound now in ways that I would soon discover. More than the resurrection energy: <u>this is the ascension</u>. A scripture ran through my mind, something Christ Jesus said just after the resurrection: "Touch me not, for I have not ascended to the Father" and the thought, purely innocent: maybe I shouldn't be touched. I went to get some water, fairly floating along. Coming back to the sanctuary, my wonderful sister friend Lee Ann stopped and looked into me, love spilling from her eyes. She said, "Do you think I should touch you?" Somewhat unsteady anyway, I nearly fell down with the rush of emotion that ran through me. Tears instantly filled my eyes and splashed down my cheeks. I stammered, "I don't know, I don't know..." Lee Ann was also teary, as she whispered, "what is your guidance, Libby?" I rushed forward and we embraced. I whispered in her ear "He said it's not a necessary instruction for those ascending alive". We giggled, made silly by the enormity of it all.

Trusting without a net

You read it; He told me the crucifixion was forever over! I heard it; I know that I know I heard it in my soul. I know that God was speaking directly to my experience. He is giving me some extreme challenges to believe it. The VERY NEXT DAY, May 9, 2003, was my last day at work. This I had known and had accepted. That chapter was most ready to be over. I didn't particularly appreciate the way it all went down (fired for asking for a review and a raise? What is that about?). I knew we could get by, for the summer at least, on what I would get from unemployment.

Driving down the driveway, I opened the garage door, and Aaron was standing in the garage, waiting for me. It turns out that May 9 was his last day at work, too. Planned obsolescence for employees: at the 90-day mark, to avoid paying for employee benefits and before the employee qualifies for unemployment, too. This is not how to love others. He had asked on May 8th when he would become eligible for health insurance. He wasn't alone; every person hired at the same time as him was let go. So Aaron's joblessness suddenly added weight to the situation. His bills I cannot handle for him. It added weight to what had previously not been a problem at all: Laura had quit her job at Wendy's a couple weeks previously, knowing her upcoming choir and youth group trips would get her fired, anyway.

I want very much to believe that the crucifixion is over for me. I have surrendered everything; that's really all I can do. I have no idea what to do next, except whatever it is I find I need to do. I am most certainly on my knees. My consciousness veers back and forth between an almost eerie calmness and naked fear. My great fear is that I am not capable of this, but the Truth is that I Am capable of this. Not too long ago, in trying to accept being fired, I stood outside my home, this big brick place of comfort and safety nestled in our enchanted, vibrantly green neighborhood, and God said *Do you see what we have together accomplished with $25,000 a year?* In that thought He projected numerous other thoughts, like *Can you imagine what we would accomplish* with *much more?* and *We could do the same with far less, too,* and *Can you see that I Am your Source in all of this?* and *This is your family's home; my beloved, and I will see that this is so as long* *as your family has need of a physical home.* All this was accompanied by a sweet comfort, that Peace that passeth understanding.

There are some difficulties I am having with ordinary consciousness; what I "should" do. The world would say (and does say) I have to get another job. But as much as I know that is true for most people, I cannot seem to intend to get another job, even though I answer the advertisements and send the resumes. I cannot see myself in another job; there is no vision in my mind of that possibility. What I most desire is to be about my purpose, to be about God's plan for my life. To speak the Word of God as God puts His Word in my mouth. For you to read these pages and accept for yourself your own destined evolution. About these outcomes I have plenty of visions! I also know that my purpose is inextricably tied to my spiritual experience, and that is entirely God's timing. My entire family has been freed up, unbound from our physical experience (school's out too!) at this time for a truly miraculous reason, but how it all plays out is the unknown factor. The unknown is the scary as hell part. I want to constantly feel cradled and protected and provided for; childlike in my trust, but the world has so successfully thwarted that kind of trust in me for so long, that to have so many challenges in my face with only trust to hold to is quite a test. I get to trust without a net. Goody.

I have noticed things, though, now that I have been remembering how to live life again, slowly, with care and patience. It's been a long while since I have been able to relax on a daily basis, and I realize this goes far back beyond "before the divorce". For example, when we moved into our house, the ground was hard and dry because Tennessee had been in a drought for a couple of years. There were only a couple of areas in the yard that were green. The green was moss, and it was blooming with miniscule white flowers. I remember transplanting a little of the moss up around the house; just a little bit, and I thought it would just dry up and blow away. I remember thinking to myself that it would be beautiful, not to mention easy, if the whole lawn were moss-covered. Every time I appreciated the moss, I imagined the beauty of my lawn, moss-covered.

I do a lot more mowing and lawn work in general since the divorce, but in the past year, have not had time to notice much. But my moss-covered lawn is manifesting; honest to God, my moss-covered lawn is manifesting! And the most moss-covered area? Right around the corner and down the lawn from my bedroom window!

Thank God (I know, it's weird) I've been able to clean my house, to restore the gleam of cleanliness to the rooms. Not that I'm a neat freak or anything; being that would drive me nuts given the age range of my children! But it's the underlying clean, the aroma of clarity, the sheen of dust-free everything. That's what I'm talking about. But here's the biggest thing. I'm utterly willing. I have no agenda. I have my desires, indeed, but no real idea how to make any of it happen. I am really like a lily of the field, neither toiling nor spinning, in the place of awareness where everything that I need is provided.

And now there is time to do things! I had the time to go to Louise's home for an advanced "class", really more of a meditation party. Her home is directly on the other side of Nashville, almost exactly as far west of Nashville as I am east, an interesting and beautiful drive. She was most delighted that I would come to her home, and this evening she unabashedly focused the entire meditation on healing my situation. Mary, the "belle of the bowls" accompanied the evening's meditation with divine sounds: she brought two crystal bowls, many singing bowls, percussion instruments, rain sticks: a wonderful collection. So it was Queen Louise, Mary and me, in Louise's emerald green, enchanted elfish woodland setting near Pegram, Tennessee. We intended for abundance, Divine Abundance, to rain down on my family and me and on the whole world.

El Morya, Master M, the tender, merciful (he wasn't always tender and merciful!) opener of God's Will in my life came then, bringing Peace. He brought a vision, too; a mountainous vista opened before me, and I saw my Self, my true being, standing on and as the pinnacle of the great central mountain. The mountain was made up of my selves, my many earth selves, family members of each self, friends of each self. Closest to my Self, nearest the pinnacle, were my children, my Unity family, my current beloveds. We were all one life as the mountain. Realization rushed into my being. Healing lack issues and opening entirely to the natural Divine Abundance that is my inheritance as the beloved child of God I Am, trusting this knowing that GOD IS MY SOURCE, will flow down and through the entire mountain, healing these issues in all those I have touched, ever. My mountain will be moved, and the movement will be to the Light. Louise spoke "Thy Will be done" and a whippoorwill trilled in response, sounding exactly like "It's her will! It's her will!" as we collectively gasped in astonishment!

Immediately returning our collective focus to Christ mind, Louise called down a pillar of Divine Light to surround and uplift my human life. Since we were three, we created a triangular pillar of light, and then simultaneously another triangular pillar, facing opposite, intersected and became one with our created pillar. It was a brilliant Light, and I knew it to be a Divine projection, the Lay-oo-esh (Hebrew for pillar of Light). I knew that we were connected with the grid of Divine Consciousness in a profound way. I was in an exalted, crystalline consciousness, while simultaneously acutely aware of the beautiful earthly place surrounding my body/mind.

Envisioning my Self once again at and as the pinnacle of my mountain, I felt myself to be covered with glass, marvelously detailed, shining, but stuck in the thinnest glass, not moving, powerless of myself to make the tiniest forward motion. There was no going back. The thought of going back was not a known option in that moment. This image of self, my entire Self "stuck" there, beautiful, glowing behind the thinnest of veils, able to see everything beyond but not yet empowered to move toward it. The image was as the exquisite moment of expectancy just before the total cosmic orgasm. Geez, I can't believe I typed that, but there it is, and that is how I appeared. Again realization swept through me: the moment I am empowered to step through this thinnest of veils, my mountain will again be lifted, each and every one, to the same Light. Such responsibility, and such ease. I need do nothing but be willing and open to follow. I am willing. I am open to follow You, all the wonderful Way. Thank God. *Thank you.*

The image shifted slightly, causing me to have somewhat more of my human appearance there on the pinnacle of the mountain. The energy of trust was very strong; I could feel myself chanting, "I am trusting. I am trusting" while the energy vibrated like the heartbeat of the mountain. The memory of a previous vision flashed through my mind; just after the divorce and before the first paycheck, I saw myself on a hill, with people in a line as far as the eye could see. Each person, smiling, happy, willing, was in line to bring me

239

money. They all held little baskets of cash! Shifting back to the wondrously beautiful ascended me (not encased in glass, either!), now I was seeing something similar, but tremendously expanded. Now on the pinnacle of a mountain, and now surrounded by a vast sea of souls, of faces, all eager to bring me their offerings of green in exchange for opening their imaginations to their own wholeness of being! The image shifted again, and my Self was in and as a flame, the flame surrounded by a fiery aura of abundant emerald green. Each life whose imagination that had opened wide after reading these words now connected to me through that auric abundance.

~~~

Thank You, God. I know I am at the end and the beginning in the same moment. I am certain the appearances in my life have jumpstarted, speeded, opened and freed me, and for that there are not enough thanks, my Wonderful Abba. I will give it away, again and again and again, Lord, until every soul that chooses freedom is also free. I see that Your Will is to give us All of the Above. I see that my path requires drama; not so much that I have to get nailed to anything (at least in a physical sense) but I get it that I have to break a bunch of perceived human bondages to really appear to become Liberty made flesh. Just to let You know, though, Father of Mercy, the miracle rescue will be most welcomed any time soon. Amen.

~~~

And so, of course, God answered my prayer with an explanation of what I'm going through and what it means. I opened a book and there it was. The book is Annalee Skarin's "Beyond Mortal Boundaries". What you need to understand here is that my copy of this book is falling apart, and about one-third of it is loose from the binding. So given that fact, when I open this book I get either the first or the last page of the loose chunk of book – this is logical and expected. But not this time. The book opened to about two-thirds of the way through the loose part. This is what appeared:

> "When your troubles have increased until your desperation
> has reached the very climax of your endurance and your
> world crumbles into dust and disintegrates into murky fog,
> then lift up your head and rejoice! This is how one becomes

strong, in the overcoming of the weakness and the utter desolation that can be increased and multiplied until the little, fighting self is completely exhausted and is licked. And in this greatest of all calamities one will be given the vision and the power to stand forth, NEW BORN, if so be he accepts the divine opportunity opened to him through such drastic testing.

"This is so simple and so beautiful it has been unbelievable up until the present time. And even now, only those who use this power will be able to prove its unutterable expanse of miraculous releasing as they become knowers of the Truth!

"So when the heaped-up vicissitudes and calamities come, and they usually come in twos and threes and fours, don't panic and start frantically grabbing at the pieces in desperation of hopeless frenzy. Be still and know that I AM God! For one brief moment stand perfectly quiet. Don't work on the fallen roof, the caved-in wall, the collapsed garage, the mangled car and the leveled fences. WORK ON YOURSELF!

"And you will become the greatest miracle of all! You hold the keys of miracles in your hands. You are a living dynamo of unbelievable power! ...... You will become fully aware that you are a glorified child of God, just as you were intended to be from the very beginning, for you will become glorious! And in that glory you will have the power and the Light and understanding to step beyond all mortal boundaries – FREE! Forever free! "

How will you greet Me?

Wow. I had to walk out of the room after just typing that little bitty chapter heading. I didn't realize I was resisting that much. God is *rapidly* expanding my consciousness. I love it, and resist it, and love it some more. There truly is the thinnest of veils. I can feel that God wants my ascension for me more than I want it for me. God knows the timing and, like a parent awaiting a homecoming, can barely stand the wait!

The visions expand me, daily life expands me too. I feel my body becoming the body of Christ, the breath of God filling every cell at all times, consciously, yet this knowing is behind active thought. There are numerous people whose thoughts I can read instantaneously and, if we are in the same room, will often voice simultaneously. In one evening's meditation I was seven for seven with Louise's thought-stream, quoting identical scriptures, hearing the same ideas, knowing at once the presence of the same beings.

I am so deeply grateful for this time of rest, renewal and rebirth, though the world (remember I live in Tennessee) sees me thus: "Divorced white female, unemployed, three kids (and their many friends) in an older home ready for some major maintenance, adult son unemployed and his car not running, daughter's boyfriend homeless, an evangelist seven year old child, part of that Unity cult, a hippie fool crazy in love with God, for all the good that does her, bless her l'il ole heart. " And me? I'll just stay in my place in Consciousness, thank you, above the fray, beyond the crazy singles ad, KNOWING THAT GOD IS USING ALL OF IT.

The physical rest is truly a good thing; it opens my capacity to God. I want All of the Above to come to all of the below, and I'm willing to try it All out first. I long, deeply, more profoundly than I could possibly express, to see God's Holy Face. I am the culmination and the fulfillment of this longing for God, for all my selves and all my ancestors. For my mountain. I long for the moment when God, seeing me at the gate, runs to me. Fill this deep well of longing, God my Father, God my Mother.

Two days following the abundance visions, a new "intermediate" (I think this labeling is such a hoot!) Christ Consciousness class met at our Unity Church. Dr. Louise focused the evening on healing, and our group experienced some miraculous healings. I don't remember much of what Louise said, really, though I followed her thought-stream again. This night she began by opening us, chakra by chakra. Breathing deeply, rapidly, chakras already open, as so often happens to me, God used the chakra opening for a higher purpose. Each chakra manifested sequentially and spun, perfectly balanced, as the beautiful flower it is, about a foot in front of my physical being, while also spinning within me. It was an awesome, beautiful thought-picture, and when I opened my eyes, I could still see the vestigial light-flower forms floating in place in front of me. Our energy centers are truly flowers that blossom in the Light! The crown chakra is so, so beautiful; a brilliant white light-flower spinning so rapidly that it appears as a luminous spiraling flame... Oh! So the full opening of the crown chakra is the "baptism of the Holy Spirit"! Christianity is not required, just willingness.

Louise then invoked angelic presences, and the room, already filled with angels of healing, was suddenly overflowing with angels, seeming to almost compete with each other in their eagerness to assist us! Archangel Michael was strongly present, his immense, blue fiery presence crackling in the air. He stood directly behind me, holding his sword to my back. I was puzzled. The sword, a gorgeous, shining combination of Star Wars technology and Arthurian legend, was point-down at the base of my spine. Michael sent me the thought "it shrinks to fit" and again, I was puzzled by what he was up to. I could feel the cold/hot of the sword against my spine from base to shoulder level, and at the same instant, I remembered the balance I am, as evidenced by the chakra flowers.

Suddenly Michael lifted the sword high above me, and plunged it directly into my crown! The cold/hot "metal" seared through each chakra individually, yet the sword deeply imbedded the earth beneath me instantaneously, and curiously remained the exact size of my spine as well. I must have gasped involuntarily, because Michael looked "down" upon me while at the same instant looked directly into my eyes, conveying "this is part of the process, beloved, a necessary part. Fear not, for this is the releasing fire you have desired." I felt myself relaxing into the process, never fearful, yet reassured nonetheless. I allowed the back of my head to rest against the hilt of the beautiful sword, noticing that the cross of the

243

hilt was exactly in the center-point of my brain. I felt the activation, the expansion then, deep in my brain: the antakarana, known as the "rainbow bridge" from pituitary gland to pineal gland. Profoundly present, deep pools of love in eyes that define blueness, Michael conveyed, "Yes, beloved, that is my purpose. What was open before is now fully activated."

I felt activated all over! I could feel/see a twelve-pointed star of incredible white light above my head, way up there, and it expanded in such a way that it became a spherical sun, while maintaining the appearance of the twelve-pointed star. The light from my own sun poured over and through me like fire and water at the same time, filling me up like the vessel of the Living Christ I am. The star also appeared at my heart chakra, then both my hands had stars in the palms, then both feet. *Everywhere you walk, everyone you greet, everything you touch, beloved, you will now consciously imprint with the Christ energy.*

My vision shifted; Louise was welcoming the presence of Jesus the Christ, and Michael's eyes morphed into the crinkling-with-mirth eyes of our brother, Jesus. My "activation" apparently amused and delighted this one; I could feel his shoulders shaking with silent laughter. His presence moved to my left. Internally I questioned that, wondering, why left? You are always at my right! And again, I could feel his delighted laughter, but no response. I felt miffed! He's teasing me, I whined to myself. He stayed there, now nearly convulsed in big brother style, I-know-something-you-don't-know laughter.

Little sister style, I ignored him. I noticed again that the sword still rested in my spine, that the chakra flowers still spun and fire still flowed. I was now completely engulfed in a gigantic flame, all other images contained in this flame. To my right, while simultaneously filling me where I sat, was the image of my Self, my astoundingly beautiful ascended Self. She had that mischievous I-know-something-you-don't-know look too! But my Self I cannot ignore, so I looked left to see what Jesus might have to say about this. He said nothing at all, simply taking my left hand, while in the same instant; my ascended Self took my right hand. There was a sensation of intense swirling energy, as if we were all inside a massive light blender. We were a blending, merging oneness, the human me, the ascended I Am, and the completion that is Jesus.

Chakras were exploding in individual brilliant flame-flowers, first the base chakra in combination with the crown, then the life creation chakra combined with the third eye, then the navel chakra combined with the throat chakra. When all the energies swirled into the heart chakra, our beings were totally, without question one creation: the meeting in the heart was the greatest flame, causing all the other flame-flowers to merge and blend. I stood tall, an enormous being, towering in strength and power and wisdom and Love, at one with my own Self who has ever been one with the Christ. The whirling, swirling energy gathered at my heart chakra, a marvelous three-fold flame, and shooting plumes of light formed the Caduceus of Light there, left side "male", right side "female", but all one wholeness – the I Am that is who I am, manifested. In that realization the great flame exploded into a pillar of light, reaching at once through the earth and far, far above, connecting forever with my own Divinity. I thought well, I guess I can quit thinking about a mystical marriage ceremony. It is already so! The feeling was so overwhelmingly orgasmic that the whole thing has been consummated, too!

Then there was total silence, and I was feeling a glorious exaltation far beyond anything ever before. I felt myself to be in a Holy place, a vast, deep, no-thing everywhere present around me, all of everything cleverly hidden as no-thing at all. I knew! I was in the presence of God, now more capable than ever before to be able to know this "place" of Holiness. Still feeling my own being as enormous and powerful, I also felt dwarfed by the immensity of this hallowed hall. I dared speak. I want to see Your Face, I said. My request reverberated, vibrating the no-thing, echoing. *And how will you greet Me, beloved?* Names of God cascaded through my mind – YHVH? Elohim? Abba? El-Elyon? Jehovah? Abba? Father-Mother? Daddy? I wanted to cry like a baby. I don't know how to greet God, and Jesus was laughing again!

Hi Daddy, I'm Home!

As you can well imagine, I spent some agonizing time trying to decide how to greet God. Somehow I got it in my head that God <u>must have</u> a proper greeting. But then my rebelliousness reared up, and I thought, how could it be that God has this requirement? God has no needs! He doesn't care how we address Him, just that we do! If I am indeed God's prodigal daughter, then the mere sight of me, coming home, is all God desires! God knows I will probably be a) utterly speechless, or b) stammering helplessly, or c) weeping uncontrollably. So I relaxed about the whole greeting thing. Thanks, Jesus, for teasing me into this realization, and I know that's what you were laughing about!

My meditation life is so much more real to me than any other time. Not that my time with my children, my daily life, are not of great importance to me; not that my love for my family and my friends is not of great importance to me; not that these are not real; it is just that my time with God is Real. Union, conscious intentional connection reveals the Eternal, the unmoved Mover. The rest is fleeting, even while the relationships themselves are forever.

While I was rinsing dishes, God Self conveyed that I might next study the natures of Light. She indicated that Light is composed of the basic elements of creation, which we see as separate, but are truly One Light. Therefore, Light is fire, water, earth (or matter) and air (or prana, life force). Dutifully, I looked all these words up in Webster's Dictionary and in Charles Fillmore's "The Revealing Word", and I even composed a paper about the subject. God Self conveyed okay, good job, but how does Light feel and behave, based on what you have discovered? This is what you need to know, not what humans perceive about the individuated elements!

So Divine Light is this: flaming, flowing, life-giving, sustaining, blowing, lifting, solidifying, singing, sighing, relaxing, rejuvenating, enlivening, dancing, spiraling, revealing, redeeming, sanctifying, quenching, bubbling, cascading, replenishing, musical, raining, dripping, laughing, reviving, nourishing, roaring, soaking, stripping away, hot, warm, cooling, cold, hard, soft, breezy, wafting, waving, lifting, nurturing, surrounding, rushing, rapid, devouring, splashing, dense, weighty, solid, liquid, gas, emptying, filling, cleansing, purifying, squishy, gooey, floating, sinking, forming and reforming, vitalizing, movement, rest, inexhaustible, inextinguishable - And I have no real idea what God is up to with this study of Light. I'm sure She's got something going on. So another group meditation time came, and perhaps I found out what the study of Light is all about. Just maybe I'm it.

The meditations are a continuing saga, a rushing rapid and astounding unfoldment, as you have certainly realized, just as life is the same. Before I even walked into the group meditation, sitting alone in my car with God, I felt an unusual, powerful energy coming right toward me, and fast! And before I could blink, a wing-ed whiteness thundered up and into my third eye chakra - I immediately knew it was Pegasus, the mythical winged horse. But I don't know anything about who or what this means, God!

The group asked this night to release all remaining fears. I wondered what extremely deep-seated, possibly past life fear I might still have lurking. Louise began to work her enchanting magic, weaving words and music, invoking our Christ selves, angels of revelation and healing. I had what I thought was an idle idea – maybe I'll greet God with "Hi Daddy, I'm Home!" and I got a kind of chuckle from that, immediately followed by a rush of fear, a cold black density that I knew – this is my fear of abandonment! Even after all the releasing, even knowing all the Love God my Father has for me, I still fear He will find a reason to leave me. I still fear He's going to pull a fast one and leave me here alone, without keeping His promises. I learned these fears from my earthly Dad and more recently, from Gilbert.

Images cascaded through my mind. Gil, youthful, vibrant, alive, waving good-bye as he drove away. I felt a momentary sadness that he looked for a reason to leave me, sadness that he saw me as unworthy of his promises and commitments. I did not feel alone, though; he does not have that power over me. I waved back. Go on, Gil; go on to your highest and best good. I will not hold you here with my thoughts. Be thou released.

Then I saw my Daddy, young and fit, jumping off the bus and running as fast as he could through the vacant lot next door, briefcase banging his knee, wanting more than anything to open the door and see my mother, my brothers, and me. I remembered times when I was first to greet him – oh what deliciousness! He would drop his briefcase, open his arms and sink to one knee, all in one movement, and with a giggling squeal of delight, I would rush into those arms, burying my face in his Old Spice fragranced neck, just so very happy to see him and know again that his presence was with us. The day was complete and all was well when Daddy came home. Everything about me was perfect and delightful to him.

Another image then; one of my daughter Laura when she was very small. She used to lift her little arms, saying, "Hold you, Mommy, hold me, hold you" with that sweet innocent knowing that it is all the same. And then immediately I was propelled back to that exalted place, back in the Holiness of God's Presence. The little child I am, the prodigal daughter who is perfect and delightful to her Father, rushed headlong, as fast as I could compel my being, into that vast, deep, soft Presence, conveying "hold me, hold You, hold me, hold You" with everything in me. Oh, such comfort, oh, such tenderness, oh, the mercy...Oh, God, I love You, I love You and in a mirroring crescendo of Divine Love, I fell into the blackness, the overwhelmingly satisfying no-thing that is God.

It seemed like I awoke inside a crystalline palace, and then I recognized this image: I was inside my own skull, looking out through my skull made of crystal. My entire consciousness-being was now contained in the center of my activated antakarana, a tiny speck of a place, after having been so expanded in God! I had the idea to feel the delicate balance of skull on spine, and then realized my entire spine was crystal as well. Louise began playing a crystal bowl. The resonating tone vibrated my skull, my spine and my bones! My bones were crystalline, too! I felt so very light, vibrating higher and higher, my bones resonating with the tone, ringing, singing...*I fill you with Light from the inside-out, my beloved child Liberty. How did you think this would manifest?* He said this with such tender mirth...*My Light is manifested from the very core of beingness, as Above, so below, as within, so without*...I could feel Divine Light filling my bones. My hands brushed together, and I felt the tones of my finger bones! *Thou art an instrument, beloved, in many more ways than you have remembered*...Oh, play me, God, in every way, use me, play me.

There was another shift, and I became aware of an intense tingling, like a shower of Light was dancing on my crown. There was a pillar of Light surrounding me, reaching deeply into the Earth and rising far above my comprehension. It was a twelve-sided column, and I was given to know that this is my shield and my connection to the Holy Spirit. I could hear the ringing, pinging tones of the shower of Light that traveled down the column and feel the tickling sensation of Light on my scalp. Dr. Louise stood over me, hands perhaps an inch over my head, and I knew in that moment she embodied Jesus. She spoke, voice deep and rich. "Jesus has claimed you as his own." The entirety I am cried out Yes! Oh Yeshua, Yes! Jesus, brother, yes!

Louise moved away from me, over to my right, and at the very instant she said "They are here" I turned my head to the right, hearing the galloping hooves of horses, coming toward me at breakneck speed. And there was Jesus, sitting tall and powerful and majestic and beautiful on a marvelous white steed, who looked exactly like I had pictured his white horse, Victor, from the book "I, the Christ", and who had wings like Pegasus, and who was also, of course, the white horse Jesus rides in Revelation. Jesus rode right up to me, never slowing, and threw down his hand as I reached up to grab it. In one graceful, flowing movement I was astride the massive white horse, so soft it felt like riding a marshmallow. I hugged Jesus to me, and he drew me into and through his being; oh, what a feeling THAT was. I now sat in front of Jesus, and he said "There, you be in front. You haven't seen Home in a while."

Spirit-filled, Dr. Louise said to the group "You are free! You are home!" and our wonderful white winged steed lifted his front legs, Jesus and I threw our hands into the glorious sky-blueness, exulting in our freedom.

I am so his own.

Okay, now I'm ready

God, I'm ready to understand. I want to talk about the antichrist. But I want to be the one to tell You about what I have come to realize about the concept. *Ahh! I love it when the kids tell Me about what they have learned! Go!* You really **are** a parent, aren't You? *I Am that.* Don't melt me now, God; I'm on a roll. *I'm listening.*

Okay. First of all, I need to say what I thought the Anti-Christ was for most of my life. I thought he was a person, a living being, a demon or an evil person such as Hitler. I thought he was someone who was coming to the earth, sent by You, to shake us up, to shake up the world. I think most Bible-believing Christians today perceive the Anti-Christ in this way, and many see Osama bin Laden and Saddam Hussein as personifications of this being right now, and many actually seem to be expecting someone even more malicious.

But I don't think so anymore. I don't believe there is such a person, although it may have been quite possible for the race consciousness to draw out or raise up such a one not so long ago. Perhaps we have done so, at least in part, in bin Laden and Hussein, and maybe in some others, but I don't think it is possible for such a person to prevail any more. I believe enough of us have remembered a greater consciousness to prevent such a person from being created now. I believe that possibility, in other words, has been defeated. But that aside, I don't think there is or was an Anti-Christ in Your Plan. Not in the Plan You made, but because of Your incessant yea saying, a possible co-creation of humanity. I just had an odd feeling. I now have no idea, no memory whatever as to why I was so fearful of this concept.

Anyway, antichrist is simply a descriptive term. It just means negative thought, anything that says no to what is Real. It is any thought that says I am not Your beloved child. It is any denial of You and of All that You Are. It is the simple act of forgetting who we are, and living from forgetfulness. The word itself, anti (against) Christ (Love of God): therefore, anything against the Love of God. Fear. Denial. Hatred. Violence. War. Harm. Abuse. Neglect. Rage. Dominance. Attack. Defense. Jealousy. Malice. God, it is difficult to think these words. *I Am diminished by these words, for if these words are intended, I Am that. It is my promise. My children ask, I answer, and the answer is always Yea and Amen.* God is whispering. We pain our God, through our selves, with these words. Oh, my Wonderful Abba, I so apologize for our errors.

Mass or race consciousness holds numerous antichrist thoughts. Especially strong are the thoughts about dis-ease and death, the ultimate attack, really, on the perceived self. Breaking through these is the trick. Yeshua did it. All the masters have done it. It is do-able, and even more so now, because of the dispensation of Divine Life that flows these days. But these thoughts are the true antichrist: thoughts that would deny that which will save us in the "twinkling of an eye", thoughts that would deny the very Life of God. God, the I Am, will not be denied! Beloved Eternal One, I offer myself to fulfill Your Limitless potential as a Divine Human. God, I banish and rebuke all thought that would deny You in any way. I accept the purpose of my being: Eternal Life. I accept my immortality. It is so. *And so it is!*

Funny. Now that I've got all that down, I think I will look up antichrist in a couple of texts. It is so unlike me to operate this way! Expressing what I have come to know before study? Hmmm. *Such behavior is a sign.* Yeah, I'm sure it is. Maybe it's even a wonder, but let's not go there now, okay? *There is no need to go there.* Huh? Anyway, have I ever even read the definition for antichrist in Fillmore's "Revealing Word"? I doubt it - I feared that word. I feel like such a dork for fearing that word! Oh good. Now I feel even dorkier! Get this:

> **antichrist** – That which denies or opposes the idea that the Christ dwells in and is the true self of each individual. The active effort in the world to exalt death and to delude men into believing that death is the way to eternal life is an instance of work that is antichrist. (!!) Such a thought is opposed to Christ. Jesus came to deliver the human race from death and to fulfill in man God's perfect will, abundant life. The antichrist thoughts must be persistently denied. The perfect will of God for all men is abundant life, not death.

I suppose now the Bible doesn't have any scary verses about the Anti-Christ; I suppose that was all a made-up scare tactic? *Are you asking, or being sarcastic?* To quote You, yes. *Good answer! But look it up yourself, anyway.* Okay, then, my wonderful Friend, let's see. First I search for the word "antichrist" in a Bible search engine – God! There are only four references to that word – NONE in Revelation, where I would have expected it. There are only four verses in the entire Bible that use that word! 1 John 2, verse 18 (Revised Standard Version) says "Children, it is the last hour; and as you have heard that antichrist (yes, lower case!) is coming, so now many antichrists have come; therefore we know that it is the last hour." Then at 1 John 2, verse 22 "Who is the liar but he who denies that Jesus is the Christ? This is the antichrist, he who denies the Father and the Son."

The next verse needs to be read in context, because this is the definitive word, I think. It is 1 John 4, verses 1-6: "Beloved, do not believe every spirit, but test the spirits to see whether they are of God; for many false prophets have gone out into the world. By this you know the Spirit of God: every spirit which confesses that Jesus Christ has come in the flesh is of God, and every spirit which does not confess Jesus is not of God. This is the spirit of antichrist, of which you heard that it was coming, and now it is in the world already. Little children, you are of God, and have overcome them; for he who is in you is greater than he who is in the world. They are of the world, therefore what they say is of the world, and the world listens to them. We are of God. Whoever knows God listens to us, and he who is not of God does not listen to us. By this we know the spirit of truth and the spirit of error."

The last antichrist reference is at 2 John, verse 7, but in context, here are verses 6-8: "And this is love, that we follow his commandments; this is the commandment, as you have heard from the beginning, that you follow love. For may deceivers have gone out into the world, men who will not acknowledge the coming of Jesus Christ in the flesh; such a one is the deceiver and the antichrist. Look to yourselves, that you may not lose what you have worked for, but may win a full reward."

Interesting! So interesting! These antichrist references aren't even prophecy, but rather excellent lessons in discernment. "They are of the world, therefore what they say is of the world, and the world listens to them." Doesn't that sound like the news media?? And how about "…whoever knows God listens to us, and he who is not of God does not listen to us." Isn't that the truth? Spiritual talk to an unspiritual person is like talking to a wall. There is no understanding. And that lack of understanding is the spirit of error – sin! Simply the error of not knowing, of not having awareness of Spirit – that is the spirit of antichrist, and not knowing is the greatest deceiver of all. *My children perish for lack of knowledge.* Oh my, God. People die simply because they have forgotten to Live. No lack is perceived; therefore solution is not sought. That is the saddest of all. Oh, God, awaken every person to his inherent Divinity. Release Your children from the bondage of antichrist thoughts now present in race consciousness. Transmute each of these thoughts into Your Truth. Release humanity to Christhood. Release me to the fullness of my own beingness, Father, and I will show them Liberty. Amen.

What <u>was</u> that dream?

I've been sleeping up until now. **Until now!** Here is the wake up to Divine Humanity: we have been Divinely Human all along. I know. Duh. But to really understand the NOW of that statement, to fully realize that statement in experience, well, that's God. And here's something else. You don't know you didn't realize until you do. And I still vacillate between knowing and forgetting, but that too will cease, because you cannot un-know something once you know!

I thought I wanted ascension to be a moment. But it isn't, and yet it is. It is every moment, and no particular moment. The Kryon teachings discuss the nature of an ascended human, a human who is personally real yet filled with Divinity. Someone who is realized. Someone who has, by her own willingness, embraced the full truth of who she is, and continually grows in realization, in wonder, in agape. This is a person who is beloved by others, someone who is sought out, someone in whose presence you feel safe and loved without condition or prejudice of any kind. It is someone who flows with Life. Kryon of Magnetic Service, (I highly recommend all these teachings) in the teaching "Through the Eyes of Ascension, Part 1" described an ascending human, a master on Earth, like this:

> "I wish to introduce you to somebody you'd really love to be with. Forget the gender for a moment, for this Human will become a good friend. Every time this person looks at you, you feel safe and comfortable. This person is so easy to be with, you'd naturally go anywhere with them and do anything. There is never any judgment or agenda. This person won't ask you for anything, either. He just wants to be with you. You're proud to be with him, and he's proud to be with you. What if I could introduce you to somebody who had all of these qualities, and they were also wise as well? What do you say? May I do this? Are you afraid? Will you run the other way? No! You'll probably knock down the door to be introduced! Who is it? It's you, in an ascended status! I've just described you!

> "Think back to what you've read in the sacred texts about the spiritual historic masters who walked the Earth. They

254

were loved! People came for miles simply to sit in their energy. Children and animals recognized their peacefulness and followed them from place to place. They weren't weird, strange, or sullen. They emanated joy. They taught love and understanding. And those who were in their influence were changed – like Elisha was changed when standing in the same vicinity of the master (Elijah) while energy shifted.

"Expect a family who will look at you differently and fall in love with you again! Expect relationships to heal, if that's appropriate. Expect old barriers to drop. Expect enemies to see you differently and for drama to disappear. Do you know what I'm talking about here? It's not just about you, it's about the energy you carry and show. It's about what happens when a graduate walks from place to place, working the knowledge of what he went to school for. The part of the Human Being that's called perception is aware and reacts to this person. This person tempers and disarms difficult situations, and shines light in dark places. Perhaps you came to hear that? Do not fear the attributes of your master hood, for it's an attribute of the love of God. "

Ascension is every moment. I cannot possibly think that God is ignoring me, that I am not His Beloved, that God does not speak to people, that regular people really can't be like Jesus, because they already are. I am that. I truly am that! I don't care anymore about ceremony. The sacred heart of the living Christ beats in me. I am conscious that every time I breathe in I take in more of God. The Light of God flows through me, constantly. I simply become aware of the flow. I shift my focus, and God is. I don't care anymore if there is a feast in Heaven in my honor. I know God is well pleased with me. Being a human is a tough act. It is the toughest act in the Universe, and God is pleased with every one of us. Every one! I do want the garment of Light, God. I do want to be Your Visible Light.

I know that I have the gifts of the Holy Spirit. I have simply not had the conscious experience of using all of them. God does not waste energy. Just because there has not been opportunity to use every gift does not mean it is not mine to use. Indeed, I must know that each gift is mine to use. I am the Christ, after all! Refer back to chapter 26 and the gifts of spirit as found in the "Keys of

Enoch". First is the "healing power of the Holy Spirit." This is not my particular area, although healing energy does flow through me. My personal healing power has most often manifested in terms of healing the mind and also through prayer, but not so much (as yet) of the hands-on variety. The second gift is the "proper attunement of spiritual instruction." Got that. Then comes the "spreading of wisdom given by the Holy Spirit." That's what this volume is all about! I am ready to spread the wisdom and to unite all wisdom traditions. Oh yeah! That's me, too! Discerning spirits? Yahoo! That's what the antichrist chapter was ultimately about.

Following that is the "prophetic preaching" – that seems connected with spreading the wisdom of the Holy Spirit, and that's covered. Next comes "the speaking in tongues that unite the body with other levels of intelligence" and then "the interpretation of tongues so as to understand how different levels of knowledge can be coordinated". I'm not certain these are manifesting in me, at least not in the recognized way these are usually manifested. However, the thought pictures in my visions and revelations are indisputably a "language" which can be understood. This seems to be the manner of manifestation of these gifts in me. The "power of miracles." Many people would say that what has been written through me is a miracle. The miraculous happens all the time in my home: witness the moss! The violet in October! The awesome miracles of forgiveness! Finally, the "gift of active faith which shows how we must progress beyond the milk of being a newborn child of God into the Messianic fiber which cultivates the Kingdom of God on earth – seeing invisible things becoming visible. Thank You, God. Faith I have. I will see invisible things become visible!

For about two weeks God has been prompting me to write this chapter. I have been extremely resistant, almost lethargic in my resistance. I would think thoughts such as: it cannot be this way; it cannot be this simple; why would You show me such different outcomes; why did You bring me to this place with such descriptions of "how ascension would be." I felt as if I were abandoning something dear to me. And I have! My own limited ideas.

In what form will your service to My Will be most effective? Certainly, the ascension status. Certainly, mastery. You cannot know how it will look, for that is a constantly transmuting, constantly transforming idea, and my Divine Humans are doing the transmuting and the transforming. Because of the willingness of many of my marvelous Divine Human children, evolution itself is transforming. My Will is being done. My Plan, the New Birth to ascension status for all the Earth is happening. It is happening gracefully, by the choices of the Terra herself and her evolving humans that Grace be the method. Personal ascension has taken on a new grace as well, a softening, a growing-into, an as-it-happens consciousness: a process of Divine Grace. In you I Am well pleased.

*I remember your excitement when you read "The Crystal Stair" which described what was, **in that moment**, the Plan for the ascension of the Earth. There were to be "waves" of ascension, where those ready would be lifted off the Earth to avoid the tribulations and to complete the process. This plan is now outmoded, the greater tribulations avoided by the intentions for Peace of so many of my beloveds. The Rapture is happening, gracefully, and every moment a greater outcome, a more beautiful Terra, is being born, by the communal intentions of my Divine Humans. To say that I Am well pleased is an understatement. To say that the Masters and Angelic Host are well pleased is an understatement. The Heavens rejoice with grateful delight in the overcoming that is happening. Revelation, the books of the Prophets, and all the negative scenarios of prophecy from every culture, have been conquered, if not nullified. And now even the most recent gloom and doom prophecies, the earth changes prophecies and the ascension wave prophecies, are no longer valid. All of these prophetic voices have served you well, however, have they not?*

Oh yes, absolutely. They have provided a sort of propulsion. *That is My Purpose.* A side benefit for me is that I simply have no need around how any outcome will look or feel (I'm not saying I don't want the feeling!!), and when any particular outcome will occur experientially. I know it is now occurring. I have the Peace of God, and that Peace is forever within. This can only be mastery. And the term "rapture" God, I have come to understand rapture as the release from race consciousness, or rising above in-the-world thought to Christ consciousness. *A very apt description. Would you not also say that such release is rapturous?* Indeed, yes, **to know** what is truly Real is rapture, it is enthralling.

I have noticed the children and animals thing, too. When I take my walks, there are numerous dogs in the neighborhood. There are no fences in this neighborhood, and most everyone allows their animals freedom. Lately, the dogs have stopped barking at me.

They just follow me with their eyes. A few of the dogs will happily bound right up to me and bury their noses in my hand, nuzzling. They all do this same thing. Rabbits will stop in their frantic races and stare at me. Deer, too. Little kids (generally 4 or under) will gain my attention with their eyes and gaze at me, then release my gaze with a smile. My family has fallen in love with me again; my own children see me differently, somehow. There is a new esteem, a new significance to our relationships. My mountain is, indeed, moving.

My meditations have changed again. More of the time, I am so deeply in no-thing, I am blissed-out. I remember nothing about those periods, and they are deepening and lengthening. Very strange to be so desirous of no-thing, but there it is. I am that! At Louise's home one evening, one of the meditation participants played an awesome crystal bowl in the tone of E. The tone was so very resonant with me, I could not control my consciousness at all, could not direct it to another thought. The resonance was so great that all I could do was to vibrate in and with the tone. When we came out of the meditation I was unable to speak, to walk, anything. I sat there and felt retarded. I could not form simple thoughts. I was resonance, I was the sound itself: intensely aware, but entirely unable to command my humanness.

The symbols and images I have been getting are more and more incredible, even for me. Integration must be happening in those no-thing periods, because otherwise I have no idea how to integrate the idea that my skull, my spine, my very bones, are crystalline: that I am of the consciousness of the crystal capstone, that I am filled with Light all the way to the bone! And how do I integrate that my meditation buddies of late are the big three: Jesus, Buddha and Krishna. How did I deserve that? In a conversation with Louise about the angst and see-sawing emotions so many beloveds are encountering now, I responded that I have been in a sort of suspended place, balanced, that I felt myself to be in integration mode. Oddly, though, I couldn't explain what I was integrating, because it wasn't just the awesome thoughts that seemed to be consuming my attention, but there was something else, something not understandable with the mind that I was integrating.

On the first Thursday in July 2003, the first class was held out on Unity Church's new property, in the house we are currently using as offices. Due to numerous unforeseen challenges, construction has not yet begun on our church building. We wanted to anchor the Christ consciousness energy on the property, however. Since I have seen an energetic vortex at the back of the land, I was pretty vocal that we needed to be there instead of the storefront church.

Dr. Louise spoke on will and power and mastery that evening, and sometime during the meditation, she directed us to "enter the hall of your own creation." I was not in a hallway, but it was rather more like a grassy path, a very beautiful pathway, lined with trees and flowers. There was a wonderful peace, but I was disappointed. I thought I had done more co-creating with my life – in fact; this pathway was really nothing except something beautiful to follow along, a place to wander. I sat down in the middle of the pathway, feeling dejected. Then walls appeared along the path, tall, imposing, important walls made of crystalline glass. There were words printed in black type on the "panes" that appeared to be 20 feet tall. I looked up at the pane to my left. The title page to this book! Enthralled, I stood and walked on, reading each pane, feeling every experience anew, recalling every thought as if freshly occurring in my mind, envisioning all the wonders Spirit has opened me to, God-moment to God-moment.

The crystalline glass panes were truly a hallway of creation: my own personal hall of remembrance. The sky was the ceiling, beloved Earth the foundation, my own book of life etched along the walls. The pathway began to rise as I walked along, my being glowed brighter and my smile bigger. The words began to look less like typewritten words, and more like fire letters and thought pictures. There were certain moments in my experience, like the Melchizedek baptism in the Gulf of Mexico, which caused a sudden and dramatic expansion of Light in my being. There were other experiences, like the crucifixion of divorce, that caused a sort of involution, but it was in these experiences that I gained the crystalline structure in my body. Another major expansion when I first saw the visible Light during the resurrection experiences. I continued to rise and expand and brighten, becoming more and more exhilarated with every step. Then I got to the beginning of 2003, and the exponentially powerful experiences since I gave myself Louise and her Christ Consciousness class for my birthday.

As I got to the 2003 pages, my being became more and more enflamed, more of a flowing flame of spirit, until NOW I began to shimmer and small explosions of light would travel out from my being, out to enlighten another made ready by intention. The flaming flowing beingness I am, the hallway, the fiery words, the thought pictures, everything in my awareness, exploded in One all-consuming Light, and there I Am, Completed. Whole. In that Light, I Am fully my Self. I AM the ascension in the Light. It is me. I have been this all along; in every moment all along the entire book of life I have co-created. Ascension is as simple as growing in realization, and as complex as being willing to grow in realization!

The Light gradually faded into no-thing. I felt so completely relaxed, so totally comfortable, at last, being in my body. There was nothing about being human, no human trait or characteristic or function that remained unworthy of God-ness, and being human was finally, totally, okay with me. Basking in this ultimate satisfaction with my being, Louise directed the group to "call down your Christ Self." I realized that I was already surrounded by a twelve-sided pillar of Light, the personal "layooesh Shekinah" of which I have recently been made aware that constantly surrounds my being. I looked "up" but my wonderfully beautiful ascended Self was not "there"! I could not figure this out. My Self is available to me at all times, I puzzled. Still gazing up, Yeshua strode into my awareness, lifting my chin with his forefinger and looking deeply into my eyes. *Here you are! Here you are, beloved Liberty!* In a powerful rush of realization, I knew that I knew: my Self, the full Truth of my eternal being, resides fully now within the human Libby. It is the fullness of my Christ Self that is integrating!

Dr. Louise asked us to invoke our Christ presences, to fervently request all Christ presences of all persons be remembered and realized. Yes, yes, yes, I agreed, nodding silently in overwhelmed knowledge of what this would truly mean to our world. Still, I made the same plea made by John the Beloved: Even so, come quickly, Lord Jesus. And of course, again he strode into my consciousness, coming straight up to me with a broad smile, and as if I were his best friend and this were a common occurrence, he kissed me full on the lips, then on the forehead. Drawing back slightly to look into my eyes, my beloved replied *For you I will come*. Without thought, without hesitation, I responded, "for you I will stay."

~~~

The next morning I set out for my morning walk, and there in the summer sunlight, the very road I was walking became **that hallway**. With my eyes wide open, the glass walls were lining my own street. My experiences have walked me unfailingly right into the Light of my own being.

My beloved Liberty, tell all My children. Go tell it on every mountain! It is every road. It is every moment. You are ever walking into the Light you are, my beloved Liberty, and will always do so. Welcome to Eternal Life.

Epilogue

Once again it is October in Tennessee. I have come full circle, in a sense, except the "circle" has never been a circle at all, but an endless upward spiral. This is the nature of eternal life.

Thank You, Wonderful God, for the ability to appreciate! The sky is again that rich, fully saturated blue with tiny wispy clouds placed just so for the contrasting effect. The trees are just beginning their colorful shout of praise to God just before they rest and sleep for the winter. This glorious world **is** heaven. This is it. Open your eyes!

I thought that I had surrendered everything, **everything, everything!** God didn't think so. If you can believe it, my life has taken even more "negative" turns, but in the spirit of mastery, I am (usually) not bothered by any of it, therefore I will not elaborate. There is no need. This can only be Grace. Now I am entirely willing to give up every idea about everything too. It's getting easier, since I am so very aware that God's solutions are **so** much better than anything I can imagine, but ego can be very subtle in masking the difference. It helps in the ego situation to know that I AM in control of ego, my ego being my own co-creation after all! I am willing to wake up every morning and stand on the precipice that is being human, stepping out in faith, watching each step form before my very eyes. I have no preconceived notion about "what happens next", but with consciousness in my Self, image-in and co-create every moment. In present human consciousness, the appearance of my perceived human condition would deem it impossible and illogical for me to be filled with Peace and Joy, with Hope, with Divine Assurance. With God all things are possible. This is Truth. This is the real deal.

I had the opportunity to receive a free book (good price, I thought) called "The Secret" by Michael Berg. It's a simple book based upon the ancient wisdom of Kabbalah. Read this book. Recommend this book. Anyone can understand this book, because Michael Berg is a powerfully simple Christ. He speaks to the heart of hearts. There is a chapter titled "Transformative Sharing" that unlocked something in me, and I thought I had read everything. I will quote the key part:

"If [a person] is sharing something of which he or she has a great deal, such as money,...transformative sharing might involve something of which he or she has less, such as personal time. It may even mean creating an entirely new category of experience – something that he or she has never done or even thought of doing. Kabbalah teaches that we are not in the world just to do the things that come naturally. We are here to expand our nature and thereby strengthen our connection to a far richer experience.

"Life's challenges are not simply mistakes that the Creator forgot to correct or remove. The obstacles we face have been put in place as part of a thoroughly positive intention, as opportunities for transformative sharing. Yet long before we do anything or give anything, whether money or love or wise counsel, our action is defined by the character of the desire that underlies it – and Kabbalah teaches that true sharing is defined by our desire for spiritual transformation."

Then another key opened another place in me, something I had forgotten because I had not truly understood. In November of 1994, a few months before my ordination, I had my first and only psychic reading, given by my wonderful teacher Ernestine. I can only now appreciate the depth of her devotion to God. At some point in the reading, she said to me with a kind of nervous giggle "You will open seals. You are a seal-breaker." Now I know she giggled because she knew what she was talking about. I giggled because I had not a clue! Later in my studies I had realized that what she meant by "seals" are the chakras. But breaking them? I also came to know that in Revelation, John the Beloved talks about the seven seals and the apparent "horror" that the breaking of these seals brings about to the earth. Perhaps I didn't forget so much as I didn't want to know!

I connected to the third key through the miracle of the Internet. God often reveals in layers of three, have you noticed? Dr. Louise had recommended a website, www.crimsoncircle.com, where channelings from Tobias, the same Tobias from the book of Tobit, are made available. The article given on August 19, 2003, said in part "When John [John the Beloved, in Revelation] speaks of the seven angels spreading changes [breaking the seals] over the world, this is a process that is taking place within you. This is the change, and it relates to the old chakras. They are being eliminated.

They are being destroyed, so to speak, so that you can have a single chakra, one chakra. So, the seven angels come, and they make the change within… It is of the consciousness, and the soul, and the heart of the world, and of who you are."

That was it. Suddenly I knew. I would share the chakra experience God gifted me with a couple of years ago, described in "Actuality" a few chapters back. This was not just a lovely experience, but also a teaching for the world! I was wide-eyed with wonder at the awesome potential, at the tremendous possibilities, at the great responsibility, at the outrageous blessing the transformative sharing of this experience would bring to my friends, to anyone willing to hear.

Full of faith and enthusiasm, I made another appointment with the minister at my Unity Church. Remember my last appointment? The difference is that we have a new minister, Denise. Remember Denise? She's the same Christ being who looked into my eyes during an experiential exercise and we became one soul. Denise said yes, and we set a date right then. Denise said Yes!! Together we decided on a one-day workshop called "Experiencing the I Am" through opening and balancing the chakras, ending in unification. And oh, my, God intensified the learning for me, creating four weeks of amplified revelatory teachings and connections within books and materials and music. It was an extended God-mind rush!

The Tuesday before my gift of transformative sharing at the "I Am" seminar, our awesome God gave me a most outstanding gift. While driving to Dr. Louise's home on a rocky hill outside lovely little Pegram, Tennessee, I noticed that my eyes were acting strangely, and thought well okay; I must be approaching a new level of vision. It seemed as though I was looking at everything for the first time, as if in actuality I were seeing the familiar world as if completely new, while also the same old familiar world. I knew the names of everything, but associations were not available to my mind. Additionally, it was as if I could see through everything, as if I were really able to see that everything that appears solid is not so after all. But I am accustomed to visual changes, so I was relaxed about all of it, and found it quite fascinating. I was rather glad when the drive was over, though, because seeing "through" a double tractor-trailer is just a little disconcerting.

I was the only meditator with Dr. Louise that evening. We both knew that God was up to something. We immediately went into a deep, intense meditation. Louise spoke only occasionally, even though her usual practice is to guide the meditations. Together we agreed and accepted our inheritance of Divine Humanity for ourselves. Both of us were fully manifesting as our Christ selves, fully in our bodies of Light, tall and imposing, powerful. There was Divine Light projecting in a white-Light flame from my crown chakra; I could feel it profoundly. Louise mentioned the great harvest that is upon us all. I could hear Jesus speaking, speaking with his human voice, "Yes, beloved, behold, for the fields are indeed white for the harvest!" Delighted with his presence, smiling with joy, I looked out from my "elevated" state, and there was a field of souls, thousands of souls, Divine white Light glowing from each crown chakra!

The harvest, this fabulous harvest of Light was such an outrageously beautiful vision: there were people I recognized, others I did not, but I loved every one of them as my own, as part of me. Separate in our individual natures, we are One Light. Louise and I stood "above" the gathering of souls, but only because we had self-chosen to lead during this time. There were other leaders, standing tall, like sentinels, like towers of strength, like Lighthouses among the Lights. Breathing deeply, accepting, gratefully accepting my role more deeply, more gladly than ever before I felt my wings appear and expand. It was an incomparable, marvelous sight: as both the observer and the observed I looked upon the harvest of many, as the Lightworker I Am.

In this breathtaking revelation a window opened, and I looked upon our sweet, adorable human reenactment of the harvest scene: our behavior of raising cigarette lighters aloft in gratitude, admiration and applause for an excellent concert or performance! The sweetness of this connection brought a sudden flood of hot tears to my eyes, tears of tender love for all of us here, making the best of our humanness. And then I could hear music, and the tears began to flow more freely, because the lyrics I knew..."It is the concert of the Age/ The Great I Am takes center stage/ The generations stand amazed/At the concert of the Age". Oh, my friends, such a Plan God has for us. The field of Lights grew brighter and brighter, expanding, until the field that is Nashville connected with Memphis and Knoxville, then Birmingham and Louisville and Atlanta and on and on and on, connecting and lighting the whole beautiful world. Let this harvest now begin!

God, why am I so resistant to writing the next part? *Ah, my beloved, it is the issue of worth. Only that. And you know your worth to Me. Still, you do not fully believe. Still, you resist the ultimate Truth of your being. We are One. You are who I AM.* Yes, it's the strange feeling I get, the "lesser than" feeling, when I read Tobias saying, "You are God also." *I have noticed. This is good.* How so? *You have reached the point of…there, do you feel it?* Yes, I can barely type. The resistance feels almost a part of my body, so primal, so enmeshed in everything I know myself to be, the resistance is…. almost irresistible. *You are God also. I have said it, again and again: Ye are Gods. You are God also. We are One. The dream is over. The separation has ended, and it was only perception. You cannot be harmed. There is no death. Heaven is here. God is good. It's all True. I AM that I AM. Everything you have ever hoped was really true is Really True. Honest to God.* Oh, I love You. I love You. Okay. I am You. The next part. Here goes.

My being continued to grow, larger and larger. During this time of expansion, watching and feeling myself growing enormous, acknowledging and becoming aware of my galactic beingness in an almost slow-motion awareness, Louise spoke of accepting Divinity, Divine Humanness, for the all the people of the Terra. She spoke of our expanding, evolving DNA as Jacob's ladder, of the spiral of completion opening our biology to our eternity. I realized that this thought, which I knew to be truth but had never seen in a book, was a shared thought in Christ mind. My awareness continued to expand. I was entirely in the living room of Louise's home, yet I was aware of our entire galaxy. Intensely, I understood our planetary system to be a mirror of the chakra system. Our sun is so obviously the crown chakra, our wonderful Mother Earth the heart chakra. I felt so very whole, so satisfied, so completely satiated. There was nothing to seek. I Am. I Am.

Utterly relaxed and limp of body, personal mind detached and still, I Am able to be I Am. There is only Light, and the Light increases and expands. The Light is all things. Ahh. *Ahhhh.* There is a spiraling energy that passes before me, crossing the screen of awareness I Am. Each time this energy passes by, the Love I Am increases; as if I grow in awareness of my Self each time the energy cycles by in the spiraling motion. *Holy I Am. Holy I Am. Holy, holy, holy.* Then I know, the personal me becomes aware: seraphim. The energy is the seraphim angels! Knowing, then I see: with the eyes of God I see the seraphim angels. **I see the seraphim angels**, wondrous, astounded, spiraling energies ever profoundly aware of God's infinitely expanding Glory. I Am God also. Ever and forever, they fly around who I Am.

I gasped. I'm not sure I was actually breathing through that vision. The physical oxygen requirement returned me to my personal awareness. I could not stay in that expanded state, not yet. And in that first gasp, I already doubted. Seraphim? Sure. Yeah, right. Louise roused herself at the same time, and together, speechless, we headed for the kitchen and some water. I could not look her in the eye. She did not look at me, either. We stretched, moved about, and then returned to our comfortable positions.

Breathing in tandem, minds following the angelic music, sinking back into meditation, consciousness again expanding, our beings held the Earth with tenderness, with compassion, with mercy. We were one mind, one heart, and one soul, One Spirit, One Voice. I cannot possibly describe the satisfaction this level of joining brings. She spoke it and I knew it: Melchizedek is before us. We were suddenly standing, tall in our physical bodies and in our bodies of Light. The fantastic Light of Melchizedek's being filled the room, our consciousness, everything, yet this time his appearance was different. Though far beyond our kindergarten spirituality, he was our peer. "I have something for you," he conveyed to me, and at the same instant, he casually yet purposefully tossed something over me. I saw and felt a substantial sort of Light falling around me with a softly rustling whoosh.

The Light covered my body entirely, all the way to the floor. Still standing, I was breathing very deeply, tremendously exhilarated, feeling this wonderful, substantial, gorgeously color-filled fabric of Light envelope my body like a robe. I opened my eyes and the Light garment remained. My hands, lifted in praise, moved to touch the fabric covering my arms. I twirled around, feeling the Light garment move with my body, the folds wrapping around my legs and falling straight again. I knew it was a seamless garment. Melchizedek's thoughts entered my consciousness; his great pleasure with my readiness, his joyful merriment billowing around me like the garment. I could feel his tender gaze upon me, yet it was not just I he gazed upon, but me enveloped in this special, wonderful Light. Then I knew. This is the coat of many colors, the woven cloak of souls, the very same garment of Light I once saw Christ Sananda wear, and know he wears forever.

Once again I could feel myself gasping, overwhelmed with the enormity of revelation, completely in awe, yet this time the moment was unbroken. Melchizedek, and now Christ Sananda, were not allowing this shared consciousness moment to be broken, nor was Liberty. Libby wasn't getting to make any choices this time. This trinity of beings, Melchizedek, Christ Sananda and Christ Liberty, were going to get this point across, all the way through my physical being.

And here is the point. I Am Christ Liberty. I Am the beloved child of God. It is all true, truth, Truth! I know, really know, and have anchored this knowing in my humanity. It is my joy, my gift, and my purpose to give this gift of knowing to everyone. The salvation of the world has become my responsibility, because as Christ I am now able to respond. I wear and bear the garment of Light, the knowledge of our ultimate Oneness. It is my joy to be fully me, fully the Christ I am. I will wear the garment of Light forever and forever, just as my beloved Yeshua, Christ Sananda, wears his. I Am worthy of this gift.

Filled with power, filled with glory, I wanted to fall to my knees, but Melchizedek caught me, saying "Hey, don't! You'll crush some of the beloveds!" And God laughed! The consciousness all around me shook and trembled, vibrating deliciously with Divine Mirth. I laughed aloud, too.

~~~

Meditation over, Louise and I walked somewhat unsteadily toward the kitchen for more water. Gathering my wits about me, I looked her fully in the eyes, and offered, "Page one, Book of the Gods?" Nodding, trembling slightly, she responded, "Yes, I think so."

In My House there are many mansions. I have prepared a place for thee, and it is ever with Me. Come, my beloved child. Come.

Namaste'

List of References in order of appearance

"Return to Love" Marianne Williamson

"A Course in Miracles"

The Bible (New Revised Standard Version)

"Emissary of Light" James Twyman

"The Book of Books", "Beyond Mortal Boundaries" Annalee Skarin

"Son of Man" Andrew Harvey

"Communion with God" Neale Donald Walsch

"Revelation: Our Crisis is a Birth" Barbara Marx Hubbard

"Resurrection" Neville

"The Aquarian Gospel of Jesus the Christ" Levi

"The Crystal Stair" Eric Klein

"Prayers of the Cosmos" and "The Hidden Gospel" Neil Douglas-Klotz

"The Keys of Enoch" J. J. Hurtak

The "White Eagle" series

"Watch Your Dreams" Ann Ree Colton

"The Complete Gospels", Robert J. Miller, Editor

"I, the Christ" Dolores Pevehouse

"The Revealing Word" Charles Fillmore

The Kryon teachings at Kryon.com

"The Secret" Michael Berg

The teachings of Tobias at crimsoncircle.com

About The Author

Libby Maxey writes from the open heart and illumined mind of the Christ consciousness she has diligently sought from the time of her "break with meaning" in the 80's. She has consumed and internalized the writings of Spirit in every form that has resonated in her heart. Through prayer and meditation, watching and listening she has developed a relationship with the God of her soul that now encompasses every thought, word and deed.

Upon her introduction to the phenomenal power of group meditation in the early '90's, she began to have astounding revelatory visions. In 1995, as a personal act of commitment, she was ordained as a Universal Brotherhood minister, a broad ecumenical ministry. She serves as a chaplain for her beloved Unity Church for Positive Living.

Libby lives outside Nashville, Tennessee.

Printed in the United States
24493LVS00002B/220-240